Downtown Los Angeles In Photographs 2014 – Broadway

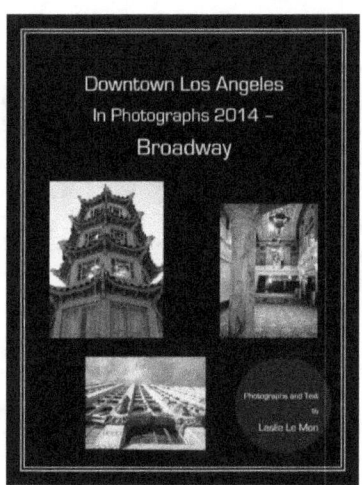

Photographs and Text

By

Leslie Le Mon

© 2014 Leslie Le Mon

TABLE OF CONTENTS

Contents

TABLE OF CONTENTS 3
DEDICATION 5
INTRODUCTION 7
MAP – BROADWAY – DOWNTOWN LOS ANGELES (2014) 9
THE PHOTOGRAPHS 11
THANK YOU 163
RESOURCES & RECOMMENDATIONS 165
ABOUT THE AUTHOR 167
OTHER BOOKS BY THE AUTHOR/PHOTOGRAPHER 167
COPYRIGHT INFORMATION 167

DEDICATION

For my father, Warren James Le Mon (1929 – 2011), a New Yorker, born in the Bronx, a man who loved the lights and shadows and music and history and poetry of great cities, particularly New York, Paris, and Los Angeles.

For my beloved mother, Sally, who is increasingly intrigued by the history of the "city of angels".

For "the amazing aunts"—Aunt Jane and Aunt Ruth.

For Amy, Julio, Craig, Maura, Ritz, Jim, Jacob, Julia, Marcus, and Andrew, always.

For Loretta, Molly, "Gramma" Sharon, and Nancy.

For cousin Margaret-Mary, the family genealogist.

For *all* family and friends—thanks for the encouragement.

INTRODUCTION

Downtown Los Angeles in Photographs 2014 - Broadway—a follow-up to *Downtown Los Angeles in Photographs 2013*—is a journey along Broadway, one of downtown LA's most significant and diverse corridors. The images in this book show how Broadway looks *today*, in the midst of an exciting revival by devoted Angelenos who include historians, artists, architects, developers, business owners, and local residents.

Photograph books, by their very nature, should be visually rich, with concise historical comments to provide context. This book is a mere taste of the history, art, foods, and adventure that Broadway offers. Readers whose interest is piqued can explore the resources listed at the end of this book to learn more. (Or better yet, grab your walking shoes and explore Broadway yourself!)

Downtown Los Angeles is a big place. Each book in this series concentrates on a specific area or theme that highlights LA's most interesting and iconic features—its historic treasures, its forgotten gems, and its promise for the future. The north-south boulevard of Broadway has always been a vital downtown artery, composed of neighborhoods as varied as Little Italy, Chinatown, the Theatre District, the Jewelry District, the Fashion District, and the Commercial/Industrial zone.

Named "Fort Street" from 1849 until 1890, Broadway took its new name from the even more famous Broadway in New York City. A stroll along Broadway is a stroll through the heart of Los Angeles history, and, thanks to recent revitalization efforts, the heart of LA's future, too.

All photographs in this book were taken in 2014. All of the photos were snapped in Downtown LA, in color, and then rendered in black-and-white. Because as stated in the first collection:

Los Angeles–the city of film, the city of noir–is a black-and-white sort of place. Dazzling lights. Deep shadows. Stark contrasts. Los Angeles is gritty even in its beauty, and lovely even in its ugliness. With color washed away, the city's patterns and lines, its darks and lights, the grit and beauty of Los Angeles emerge in their purity ...

Enjoy this time-travelling jaunt from LA's distant past toward its thrilling future.

Leslie Le Mon, Los Angeles, February 2014

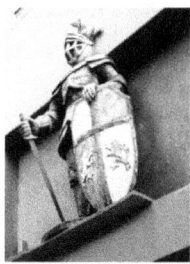

MAP – BROADWAY – DOWNTOWN LOS ANGELES (2014)

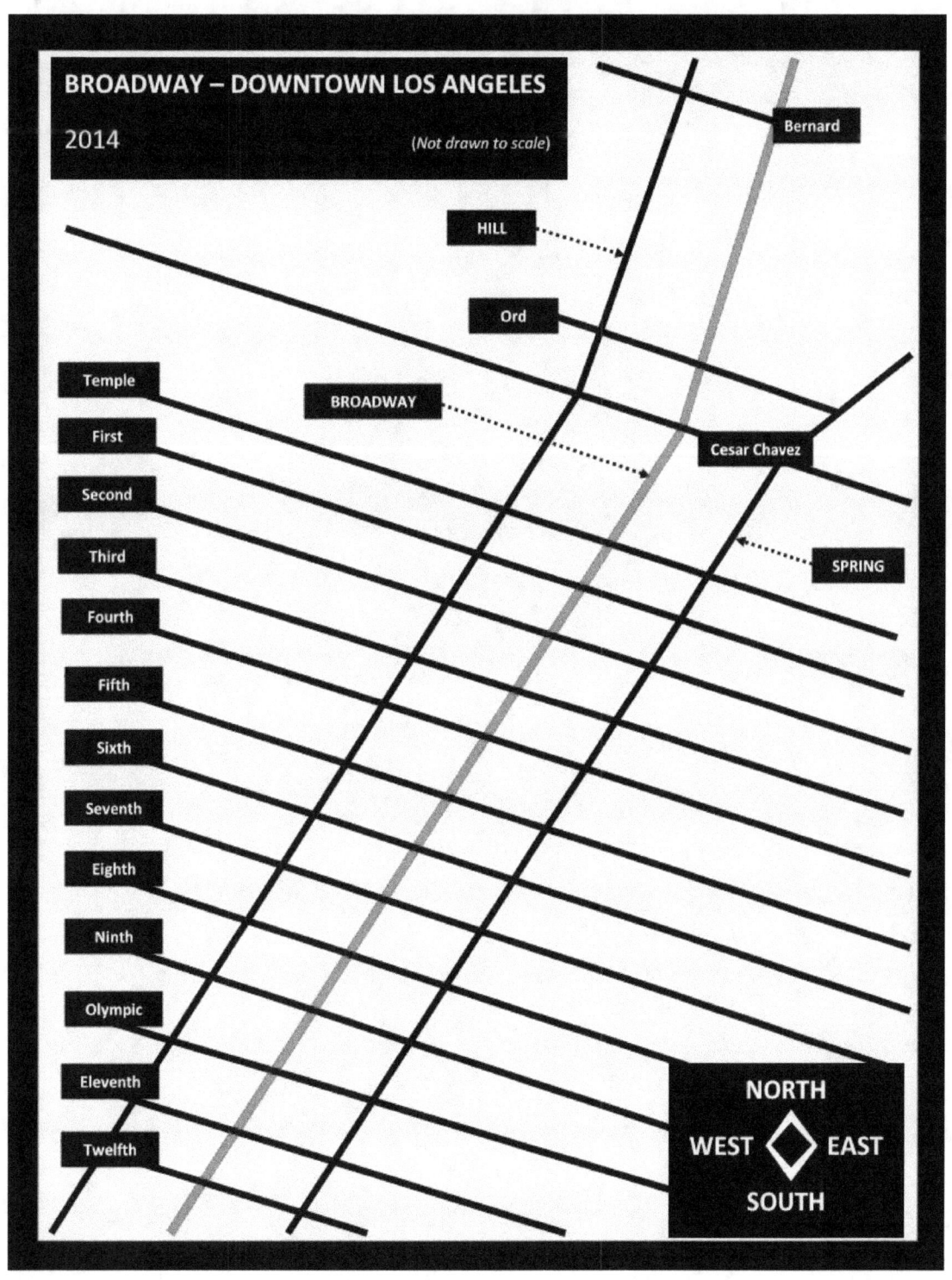

THE PHOTOGRAPHS

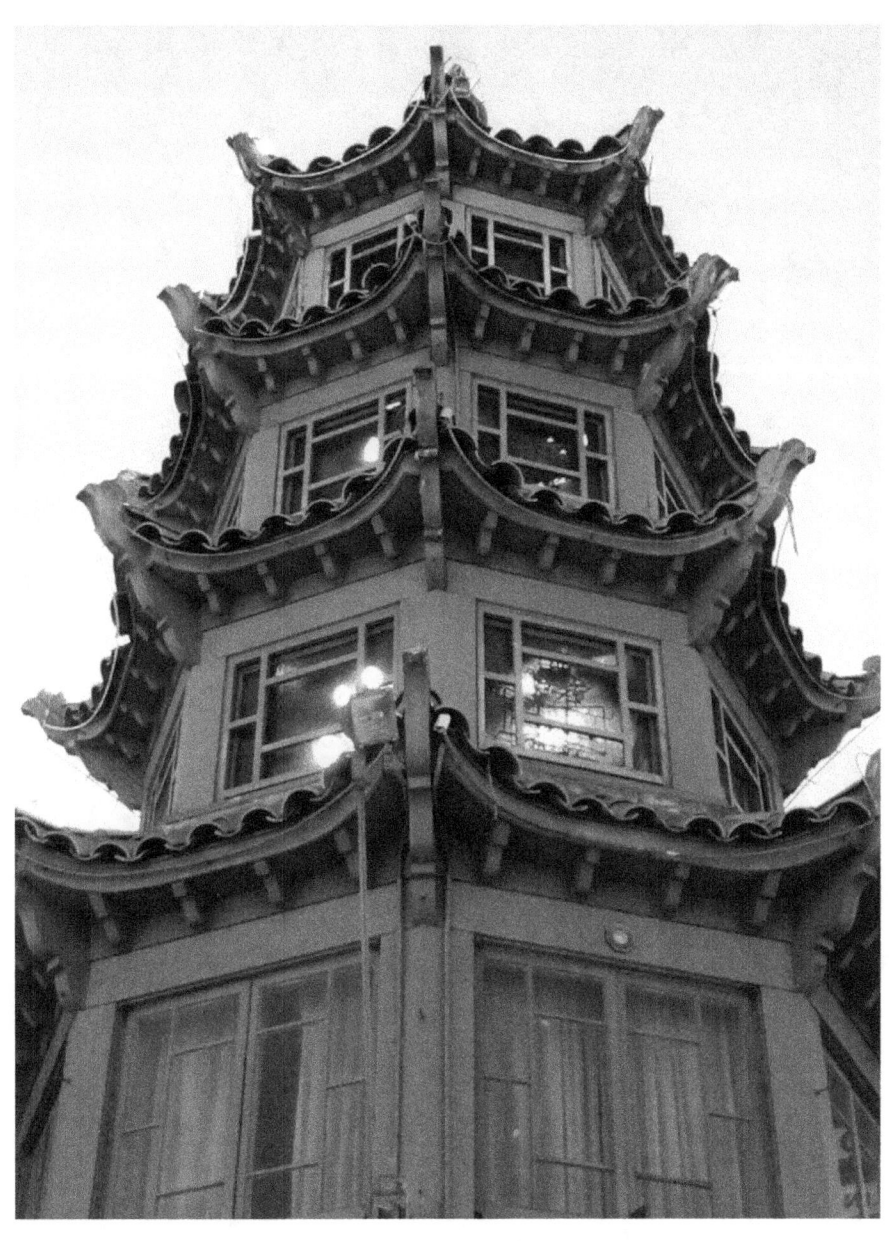

NORTH BROADWAY – LOS ANGELES

1100 Block of N. Broadway

North Broadway flows south from Lincoln Heights to Downtown Los Angeles, skirting the great rail yards and industrial zone northeast of the downtown area. The view here is from North Broadway, looking northeast. In the foreground are pallets and vehicles, and just beyond them the tracks of the LA Metro Gold Line. Beyond the tracks are the minimally landscaped grounds of the new Los Angeles State Historic Park, where fitness-minded Angelenos stroll or run, and entertainment events like the HARD Summer Music Festival are hosted on multiple stages. In the distance we see one of LA's famous arched bridges (top left) spanning the LA River's concrete canyon, and some of LA's manufacturing buildings (center and right) including a boiler works. It takes a lot of material to keep a city like LA operational; much of it is produced (or arrives by rail) in LA's manufacturing and transportation corridor just east of downtown. In the far distance: A typically sunny So Cal sky.

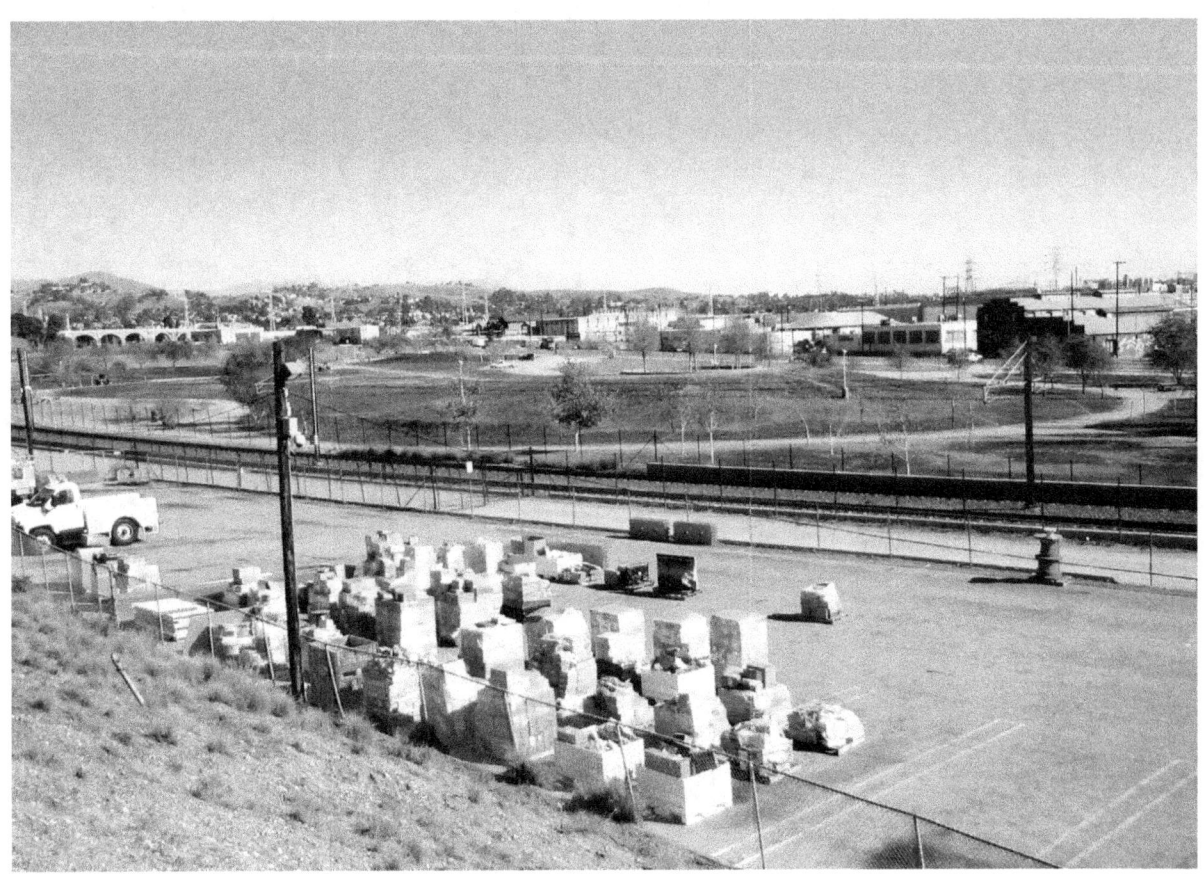

LITTLE ITALY

1051 N. Broadway

Pictured here is Casa Italiana, founded in 1972 to serve as "the crib of the Italian community" in Los Angeles, as well as the event hall for St. Peter's Italian Church. (Casa Italiana is adjacent to the church.) Feast celebrations, dances, and seminary banquets are among the events hosted here. The Italian Woman's Club, the Sons of Italy, and the Casa Italiana Opera are among the organizations that meet at Casa Italiana. LA's Cathedral High School is west of Casa Italiana, off Bishops Road.

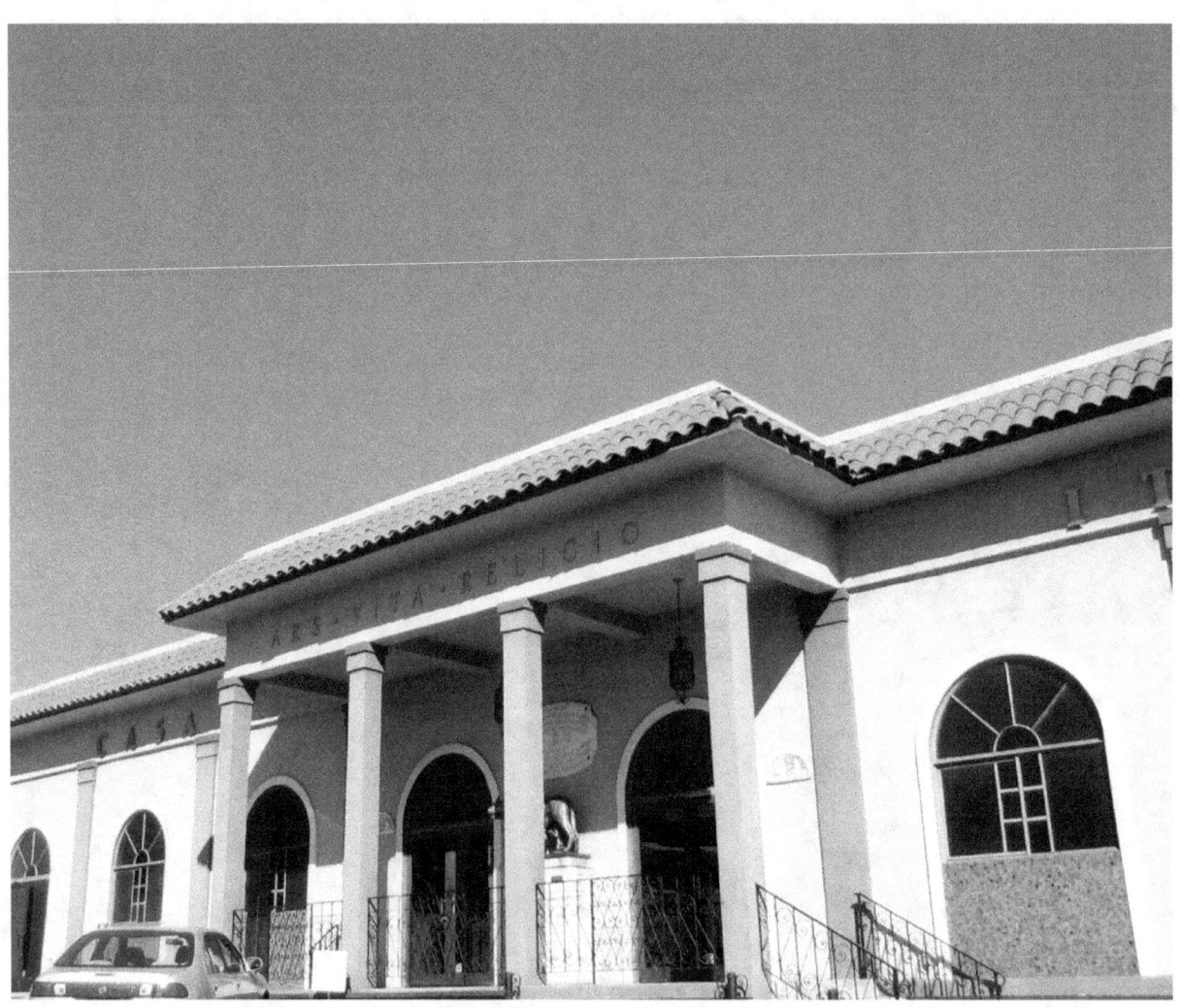

LITTLE ITALY

1051 N. Broadway

Why is Casa Italiana located on North Broadway? This area, in what is now Chinatown (and the neighborhood of Lincoln Heights across the river) formed the city's "Little Italy" district in the early 20th century. Although "Little Italy" no longer exists, organizations such as Casa Italiana continue to celebrate and preserve the history of LA's Italian and Italian-American residents. .In front of Casa Italiana stands a Capitoline Wolf statue—a sculpture of a wolf nursing legendary twins Romulus (Rome's founder) and Remus. Above the statue, a plaque proudly proclaims Italian achievements. Below the statue, another plaque reads "Roma Caput Mundi"—"Rome, Capital of the World".

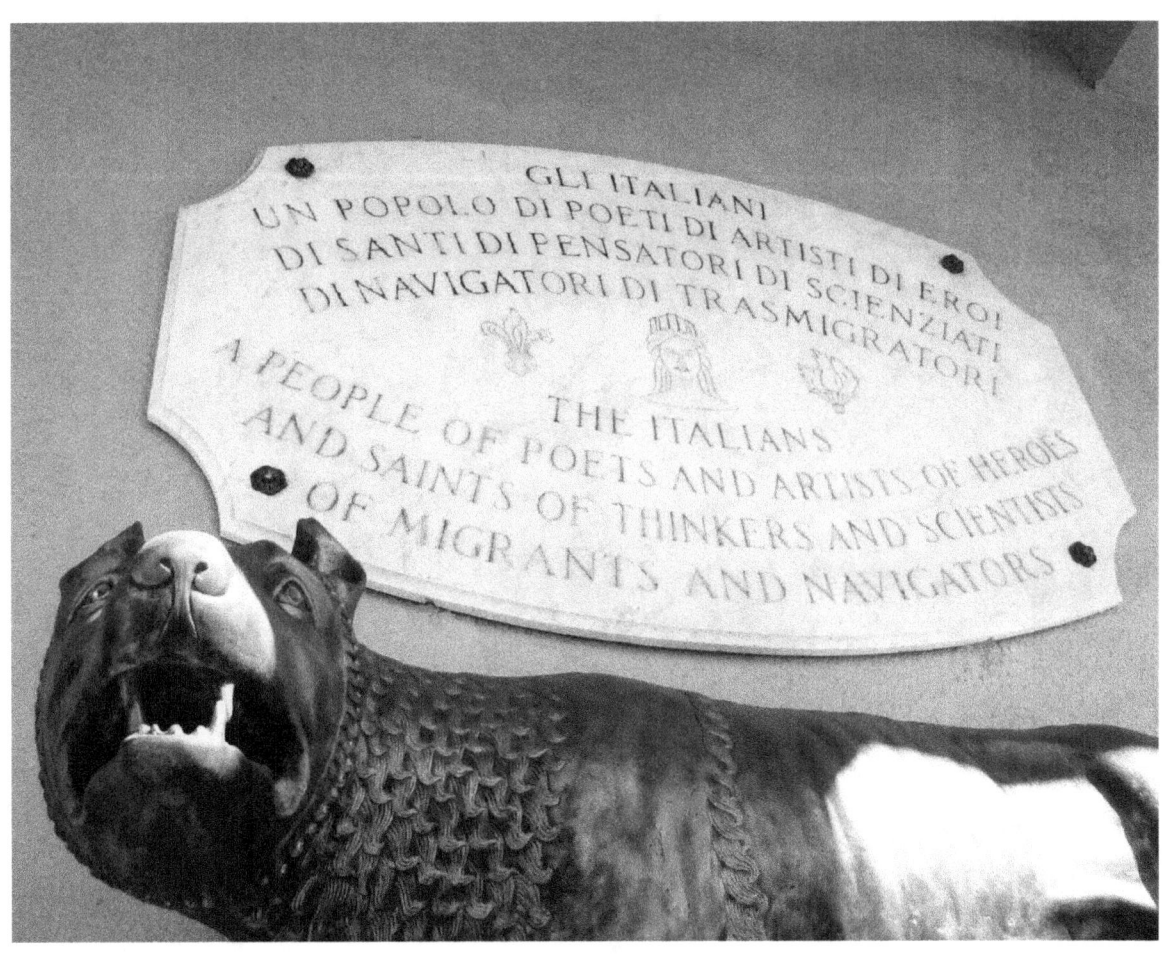

LITTLE ITALY

1039 N. Broadway

St. Peter's Italian Church is one of the centers of LA's Italian and Italian-American community, but as the church makes clear on its website, St. Peter's welcomes everyone. During the last decade of the 19th century, and the first decade of the 20th, multiple waves of Italian immigrants settled in Los Angeles. St. Peter's Church was established on N. Spring Street in 1904 to serve LA's expanding Italian population. In 1915, parishioners moved from the Spring Street space to a chapel on North Broadway, worshipping there until the chapel burned in 1943. The present church, with its striking tower, was constructed between 1946 and 1947. It remains an active Catholic church.

LITTLE ITALY

1039 N. Broadway

Over the years, St. Peter's has vigorously resisted periodic efforts to shift its focus from LA's Italian and Italian-American parishioners. However, in deference to LA's multicultural diversity, confession is now offered in English and Spanish, as well as in Italian.

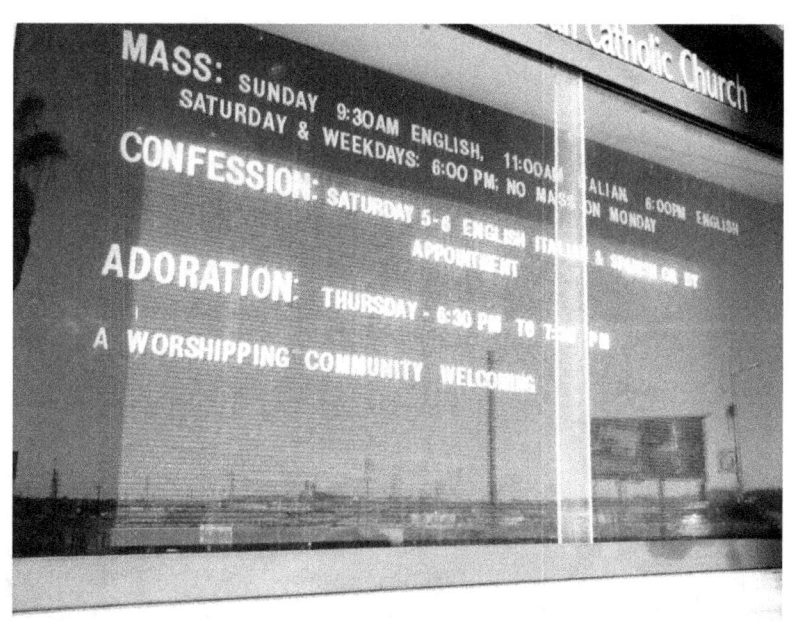

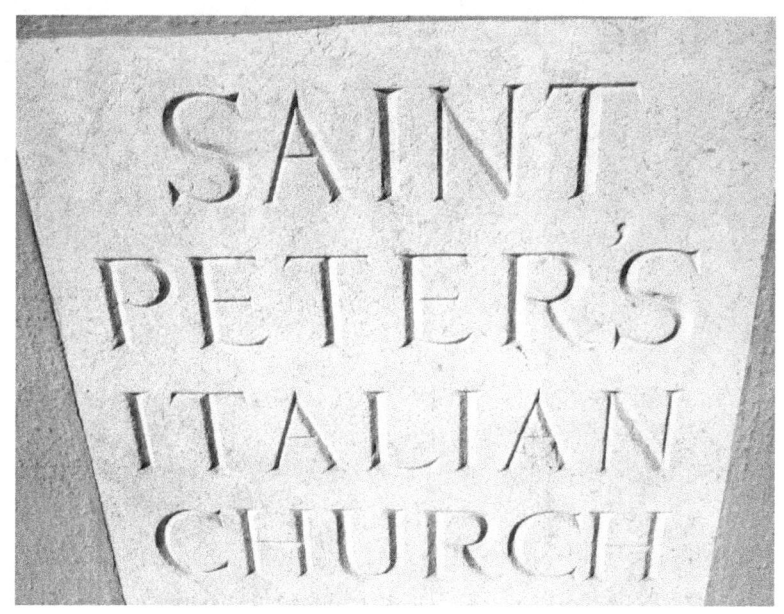

NORTH BROADWAY

1000 Block of N. Broadway

Standing on North Broadway in front of St. Peter's Italian Church one gazes southeast over the railroad tracks. Visible landmarks include the LA Metro tower (the high-rise on the left) and LA's City Hall (the pyramid-topped tower on the right of the vista), two power centers in "the city of angels".

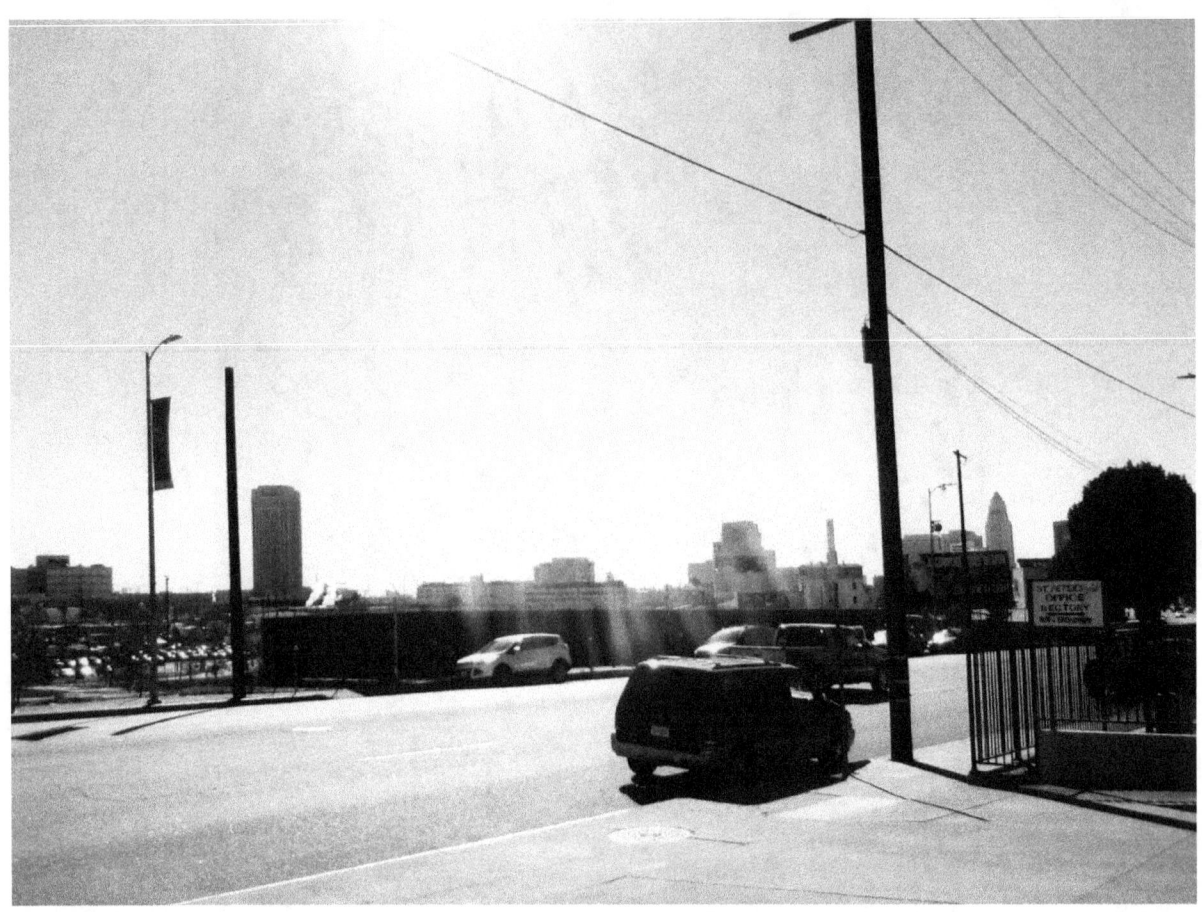

CHINATOWN

N. Broadway & Bernard Street

Traveling south of St. Peter's Church, to the intersection where Bernard Street crosses N. Broadway, it becomes apparent that "Little Italy" long ago gave way to Chinatown. Looking south along Broadway, note the Far East National Bank (center), the sign for the Royal Pagoda Motel (center right), and the motel's tiled roof, with its curving roofline, characteristic of traditional Chinese architecture.

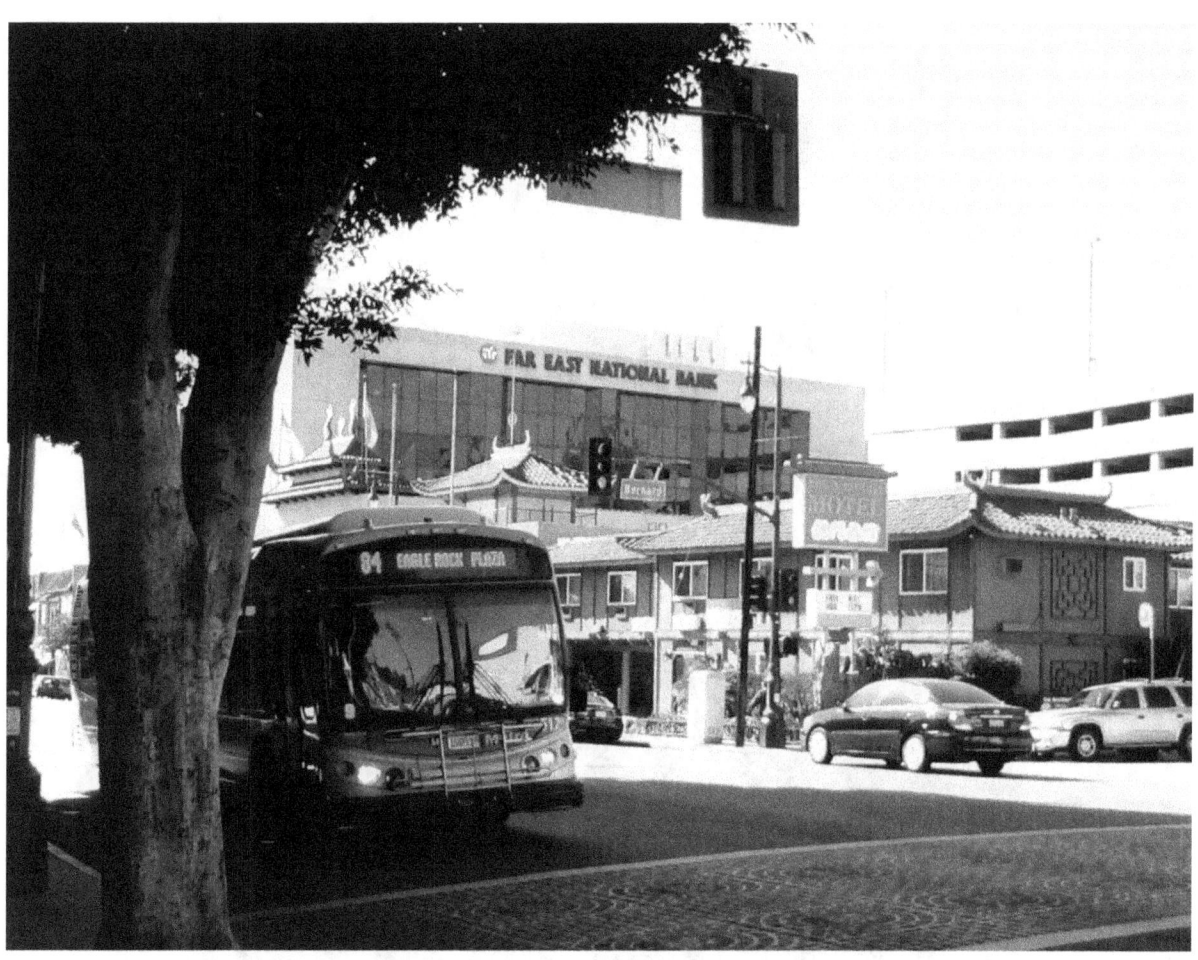

CHINATOWN

415 Bernard Street

Just off N. Broadway, on Bernard Street, the Chinese Historical Society of Southern California (CHSSC) occupies a small lavender house. Founded in 1975, the organization is dedicated to preserving Chinese and Chinese-American history in Southern California, and serving as a community resource for historical education and multicultural awareness and appreciation. Given the society's modest building and its location on a sleepy cross street, this qualifies as one of Chinatown's hidden gems.

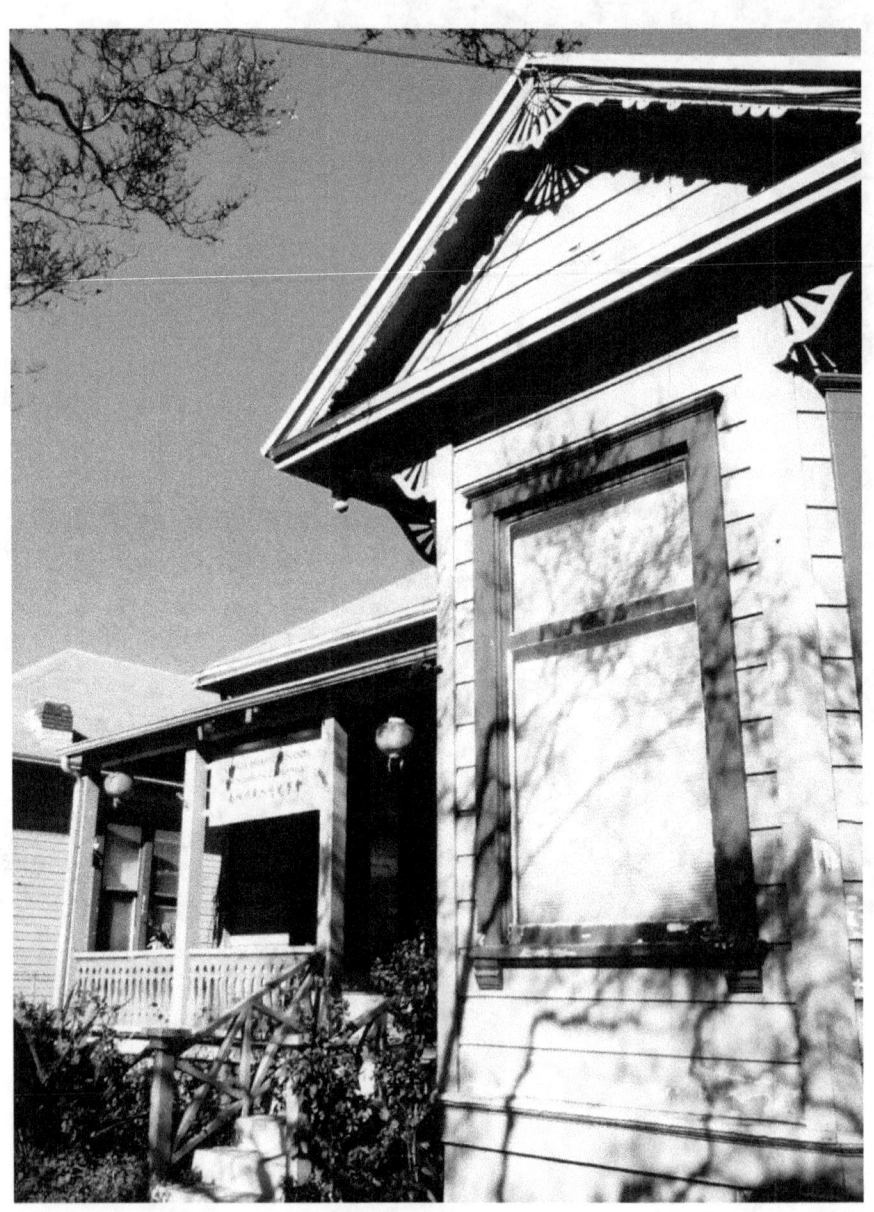

CHINATOWN

Bernard Street & N. Broadway

If this abandoned gas station on the northwest corner of Bernard Street and N. Broadway doesn't look like a film noir or neo-noir location, nothing does. Oil and gas have always been big business in LA (and drive the plot of "The Two Jakes" (1990), a sequel to "Chinatown" (1974)).

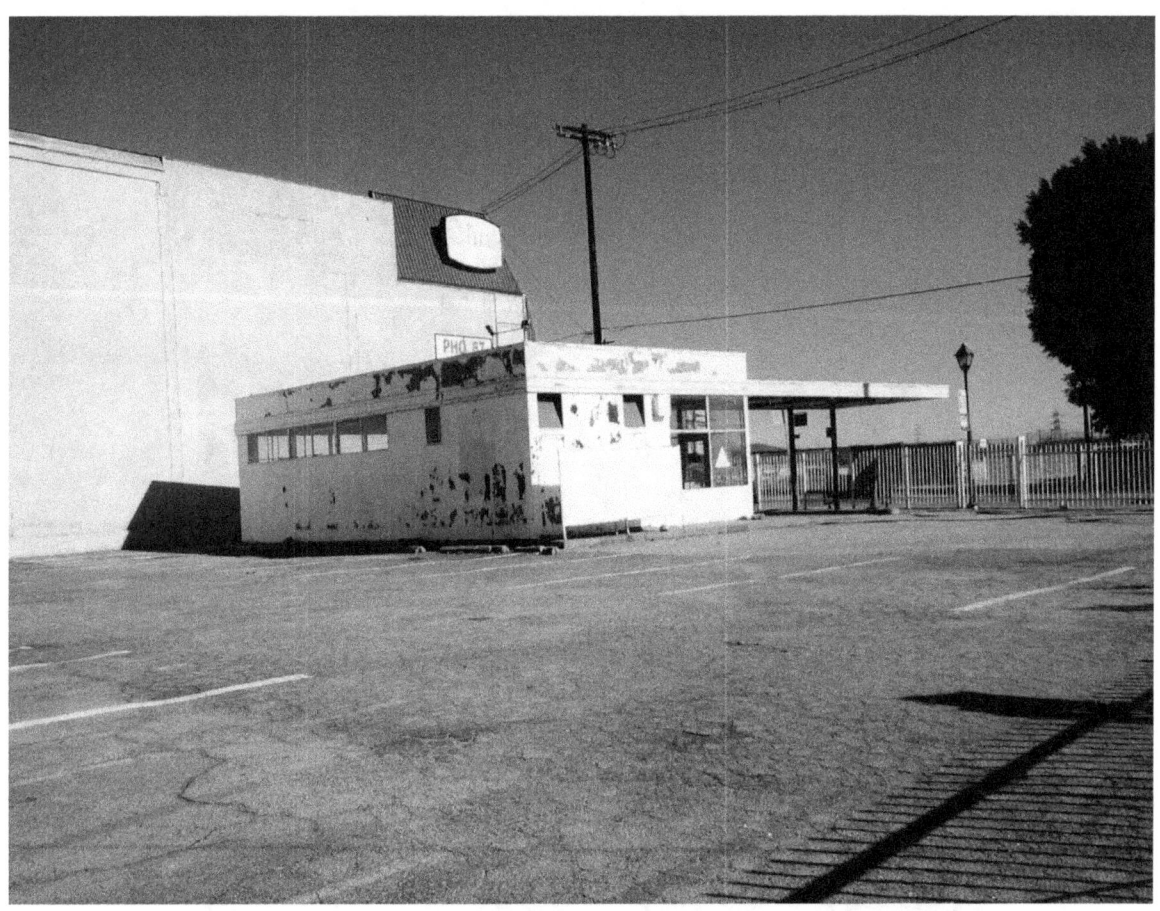

CHINATOWN

969 N. Broadway

A Chinatown landmark since 1938, the Phoenix Bakery, run by the Chan family, serves up treats like dim-sum, chocolates, and a variety of pastries—including one dubbed "Pineapple Express"—as well as their legendary birthday cakes.

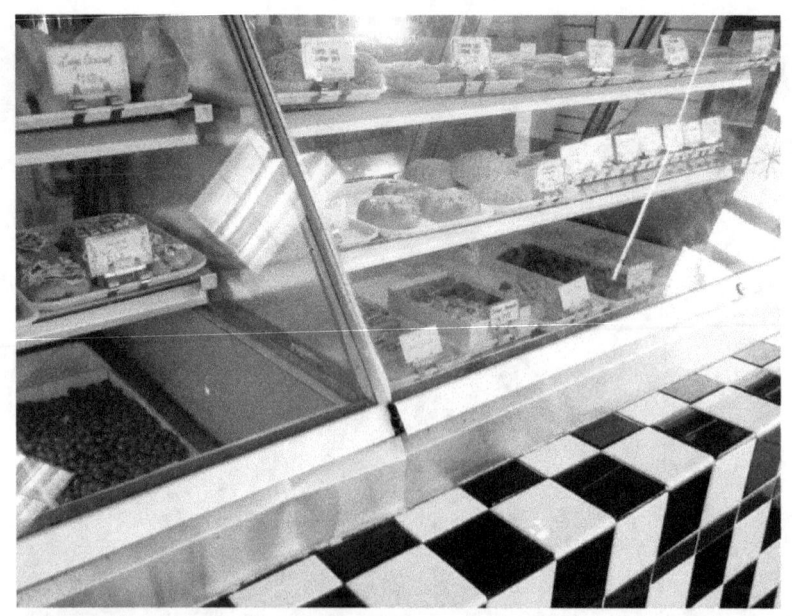

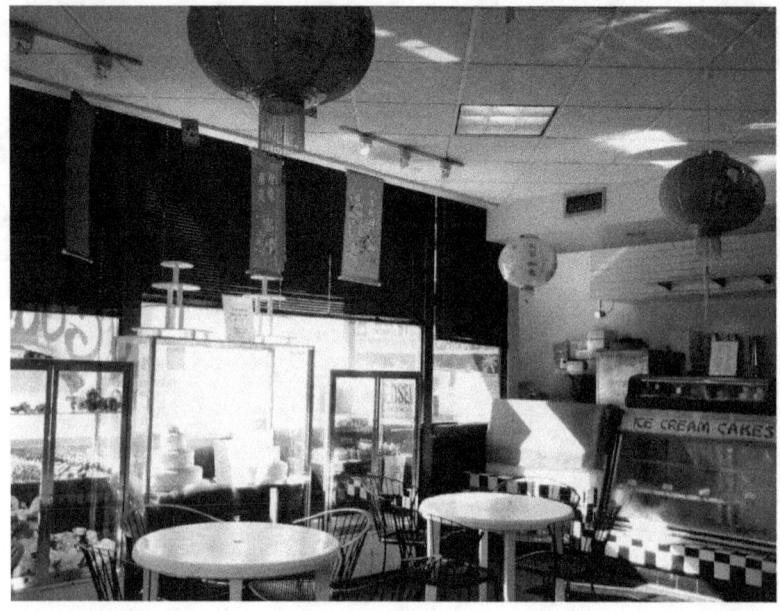

CHINATOWN

N. Broadway

Chinatown vendors sell Chinese-language periodicals, displaying them in newspaper racks outside the shops. Most business signs in multi-lingual Chinatown are printed in English and Chinese, and sometimes in Vietnamese, Korean, Cambodian, or other Asian language as well.

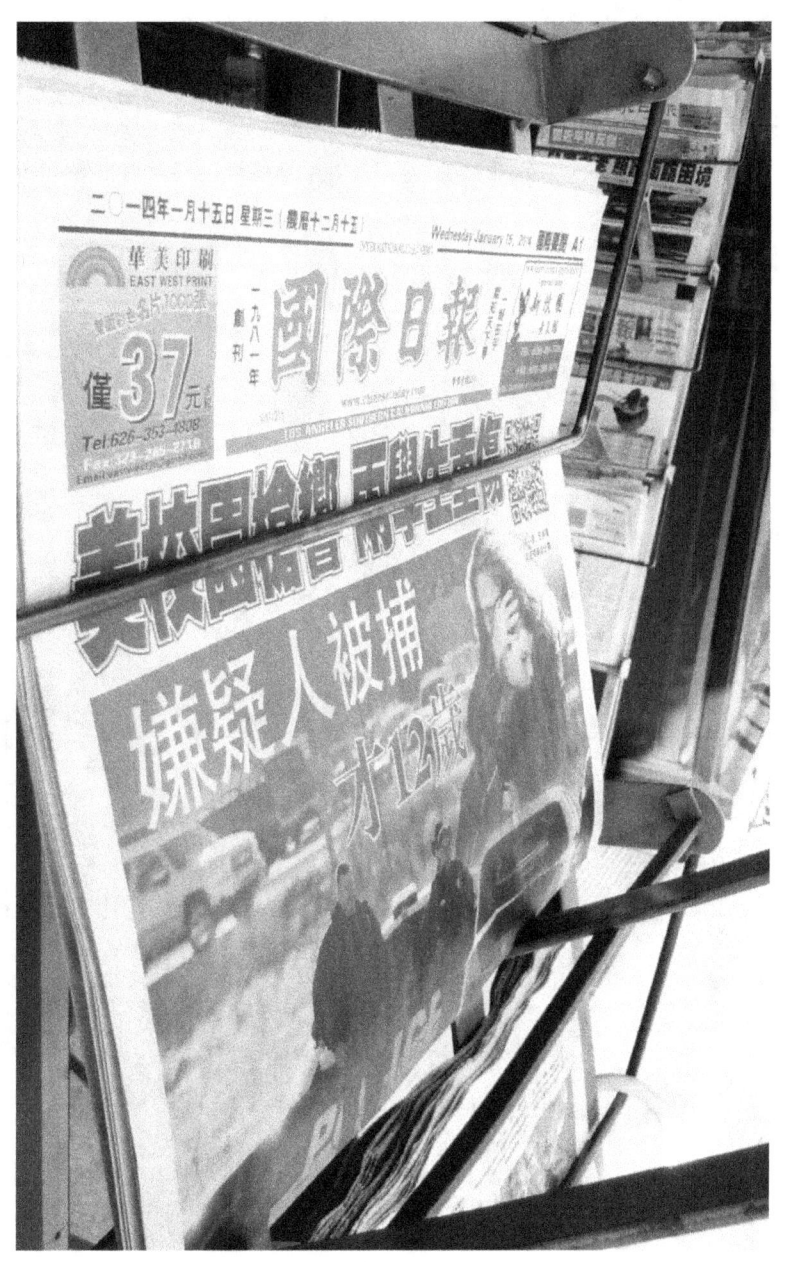

CHINATOWN

943 N. Broadway

When most people think of Chinatown in Los Angeles, they visualize the city's "Old Chinatown" and its Central Plaza between N. Broadway and N. Hill Street. Pictured here is the grand "East Gate" through which tourists and residents enter the plaza. At night the gate—the entire district—is ablaze with neon. Chinatown in Los Angeles was originally located around the present site of Union Station, near Alameda Street. The Chinese community was displaced to make way for rail yards, Union Station, and a modern transportation hub. The Chinatown Central Plaza we know today debuted in 1938, and it was a Chinese and Chinese-American-planned and run effort both then and now. It should not be confused with "China City," a project organized by leading citizen Christine Sterling, who also drove the development of Olvera Street. Picturesque and exotic "China City" co-existed with the Central Plaza from the 1930's through the 1950's when fires eventually finished "China City".

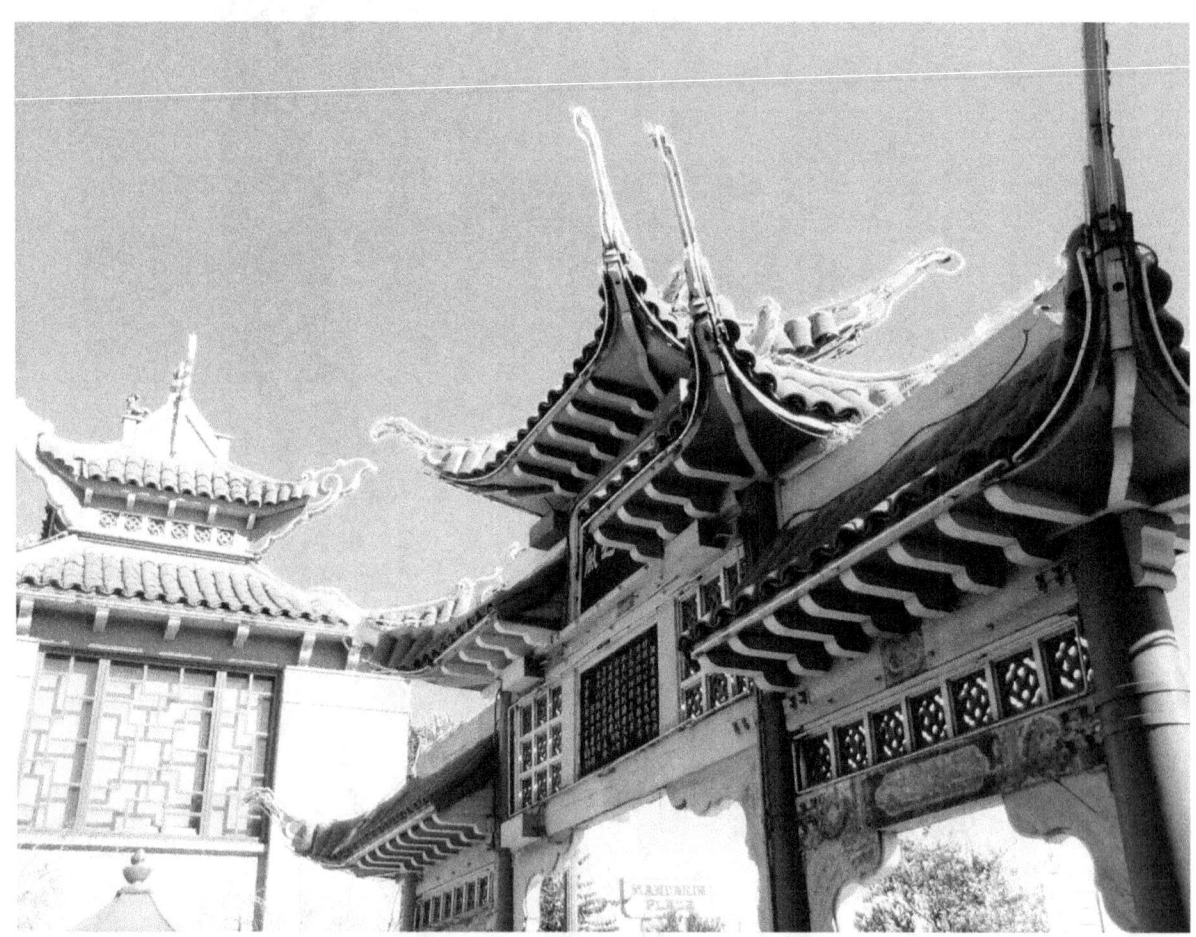

CHINATOWN

943 N. Broadway

Known as "New Chinatown" when it opened in 1938, Chinatown's Central Plaza has always featured paper lanterns, traditional Asian architecture painted in cheerful colors, Chinese food and Chinese products, gift shops, pagodas, wishing wells, and fortune tellers.

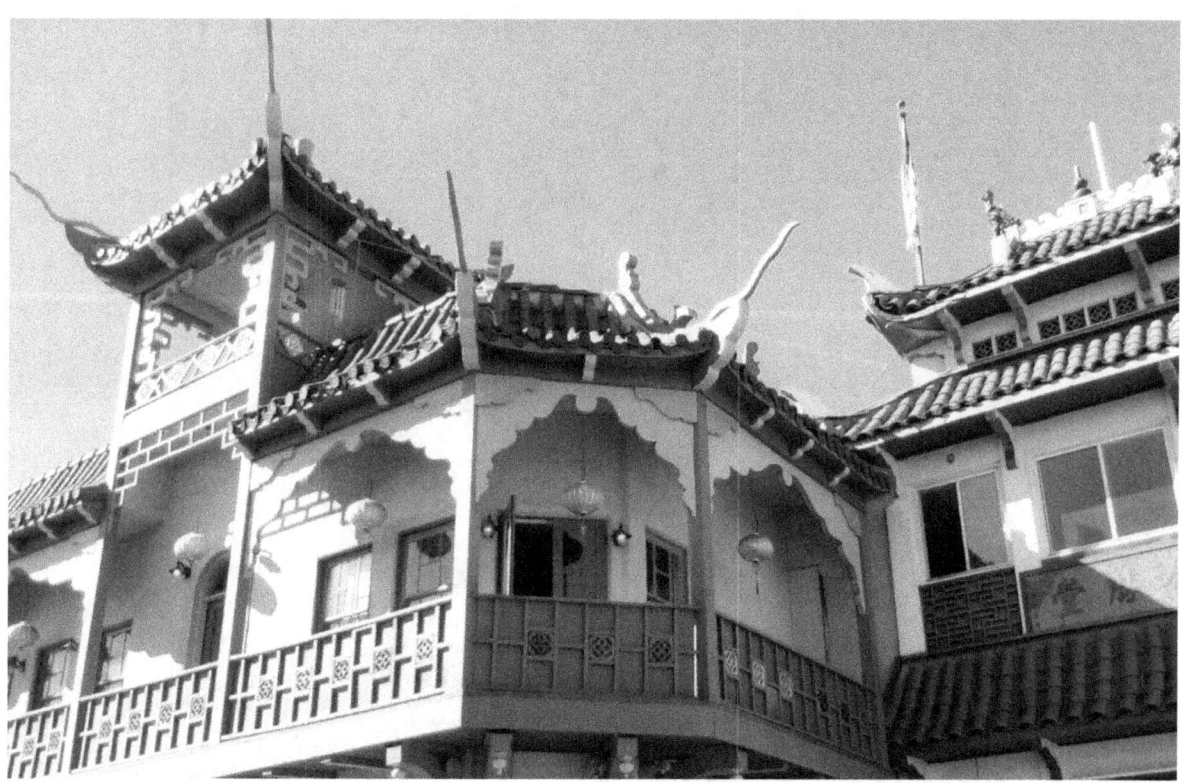

CHINATOWN

943 N. Broadway

A statue of Dr. Sun Yat-Sen, founder and first president of the Republic of China, greets visitors who enter the Central Plaza via Broadway's East Gate.

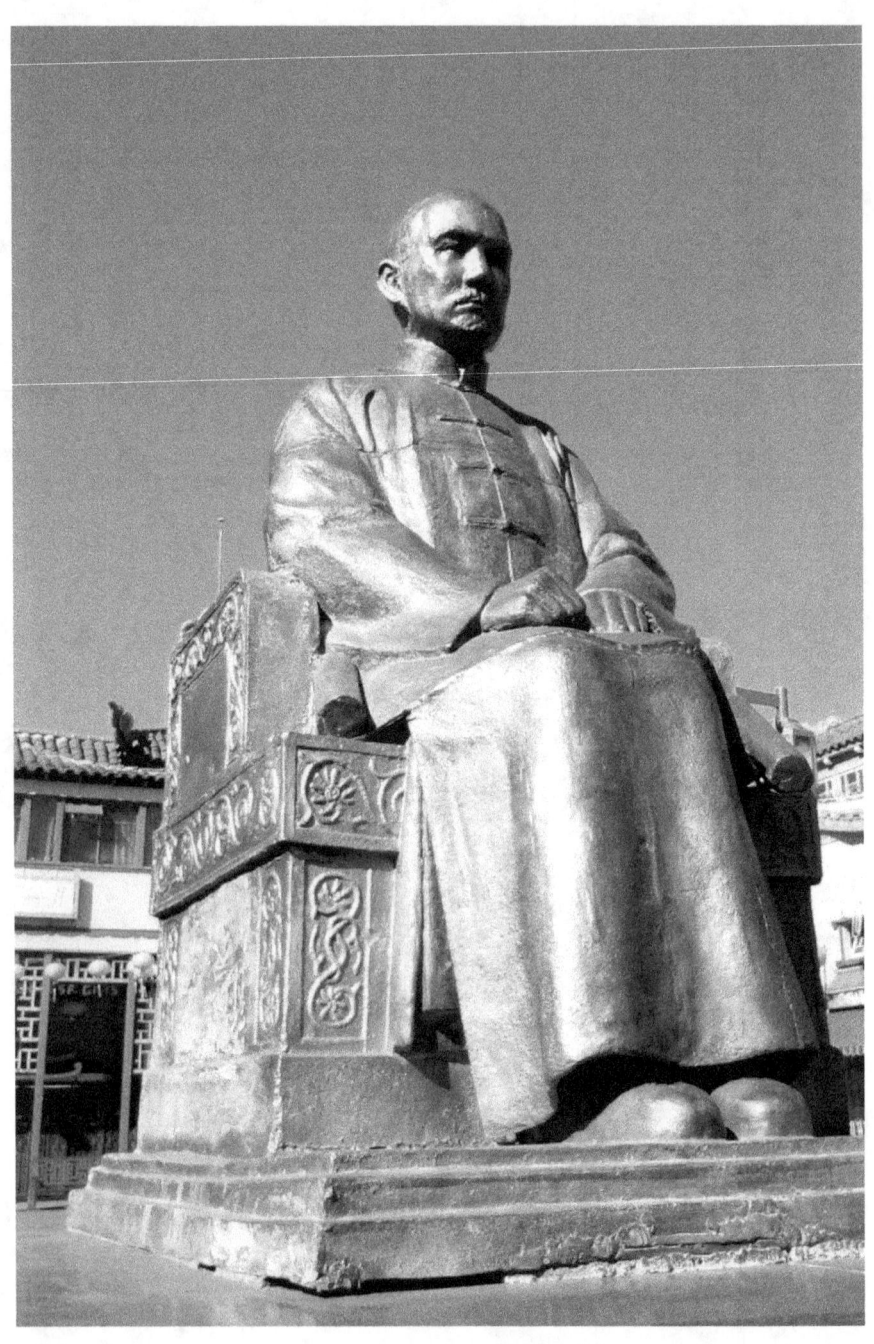

CHINATOWN

943 N. Broadway

Many motion pictures and television programs have been filmed in the Central Plaza, including "Hart to Hart," "Hunter," "Melrose Place," "The Rockford Files," "Lethal Weapon 4," and "Rush Hour". The most famous film to feature scenes in Chinatown is the 1974 Roman Polanski film "Chinatown". Set in the 1930's—a time of tumultuous growth in Los Angeles, including the displacement of the original Chinatown—the Academy Award-winning drama explores corruption among LA's elite, especially in water, power, and land development. Old Chinatown serves as a metaphor for a place or situation which is so opaque and complicated, outsiders should do nothing rather than risk causing harm.

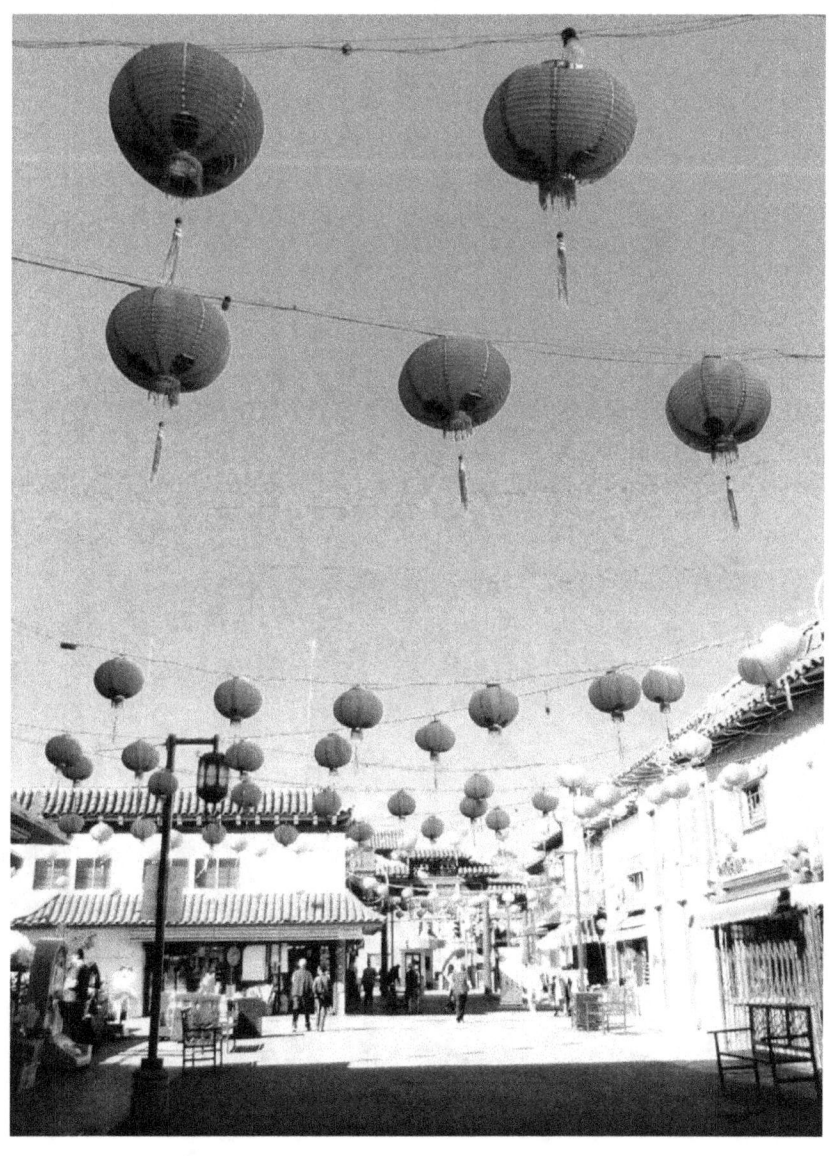

CHINATOWN

943 N. Broadway

Hop Louie (street address 950 Mei Ling Wei) is located in the southwest corner of the Central Plaza. A visually striking landmark, Hop Louise is a popular—even beloved—restaurant and bar. Although Hop Louie is famous for its tiered pagoda exterior, it's known locally for affordable appetizers, old-school drinks, the jukebox, and a genuine retro vibe. Many a film has used Hop Louie as a backdrop since it opened in 1941, particularly when the pagoda comes alive with neon at night.

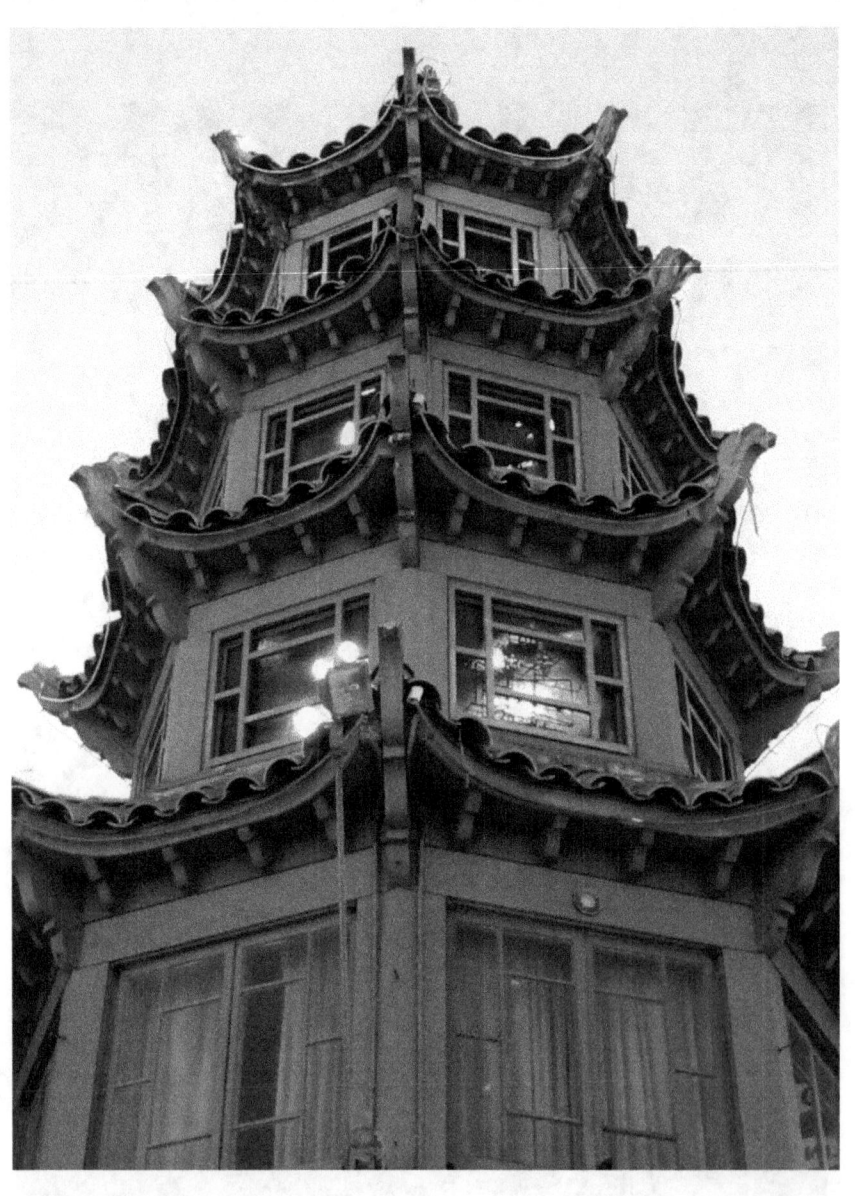

CHINATOWN

943 N. Broadway

Hop Louie's glass door reflects foliage that separates the plaza from N. Hill Street to the west.

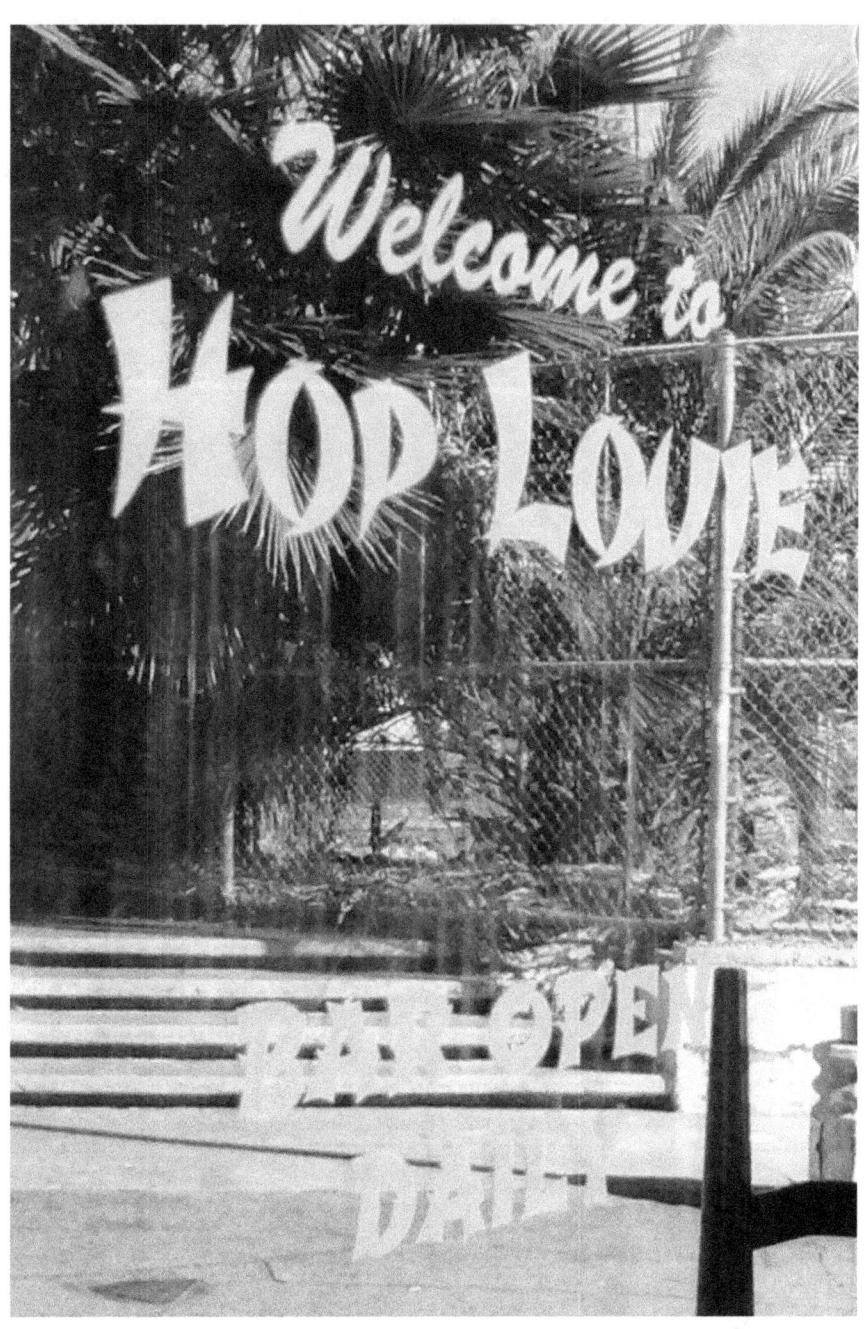

CHINATOWN

943 N. Broadway

Some of the businesses in Chinatown's Central Plaza are still owned and managed by the same families that opened them in 1938. Sincere Imports, for example, is still owned and run by the daughter-in-law of the man who launched it in the 1930's. She took over the shop in 1980, and continues to run it, as well as a second store across the plaza. Knowledgeable about local Chinatown history, she relates a tale of lost treasures; early Chinese immigrants cleverly hid their wealth in vases within vases, but the vessels holding the treasure were subsequently entombed in earth and concrete during construction of the nearby freeways. Pictured here is the Central Plaza's West Gate, which leads visitors to Hill Street. Tourists often snap photos of this Chinatown landmark.

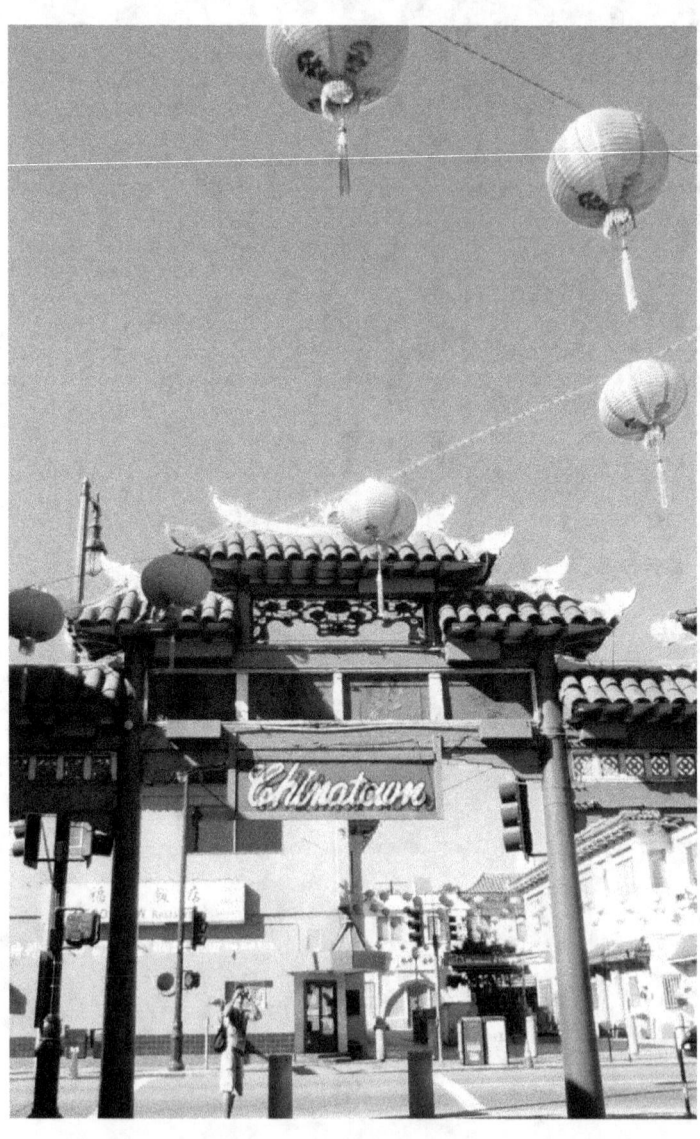

LITTLE ITALY

N. Broadway & College Street

This decrepit-looking building behind the construction fence was Little Joe's Italian Restaurant, a well-known Chinatown landmark and one of the neighborhood's many clues that this district was once "Little Italy". The "Joe" was Joe Vivaldi, who opened a grocery store at this location in 1927. He sold sandwiches and lunches to the workers (many of whom were Italian) who built Union Station. Simple meals sold over the grocery counter led to the construction of a restaurant that operated until 1998 under the ownership and management of the Nuccio family—three generations of stewardship.

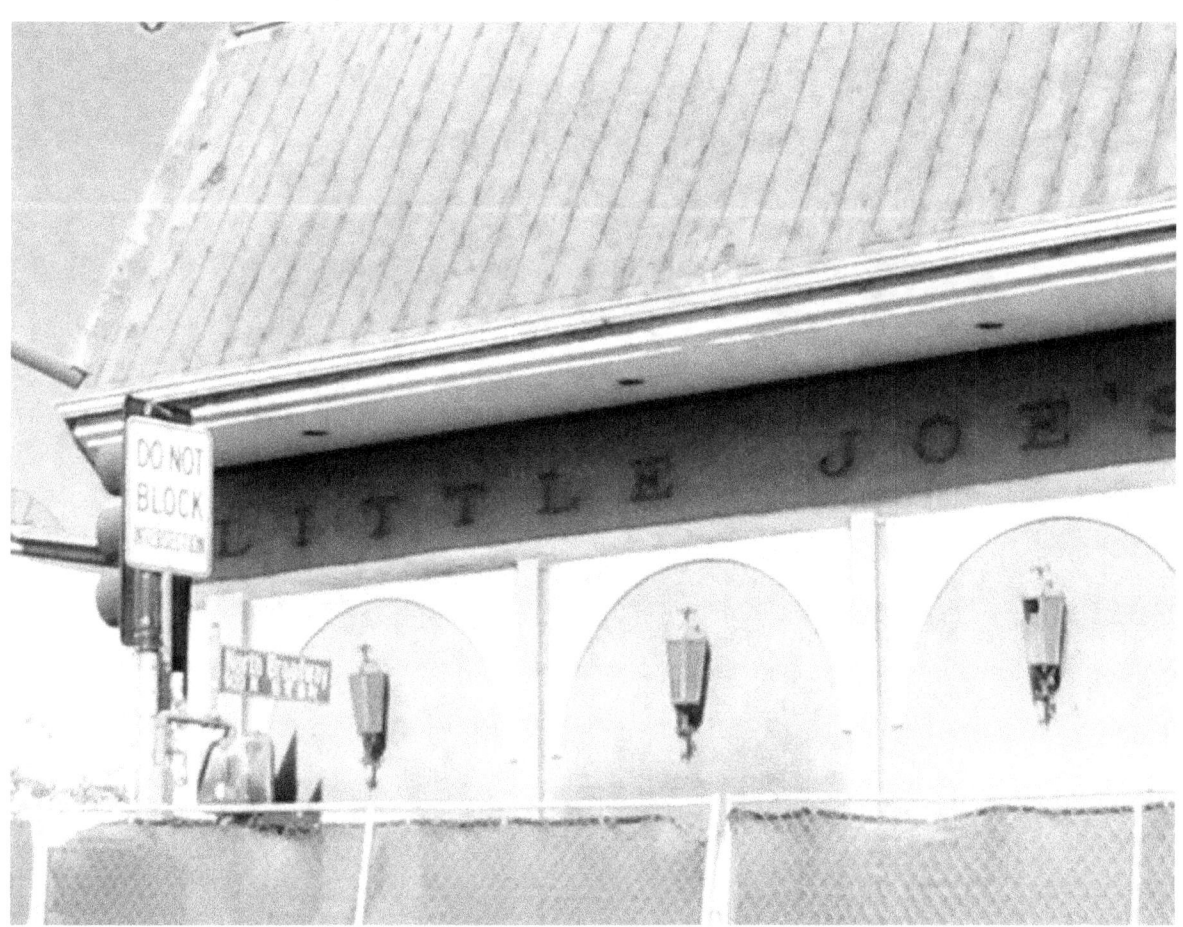

LITTLE ITALY

N. Broadway & College Street

Many generations of Angelenos recall dining at Little Joe's. By the late 1990's, however, Downtown L.A, including Chinatown, had faded as a popular nighttime destination. And Old Town Pasadena's late-1990's revival further diverted diners. The Nuccios closed Little Joe's in 1998. It sat vacant until December 2013, when demolition began. These photos, taken in January 2014, show demolition in progress. These are among the last photos taken of Little Joe's before it was razed. What will replace it? This corner will be the site of a new mixed-use project that includes apartments and retail spaces.

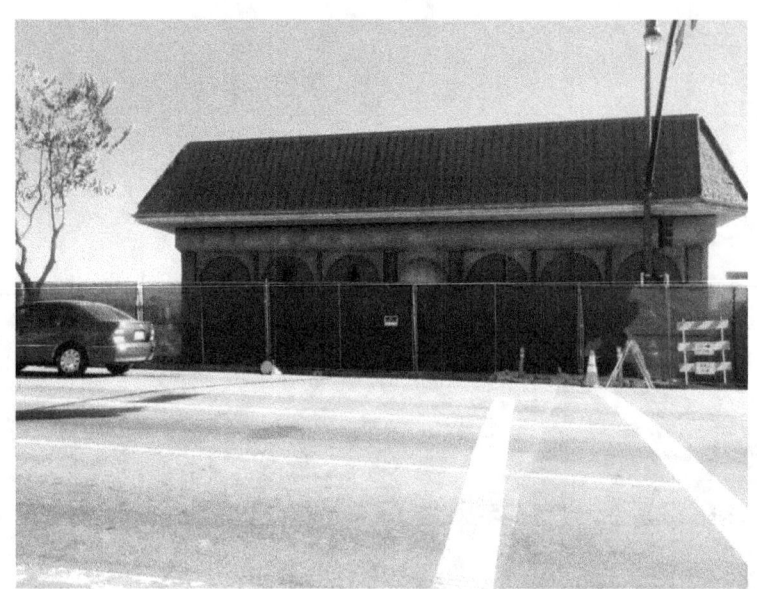

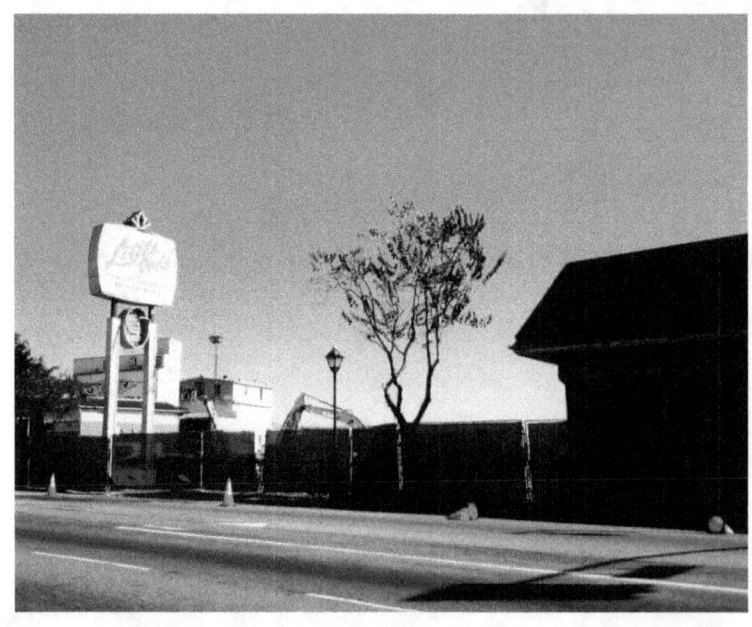

CHINATOWN

N. Broadway

Visitors strolling south on North Broadway from the Central Plaza to Cesar Chavez Avenue will encounter numerous businesses, from banks to jewelers to dentists and optometrists, Chinese restaurants, bakeries, grocers, seafood mongers, florists, and myriad gift shops. It feels like you can buy anything in Chinatown. The air is scented with freshly cut oranges, and incense burning in rooms just off the shops. You'll find T-shirts, Irish caps, herbs, shoes, sunglasses, hats, purses, lucky bamboo plants, live crabs, and roasted pigs. Chickens cluck frantically behind a fence labeled "Pollos Vivos" ["Live Chickens"] and "No Entry". It's "no entry" for visitors, "no exit" for the fowl.

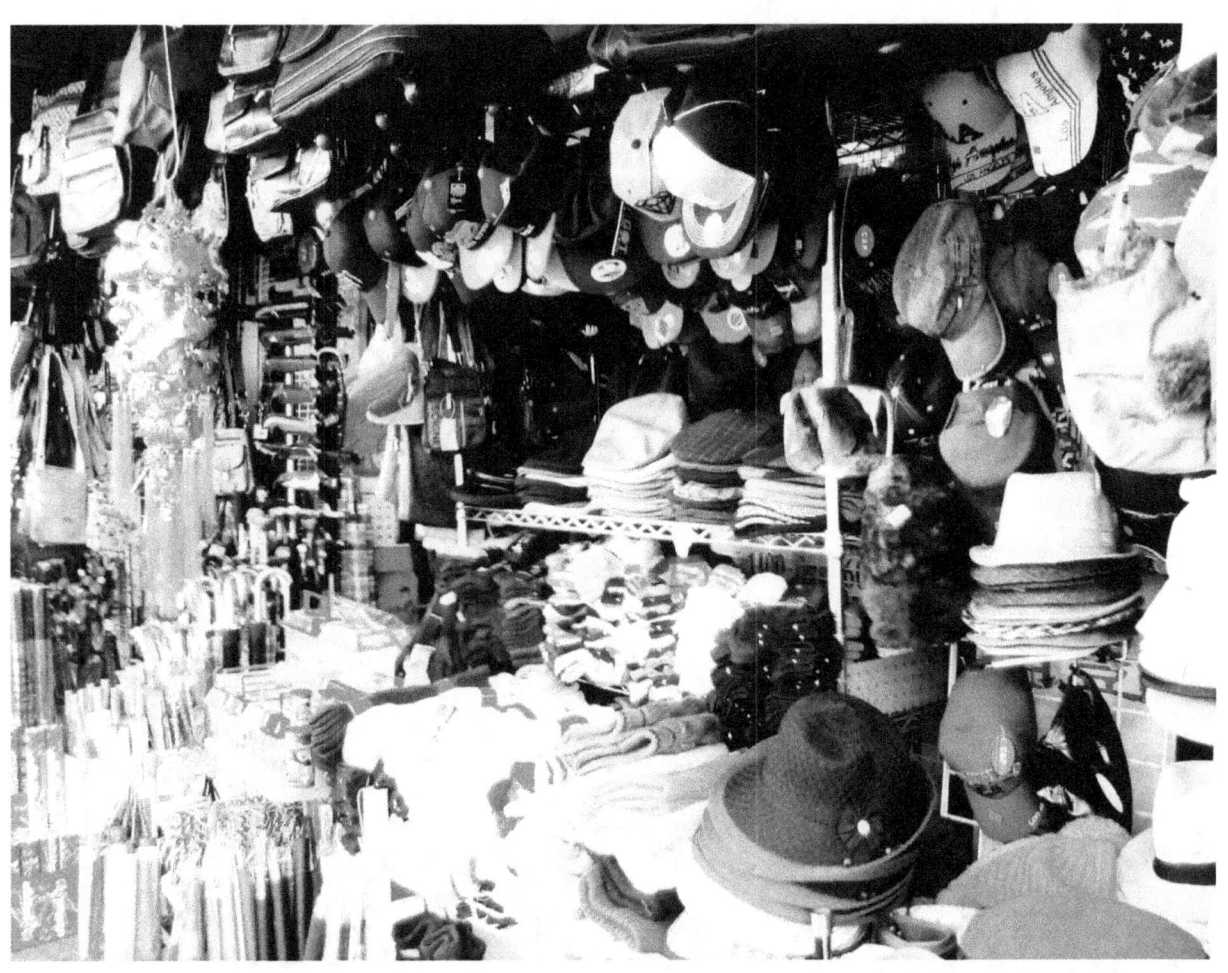

CHINATOWN

N. Broadway & Cesar Chavez Avenue

The Dragon Gate at Broadway and Cesar Chavez marks the southern border of Chinatown. Fantastic golden dragons face-off high above the street, and glow with neon at night. Note the brand new residential building beyond the gate (bottom right corner of the top photo), one of many signs of Chinatown's continued vitality. In the shadow of the Dragon Gate, Chinatown's elderly citizens stroll or relax on benches near the senior center on the northeast corner of Broadway and Cesar Chavez.

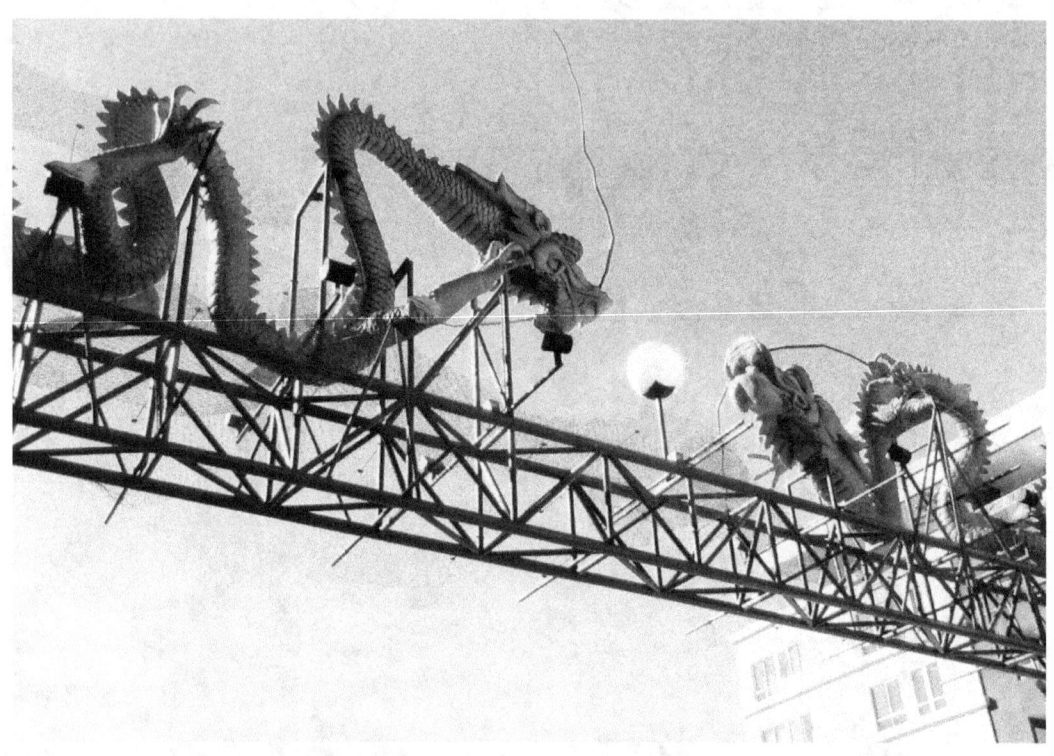

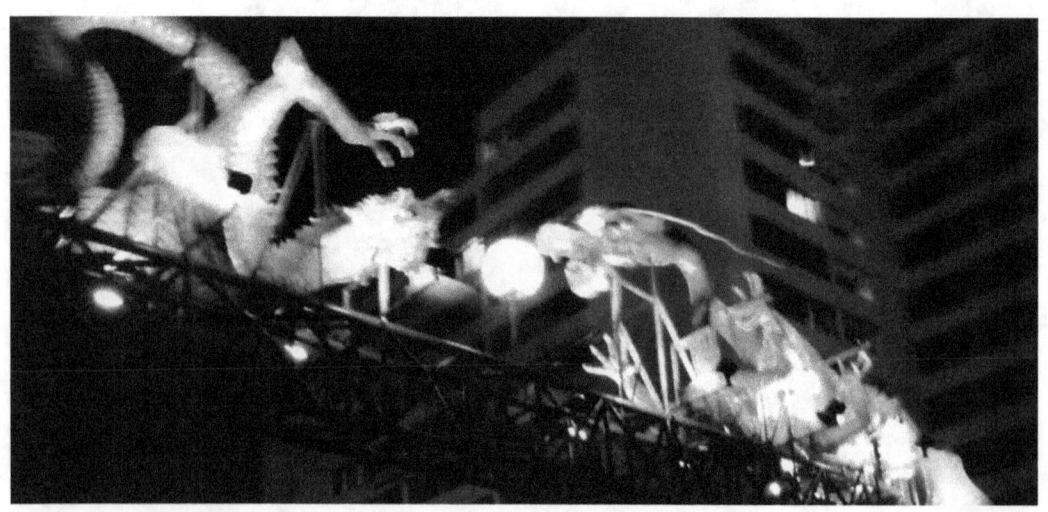

CHINATOWN

N. Broadway and Cesar Chavez Avenue

A vibrant sign on the Dragon Gate's west support post. A note about Cesar Chavez Avenue: Originally the eastern portion of Sunset Boulevard (as well as Macy Street and Brooklyn Avenue in East LA), Cesar Chavez Avenue was created in 1994 in honor of union leader and farm workers' rights crusader Cesar Chavez.

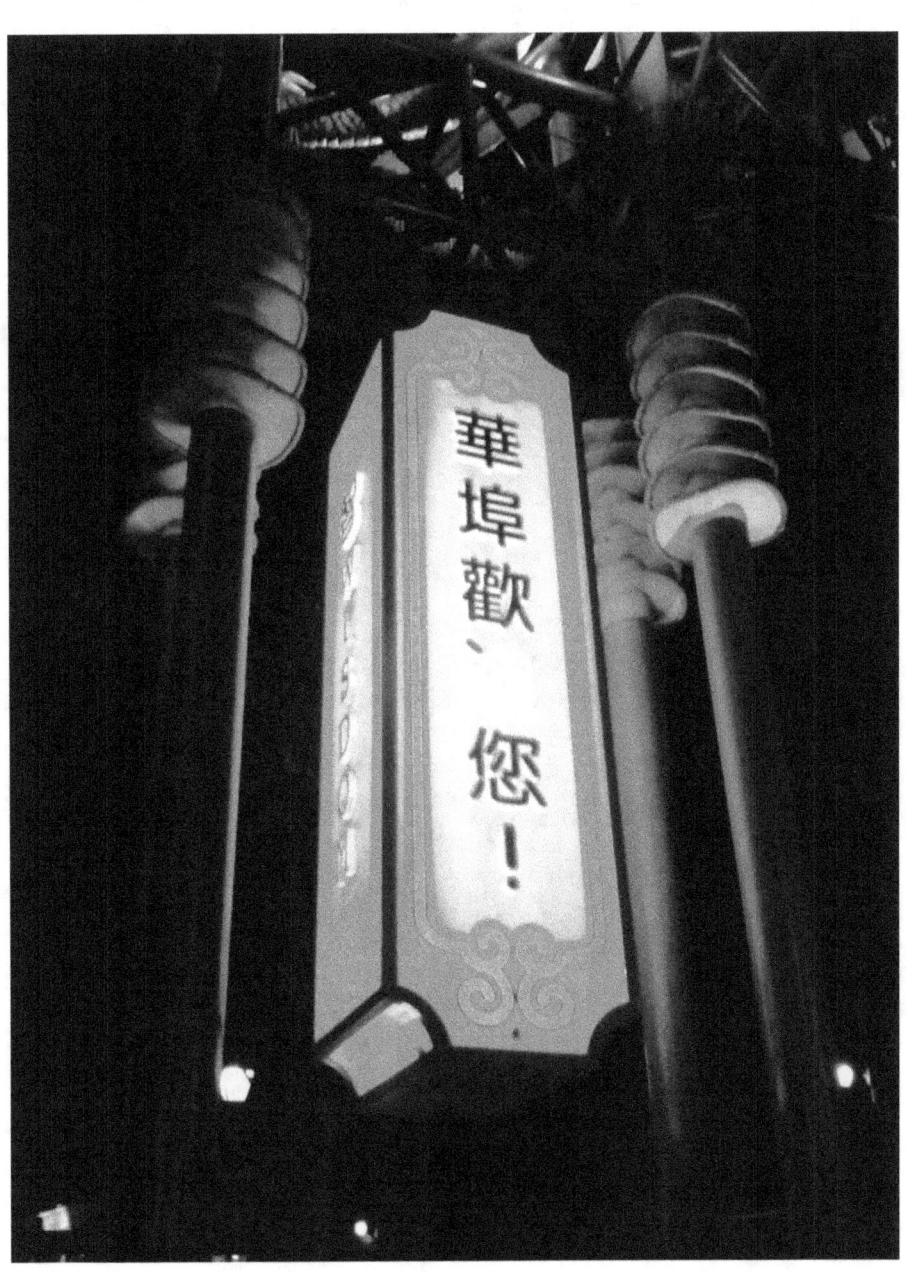

FORT MOORE HILL

400 – 300 Blocks of N. Broadway

Broadway wasn't always called "Broadway". In 1849, Fort Street, laid out by surveyor Lt. Edward Ord, became a connecting corridor between the downtown district and Fort Moore, perched high atop Fort Moore Hill. The fort had been very recently constructed (in 1847) during the Mexican-American war, built to protect U.S. soldiers under frequent attack by local Californios. Wealthy landowners like Pio Pico had no interest in ceding Alta California to the United States. However, Mexico lost the war. California became part of the U.S.; and Fort Moore soon served no purpose. The fort quickly fell into disuse and disrepair, but the name "Fort Street" remained until 1890. Pictured here: A 2014 view looking south along the 400 – 300 blocks of North Broadway. Note the Federal Courthouse (left), LA City Hall (center), the columned Hall of Justice (center-right) with the more modern Criminal Courts building peeking out behind it, and the Hall of Records (far right).

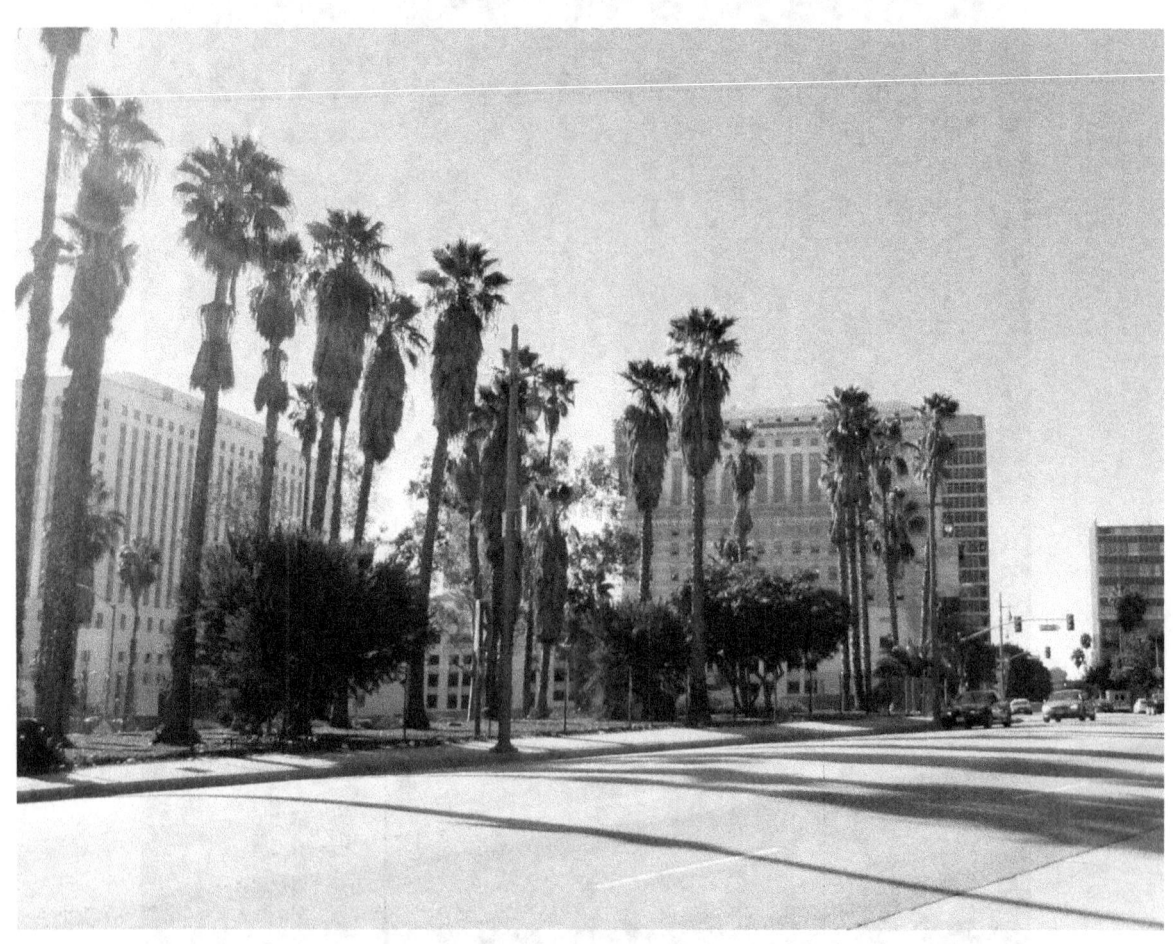

FORT MOORE HILL

400 – 300 Blocks of N. Broadway

After the fort was decommissioned, a beer garden and a cemetery were built atop Fort Moore Hill, providing ease for both the living and the dead. In its heyday, the hill blossomed into an elite neighborhood featuring mansions inhabited by the likes of Mary Banning (Phineas Banning's widow), a grande dame of early Los Angeles society. But gradually the rich moved westward, the mansions became boarding houses, and the hilltop neighborhood lapsed into shabbiness, except for Los Angeles High School on the western edge. Over time, Fort Moore—and most of the hill on which it stood—was removed. Bodies that had been buried in the hill were repeatedly unearthed during construction projects, even after the city moved what they had believed to be all of the remains to other LA cemeteries. Fort Moore Hill has always attracted rumors of buried Mexican and Spanish treasure caches. The tantalizing stories persisted; every few decades, people caught gold fever and went digging. No treasure was ever discovered, but diggers continued to uncover bodies (most recently when LA's High School of the Performing Arts was built). All that presently remains along this stretch between N. Broadway and N. Hill Street is a gently sloping rise cordoned off with chain link fences. On the west side of N. Hill Street is a rather neglected memorial to Fort Moore (the obelisk and flag).

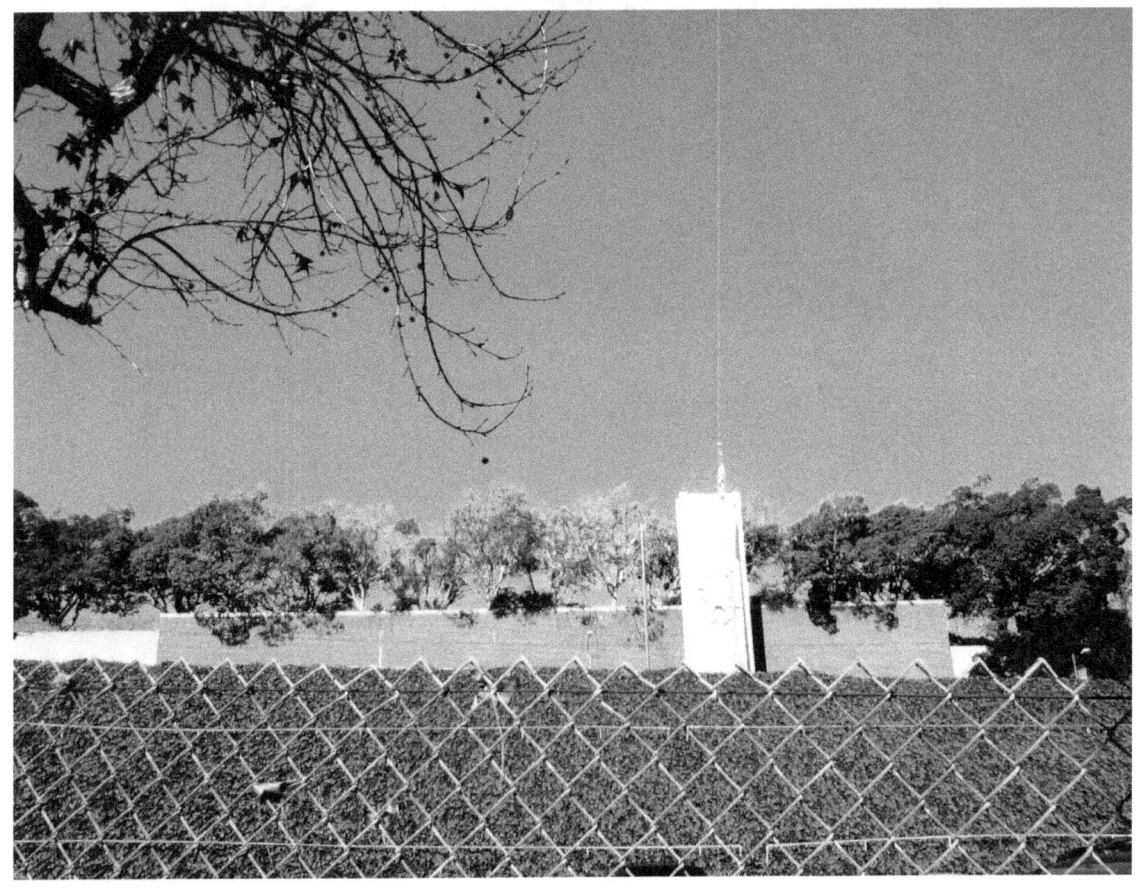

FORT MOORE HILL

400 – 300 Blocks of N. Broadway

This steep staircase leads from N. Broadway to the Fort Moore Pioneer Memorial. The view is facing westward (and upward) from N. Broadway to N. Hill. Though difficult to see in this photograph, there's an abandoned shopping cart near the top of the steps. This area is nearly devoid of regular pedestrian traffic, and a haven for LA's homeless.

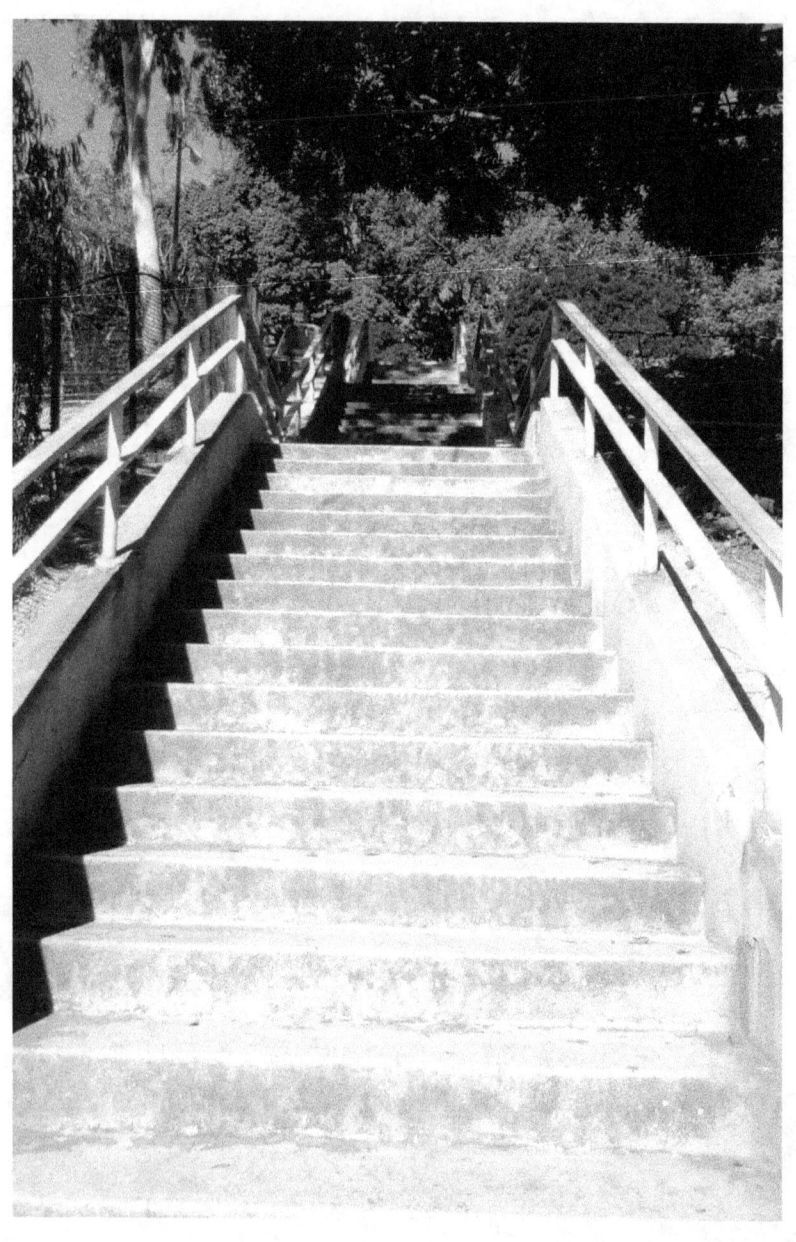

FORT MOORE HILL

400 – 300 Blocks of N. Hill Street

In 1957 the Fort Moore Pioneer Memorial was unveiled. As the multiple bas-relief sculptures show, it was designed as a tribute not only to the U.S. soldiers who built the fort but also to the ranchers, the pioneer settlers, and the water-and-power magnates (shades of "Chinatown") who made Los Angeles a habitable community. Although much of the monument has a weary and neglected air, these bas-relief panels remain in good repair.

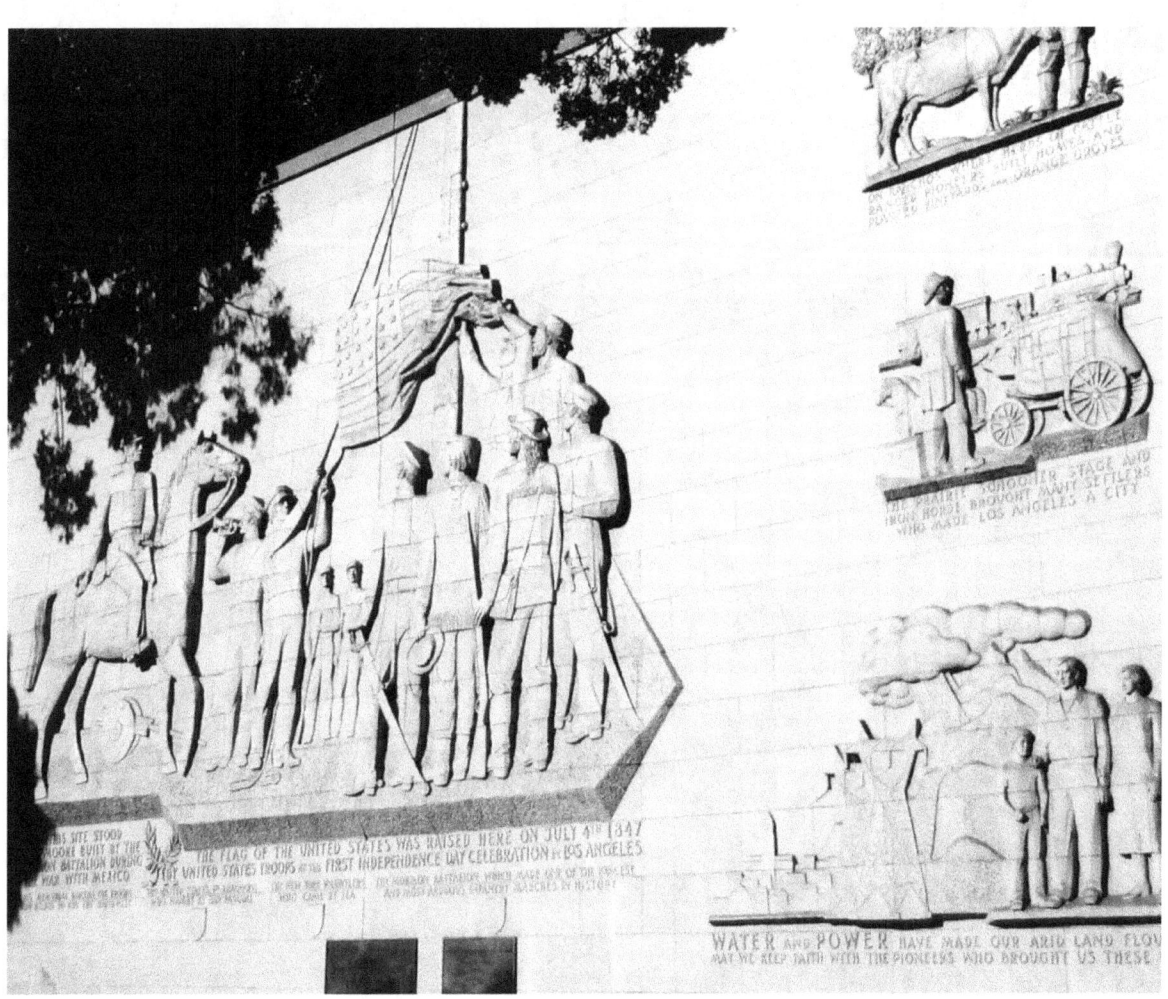

FORT MOORE HILL

400 – 300 Blocks of N. Hill Street

Originally the memorial featured a waterfall that flowed past a tiled wall into a pool 80 feet below, certainly a fitting element for a memorial that celebrated the might of LA's water-and-power magnates. Ironically, the water was turned off in 1977 due to severe drought—and the tap was never turned on again. Chipped and missing tiles, dry as a bone, look forlorn under the hot Southern California sun.

FORT MOORE HILL

400 - 300 Blocks of N. Hill Street

The Fort Moore Pioneer Memorial obelisk and flagpole draw the eye upward, toward the crest of what remains of the Fort Moore Hill.

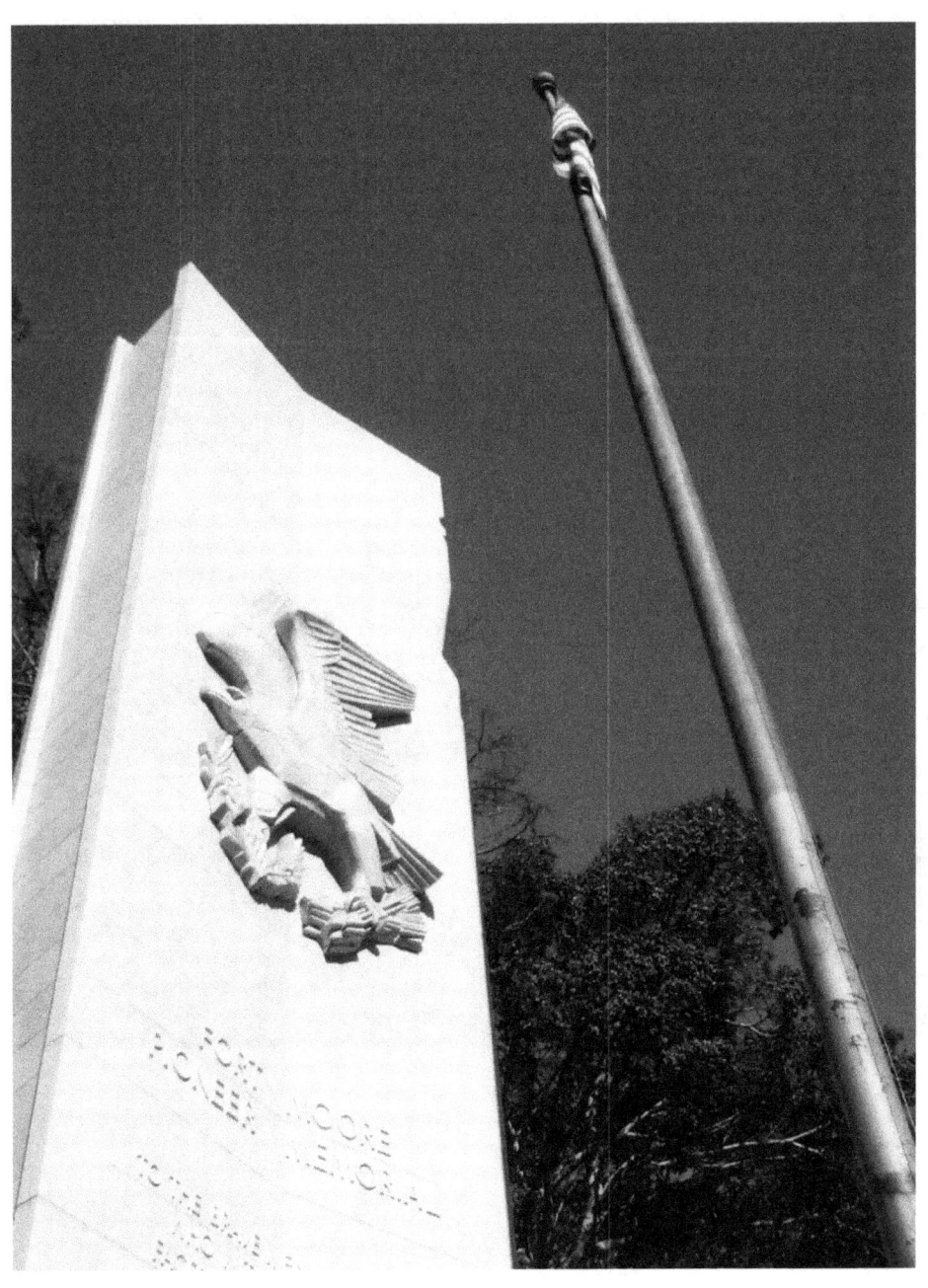

NORTH BROADWAY

400 – 300 Blocks of N. Broadway

Turning from the memorial to gaze east, here is the view looking down at N. Broadway, where a bus and car can be seen traveling from Chinatown (north) toward LA's Civic Center (south). Beyond Broadway are the Moorish turrets of the Postal Annex (left), the soaring LA Metro tower (center left), the Mission-style tower of Union Station (center), and the western wall of LA's original church "Our Lady, the Queen of the Angels" (right). The parking lot just beyond N. Broadway accommodates visitors to the Olvera Street district of which the historic church is a key feature.

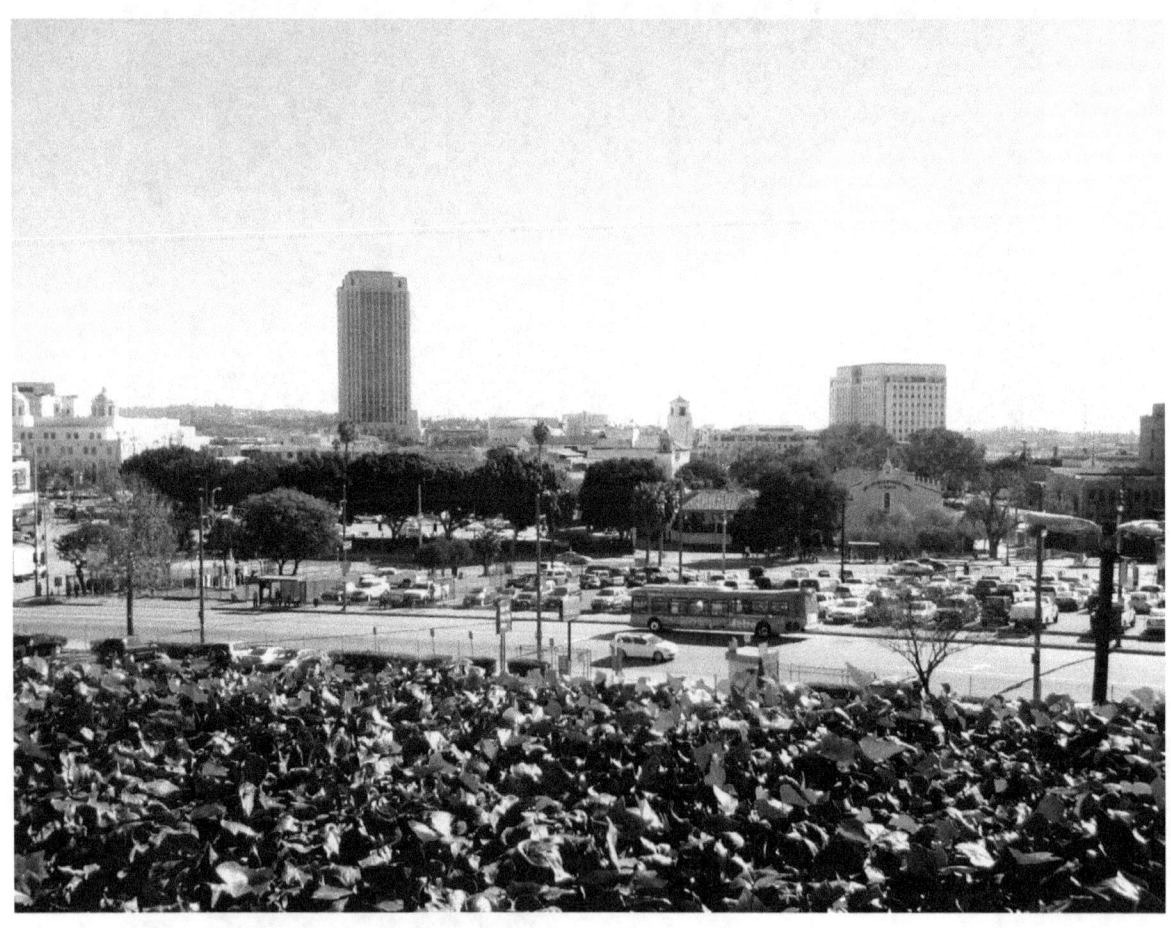

NORTH BROADWAY

300 – 200 Blocks of N. Broadway

Just south of the old site of Fort Moore, N. Broadway crosses the 101 (Hollywood) Freeway that cuts through Downtown LA. This is the view from N. Broadway looking west. The overpass in the near distance (center) is N. Hill Street; it runs parallel to the N. Broadway overpass from which the photograph was taken. To the north (right), not visible in this photo, is what remains of the historic Fort Moore site, now the property of the Los Angeles High School of the Performing Arts. To the south (left) in the photo, the Cathedral of Our Lady of the Angeles is visible—look for the pale stone cross in the dark glass window, and then to the right of that, the cathedral's campanile.

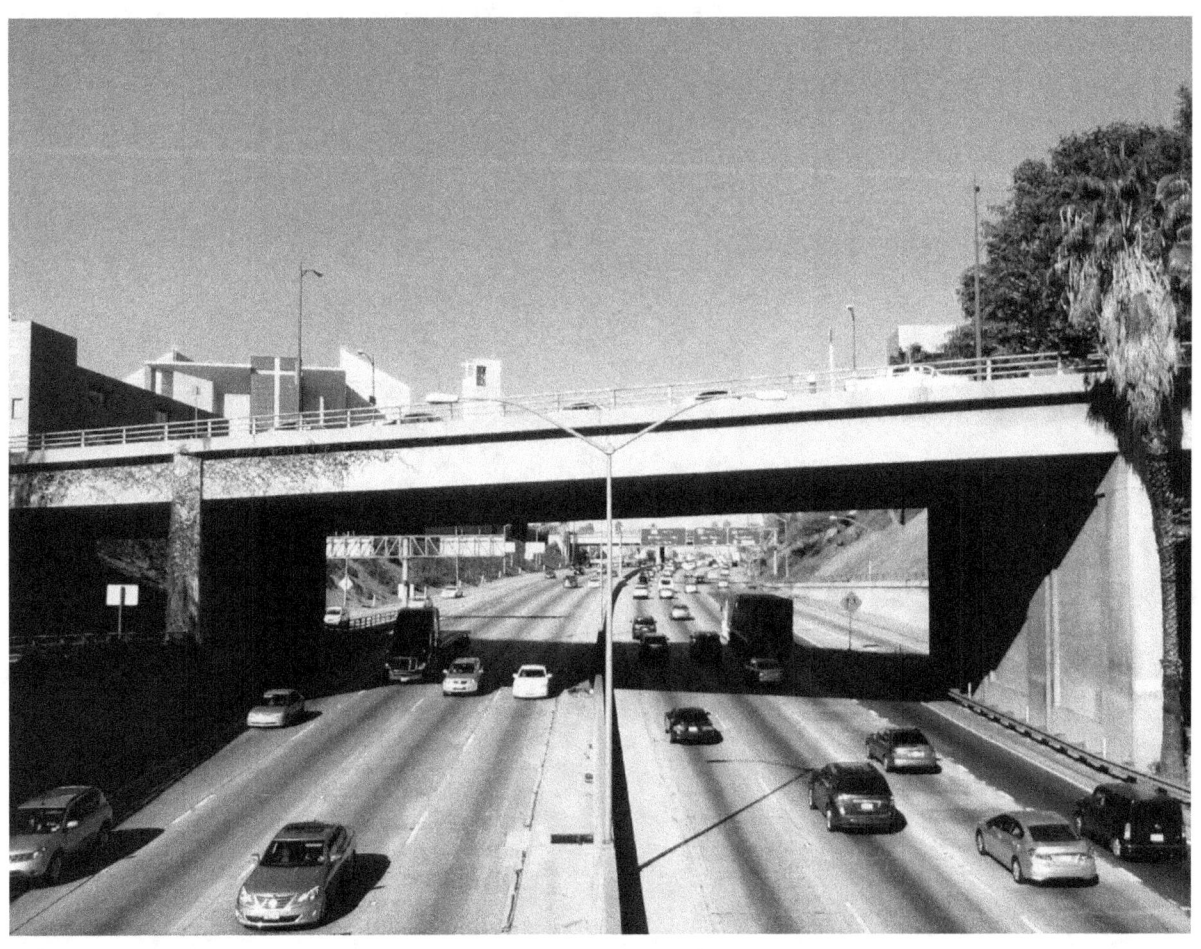

CIVIC CENTER

N. Broadway and Temple

Once it crosses the freeway, N. Broadway meanders through LA's Civic Center. Here the buildings become monumental, a symbol of LA's civic majesty. This photo shows the N. Broadway (west) side of LA's Hall of Justice. Completed in 1926, the Hall of Justice contained LA's courts, its coroner's office, and, on the top levels, its county jail. In early 2014, when this picture was taken, the Hall of Justice was just coming out of its "cocoon" following an extensive refurbishment. (The Hall of Justice had been closed in 1994 due to Northridge quake damage.) The N. Broadway side of the building is free of scaffolding, but scaffolds remain on the north face. Note the grandeur of the ornamentation and the columns. From its earliest days, Los Angeles sought to be recognized as a significant American city, and commissioned architects who designed the civic buildings with that gravitas in mind. The Hall of Justice reopens in 2014 as HQ for the Sheriffs and DA's office.

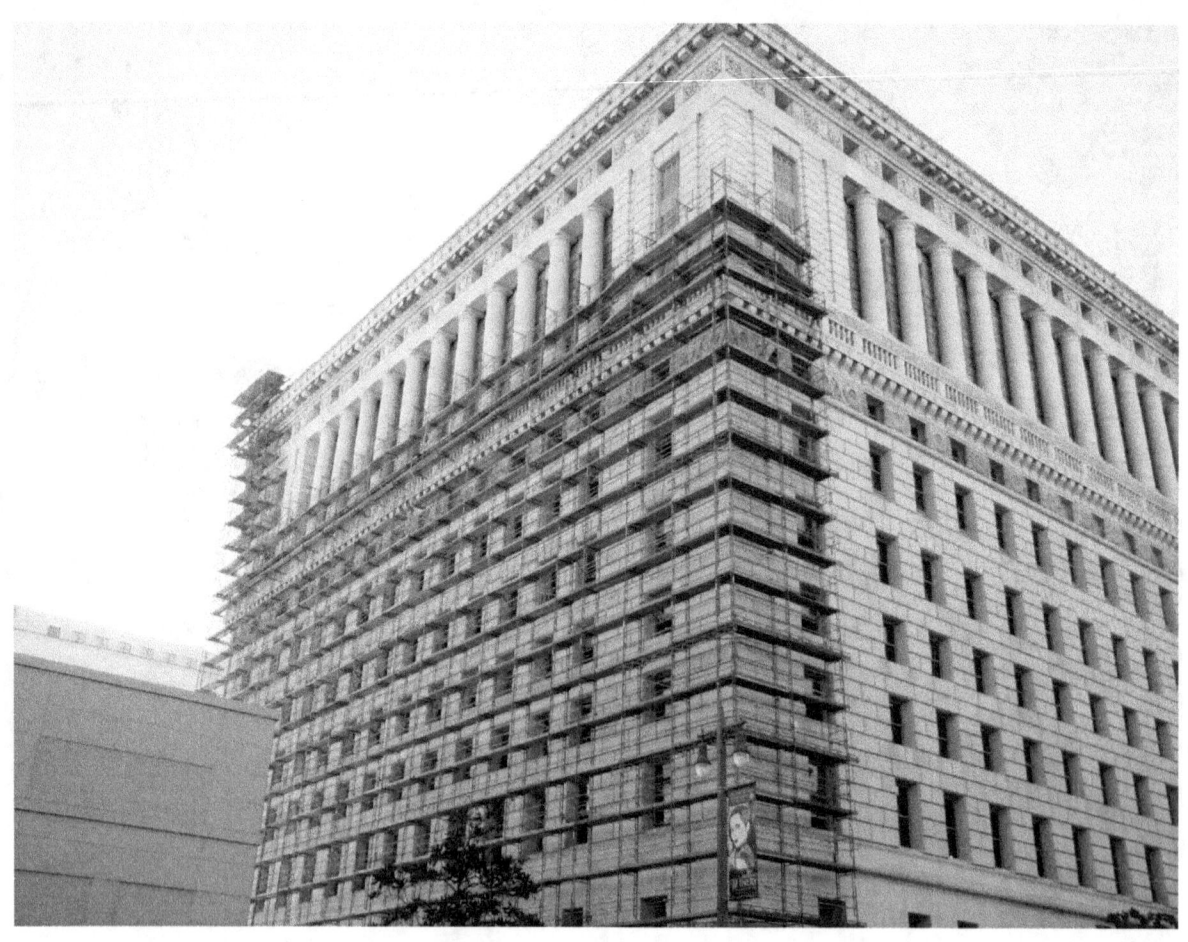

CIVIC CENTER

N. Broadway and Temple

On the upper levels of the Hall of Justice—photos of which often appeared as establishing shots on the "Perry Mason" TV program in the 1950's—prisoners awaited their trials, which would unfold in the courtrooms below. Following his arrest for orchestrating the terrifying "Helter Skelter" murders, Charles Manson spent time in this jail; he was assigned his own cell, away from the other prisoners. During the 2014 refurbishment, the jail cells were removed. Like the jail, the coroner's office has had its share of famous "visitors". Marilyn Monroe was brought there after her death.

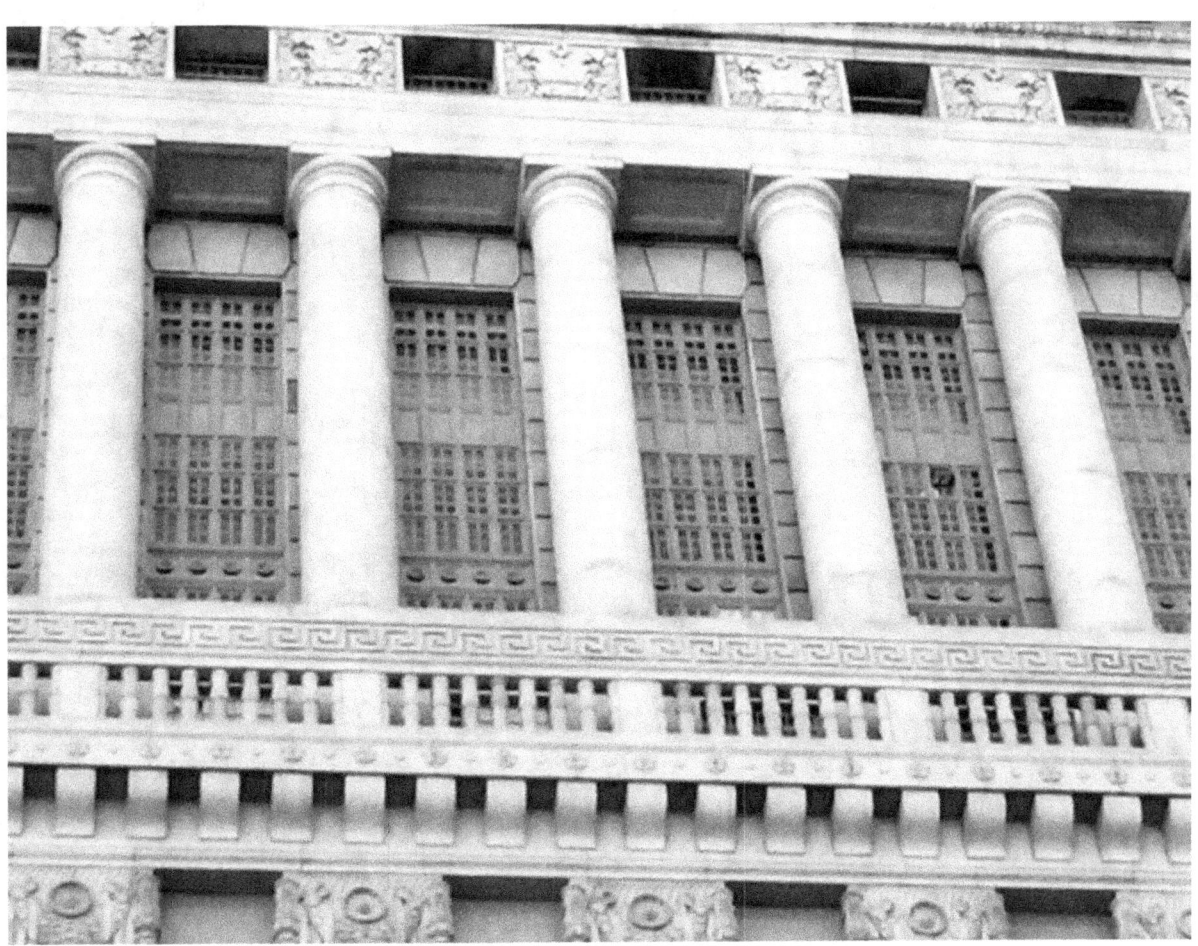

CIVIC CENTER

N. Broadway and Temple

On the north side of Temple Street stands the Hall of Justice (left). On the south of Temple Street stands LA's present criminal courts building, the Clara Shortridge Foltz Criminal Justice Center (right), which opened in 1972. Notice the shady old trees that line the sidewalks in the Civic Center district. This historical touch reminds us of what the district would have looked like in its early days.

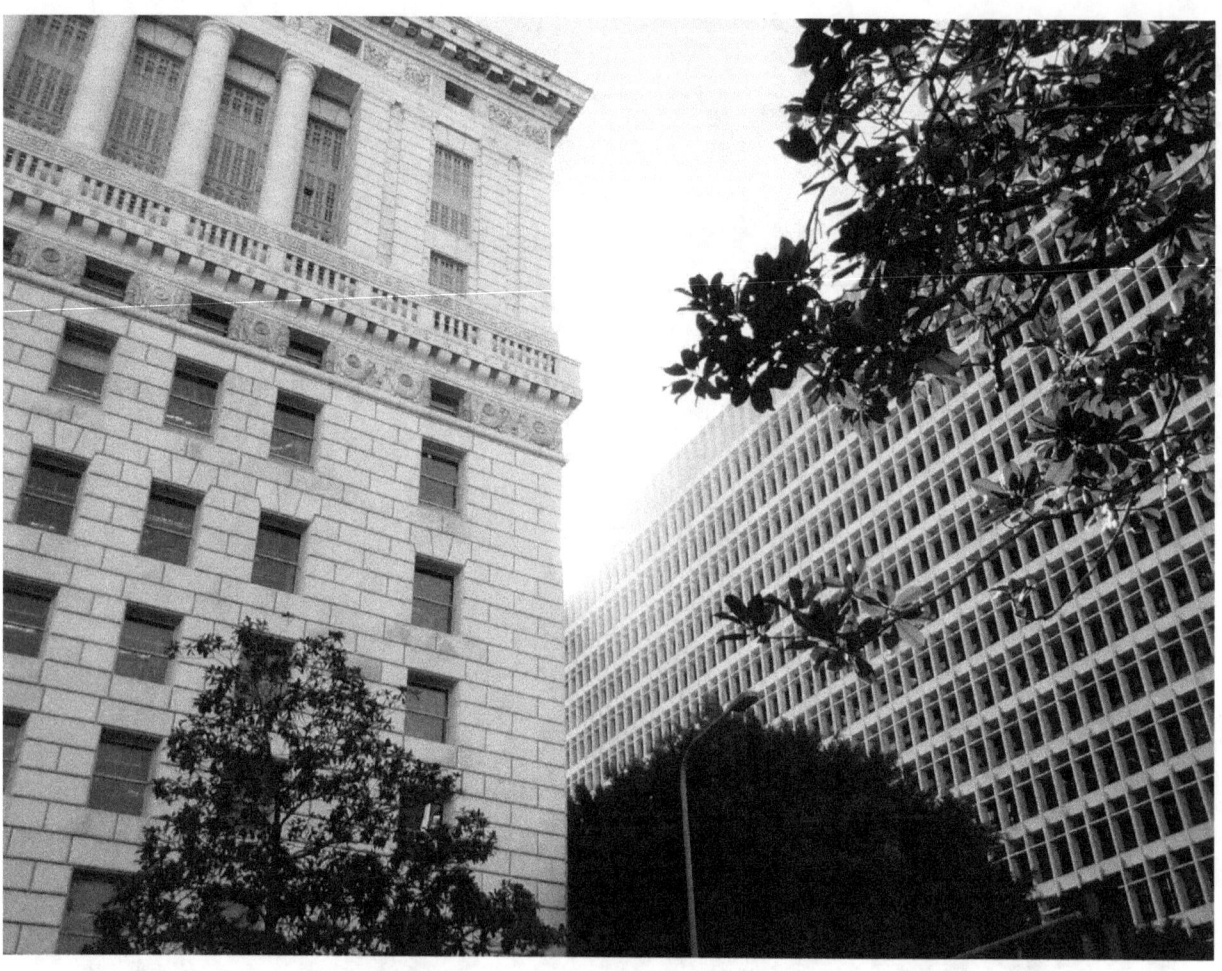

CIVIC CENTER

N. Broadway and Temple

This view of the N. Broadway side of the Hall of Justice highlights the beautiful trees that shade the Civic Center's sidewalks along Broadway, not only providing a glimpse of a past LA, but also balancing the monumental strength of the civic buildings. Note the corner of an industrial-style building (bottom left) across the street from the Hall of Justice: LA County's Central Heating and Refrigeration Plant.

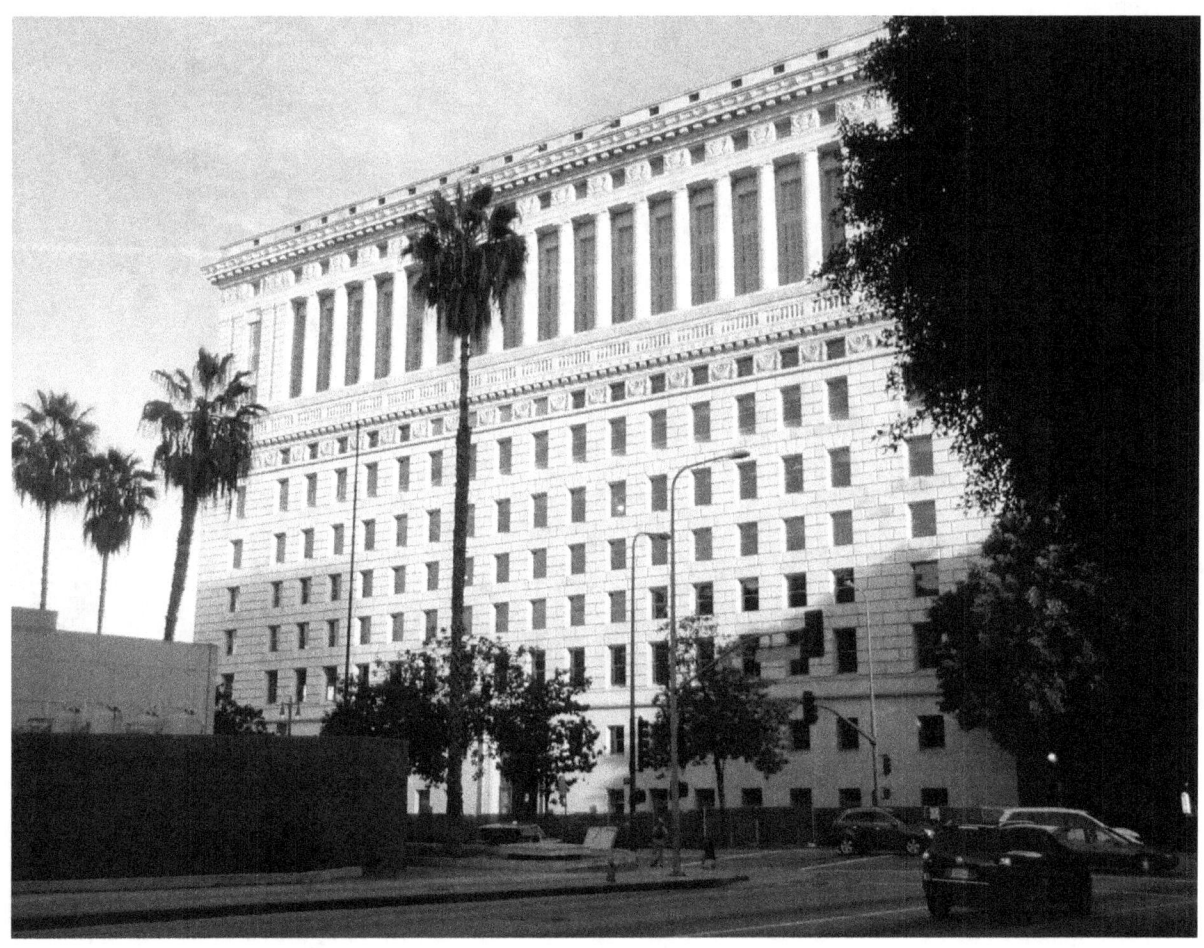

CIVIC CENTER

N. Broadway and Temple

Los Angeles County's Central Heating and Refrigeration Plant stands on the northwest corner of N. Broadway and Temple. Built in the 1950's at a cost of around $3.5 million, the sleekly simple lines of this plant set it apart from the surrounding civic buildings. Cutting-edge in its day, the automated Central Heating and Refrigeration Plant, which opened in 1958, serviced LA's county buildings.

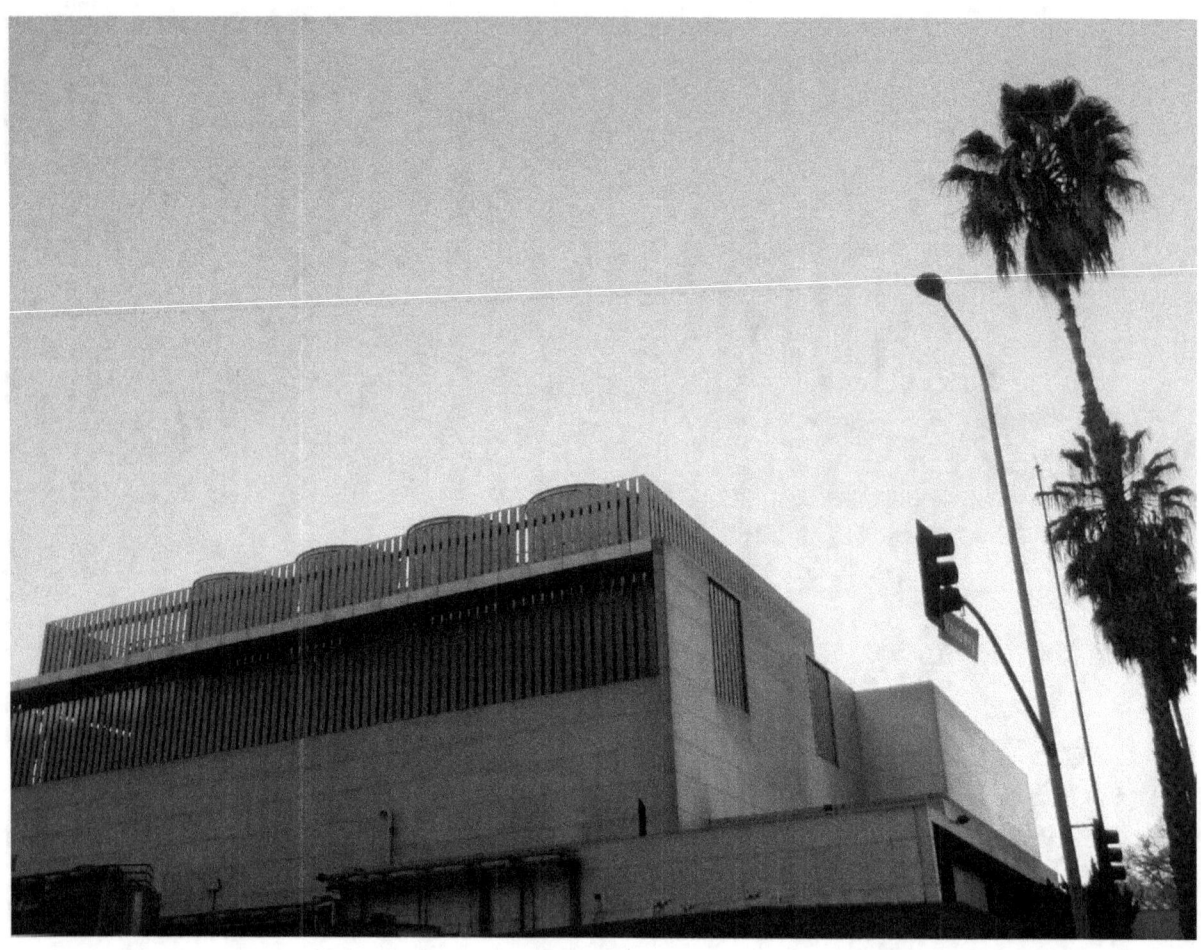

CIVIC CENTER

N. Broadway and Temple

Situated on the southwest corner of N. Broadway and Temple, LA County's Hall of Records opened in 1962 and has a distinctly 1960's look. Modern and energy-efficient for its time, it now evokes a bold "vintage" tone as strong vertical lines contrast with the horizontal balconies.

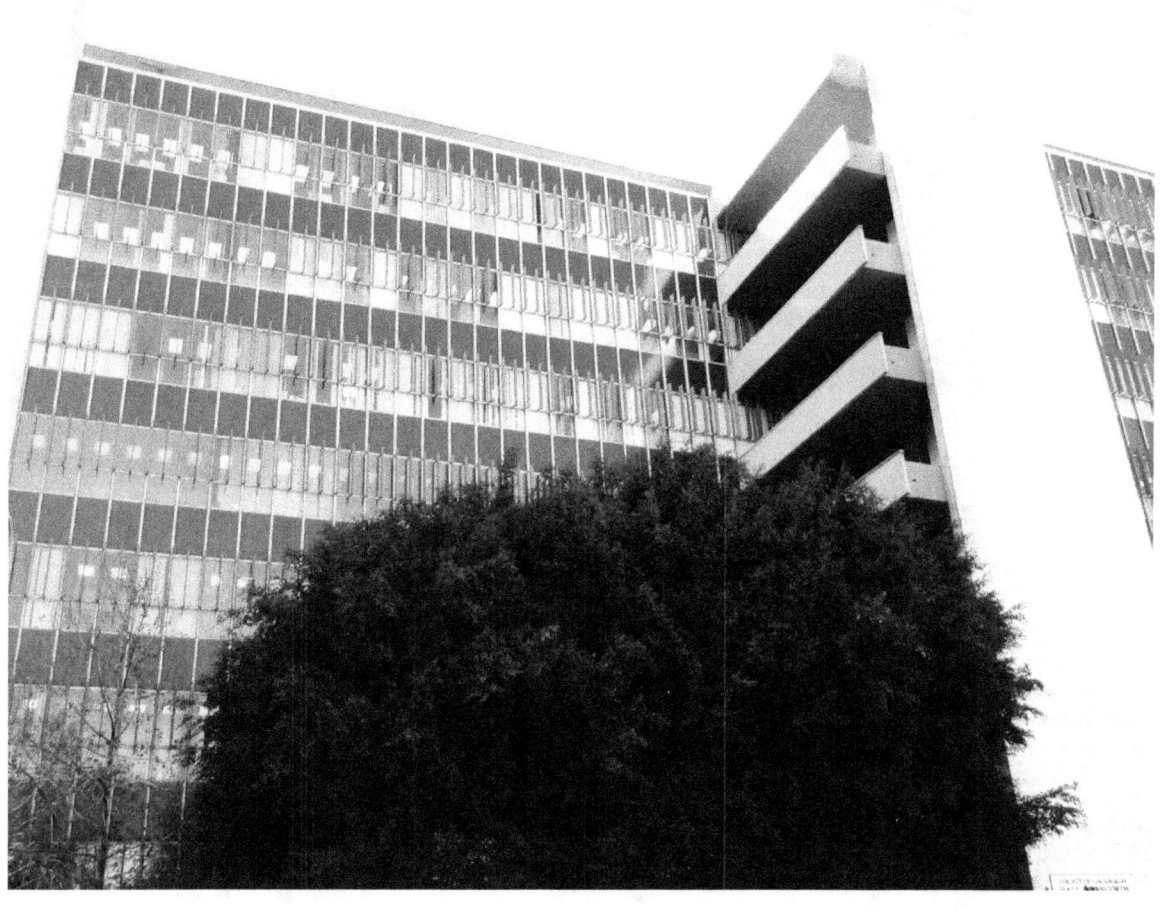

CIVIC CENTER

N. Broadway and Temple

The Hall of Records was designed by architects Richard Neutra and Robert Alexandra. Richard Neutra (1892 - 1970) was a prolific genius among modernist architects. Pictured here are the building's north face (top photo) and east face (bottom photo).

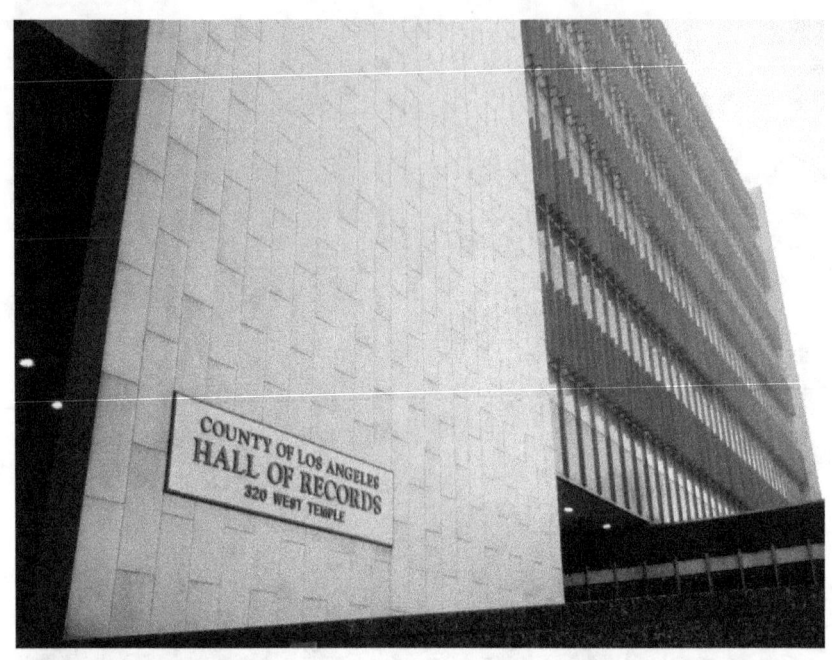

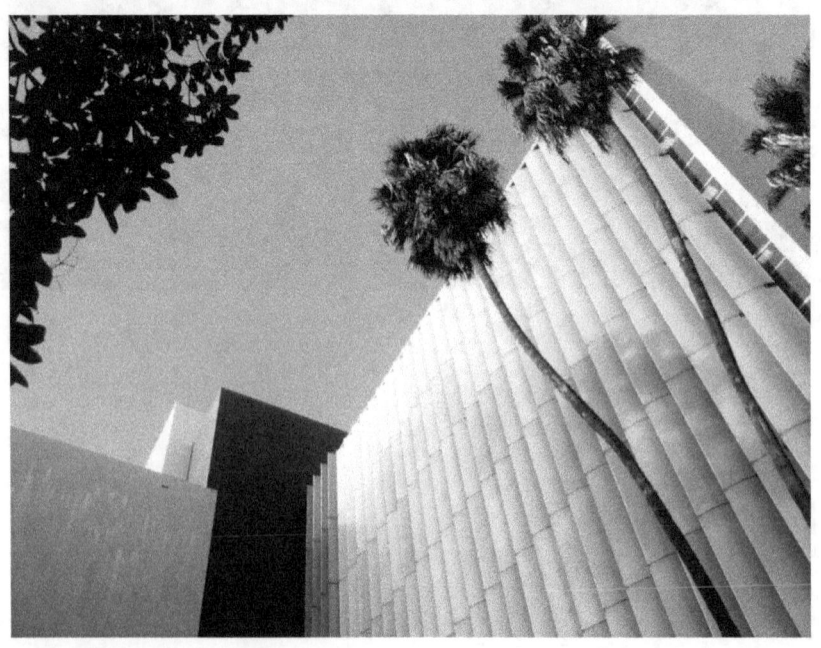

CIVIC CENTER

N. Broadway and Temple

The Clara Shortridge Foltz Criminal Justice Center (left) on the southeast corner of N. Broadway and Temple opened in 1972. It replaced the handsome sandstone county courthouse that had sat atop Poundcake Hill from 1893 - 1936, until it was razed due to damage sustained during the quake of 1933. Poundcake Hill hosted LA's first high school (1873 - 1886). Poundcake Hill was never more than a hillock, but it was reduced even more when the present criminal justice center was constructed. Notable trials held in the Clara Shortridge Foltz criminal courts included the OJ Simpson and Phil Spector trials. Clara Shortridge Foltz (1849 - 1934) was the first female lawyer in not only Southern California but on the entire west coast. LA's City Hall (right) is visible just east of the criminal courts.

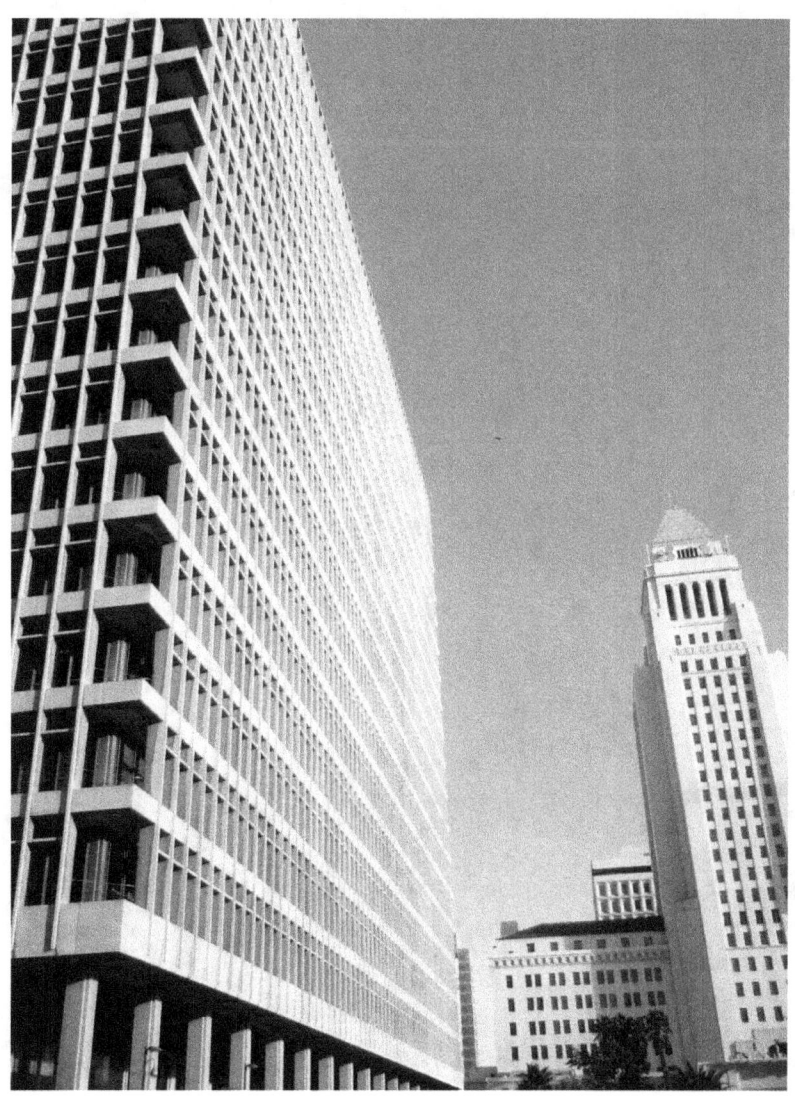

CIVIC CENTER

100 Block of N. Broadway

LA's City Hall dominates this view looking east across the 100 block of N. Broadway. After they've crossed N. Broadway, pedestrians can stroll through the Broadway-to-Spring Street section of Grand Park (the Event Lawn)—one of LA's new green spaces—before visiting City Hall.

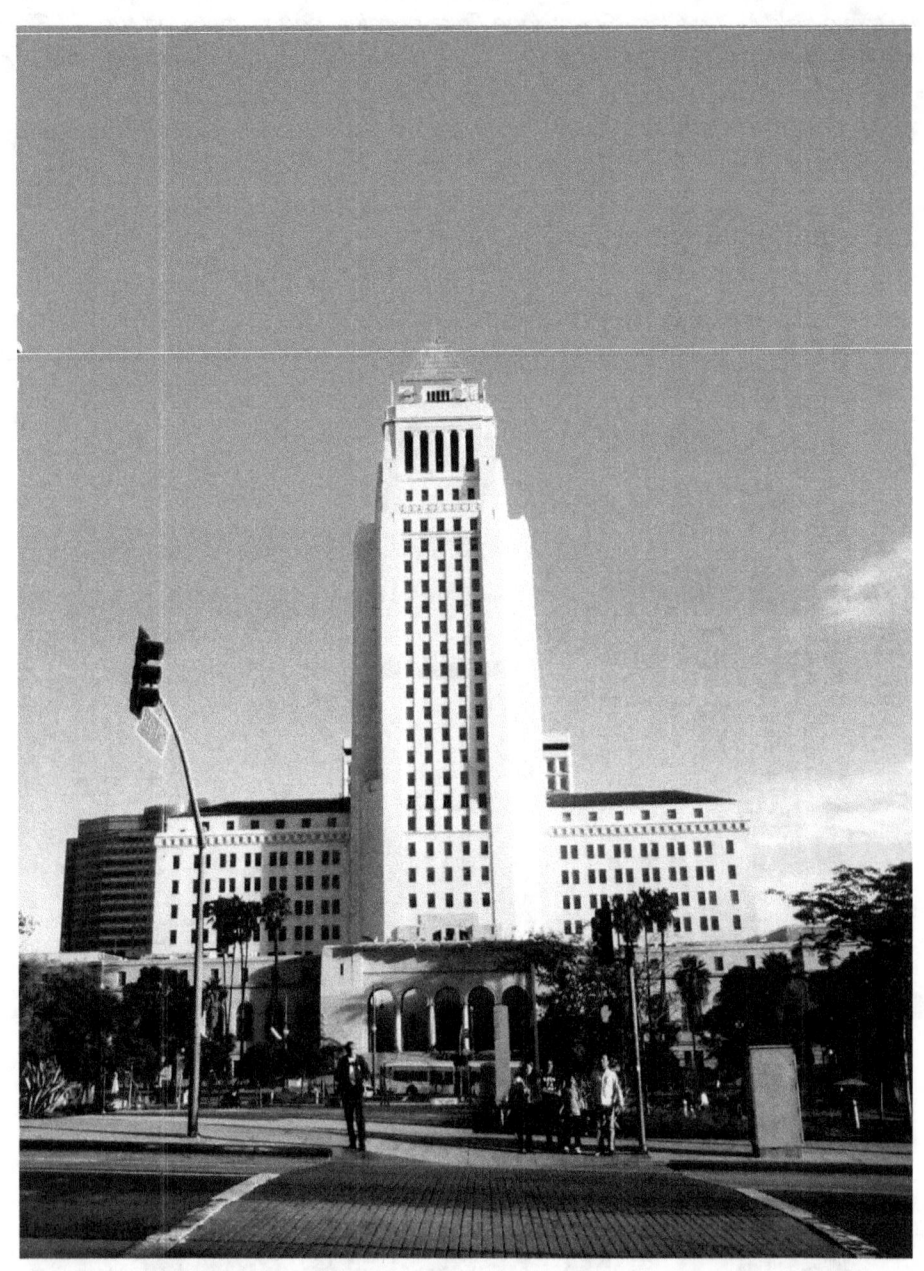

CIVIC CENTER

100 Block of N. Broadway

On the west side of N. Broadway, the Broadway-to-Hill Street section of Grand Park (the Community Terrace) beckons with its patriotic and historic Flag Court. The building in the distance (left center) is the Kenneth Hahn Hall of Administration on W. Temple. The southern face of the Hall of Records is clearly visible on the right.

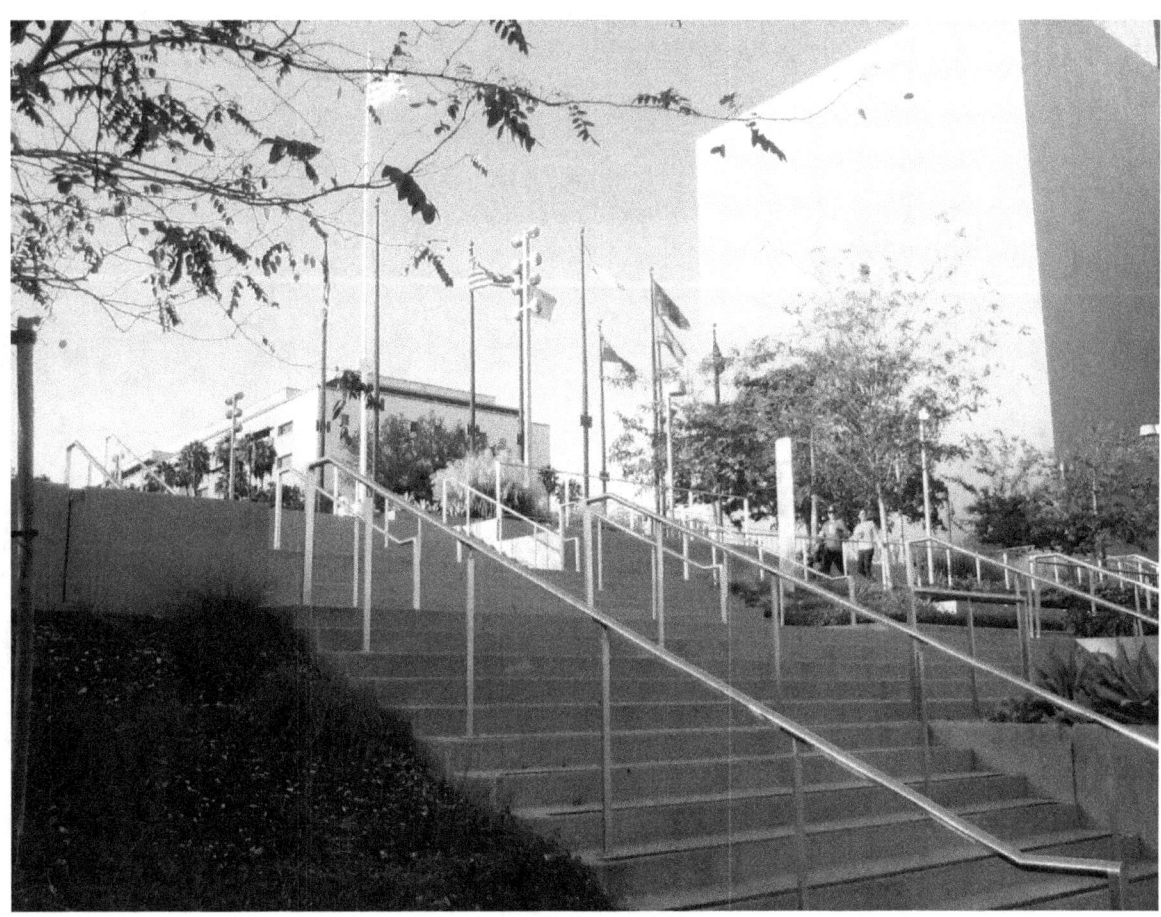

CIVIC CENTER

Broadway and First Street

Continuing south along N. Broadway, one comes to another interesting intersection: Broadway and First Street. Across First Street, "N. Broadway" becomes "S. Broadway". On the northwest corner, just south of the Court of Flags, stands the LA County Law Library. LA's law library has been around for more than one hundred years, but this building, completed in the new millennium, is a newcomer to the neighborhood. The more venerable Stanley Mosk Superior Court visible to the west (top left), for example, opened at 111 N. Hill Street in 1959. It is presently the largest courthouse in the United States. The new LA County Law Library is vast as well; it contains around 800,000 volumes and boasts free Wi-Fi—but (to the chagrin of some lawyers and clerks) it closes by six pm.

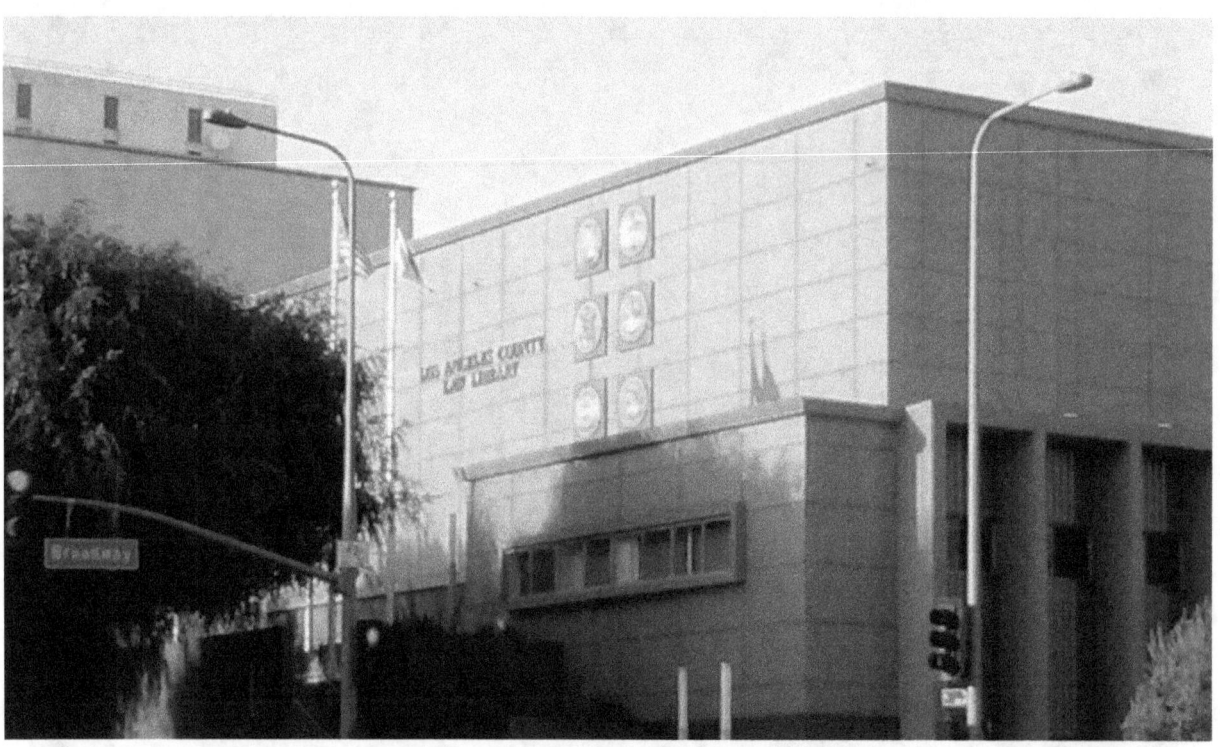

CIVIC CENTER

Broadway and First Street

The southwest corner of Broadway and First—designated "107 S. Broadway" by a mailbox hanging on a chain-link fence—is an enormous crater of an empty lot. Once the site of the Junipero Serra State Office Building (razed in 2007 due to quake damage), it will soon be the location of LA's newest federal courthouse. (The towering buildings to the southwest (top left and center) signify the start of LA's Financial District.) Historical note: On this block, at 127 S. Broadway, the Mason Opera House (later called the Mason Theatre) was an elegant presence from 1903 until 1956. Sarah Bernhardt performed at the Mason. The theatre was torn down in 1956 to make room for the state office building; as previously noted, the 1950's were a key era for LA's civic building projects.

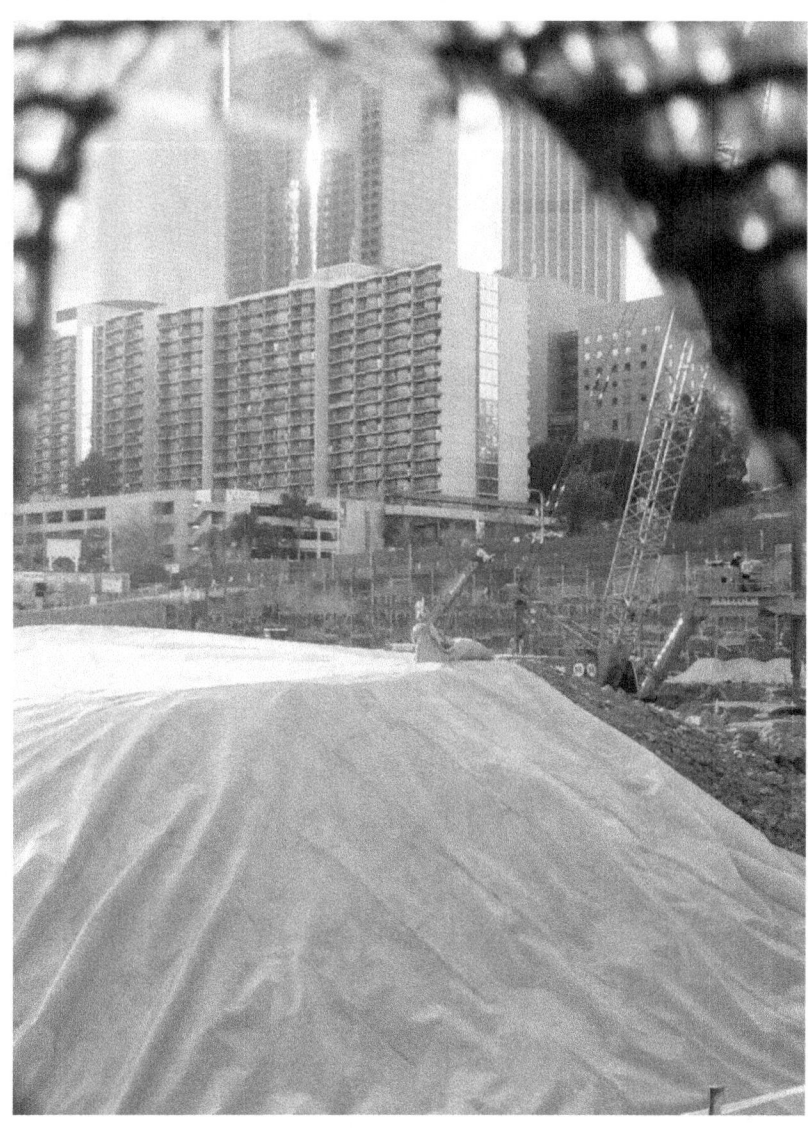

CIVIC CENTER

Broadway and First Street

Across Broadway, opposite the construction lot, the southeast corner of Broadway and First is dominated by the "Los Angeles Times" newspaper block. The venerable "LA Times" (founded in 1881) is presently housed in a complex that includes a massive parking garage. Pictured here is the First Street entrance of the main building. As the cornerstone states (bottom right), "This stone was set ... in 1934 by Harry Chandler publisher ...". In 1935 the building was completed.

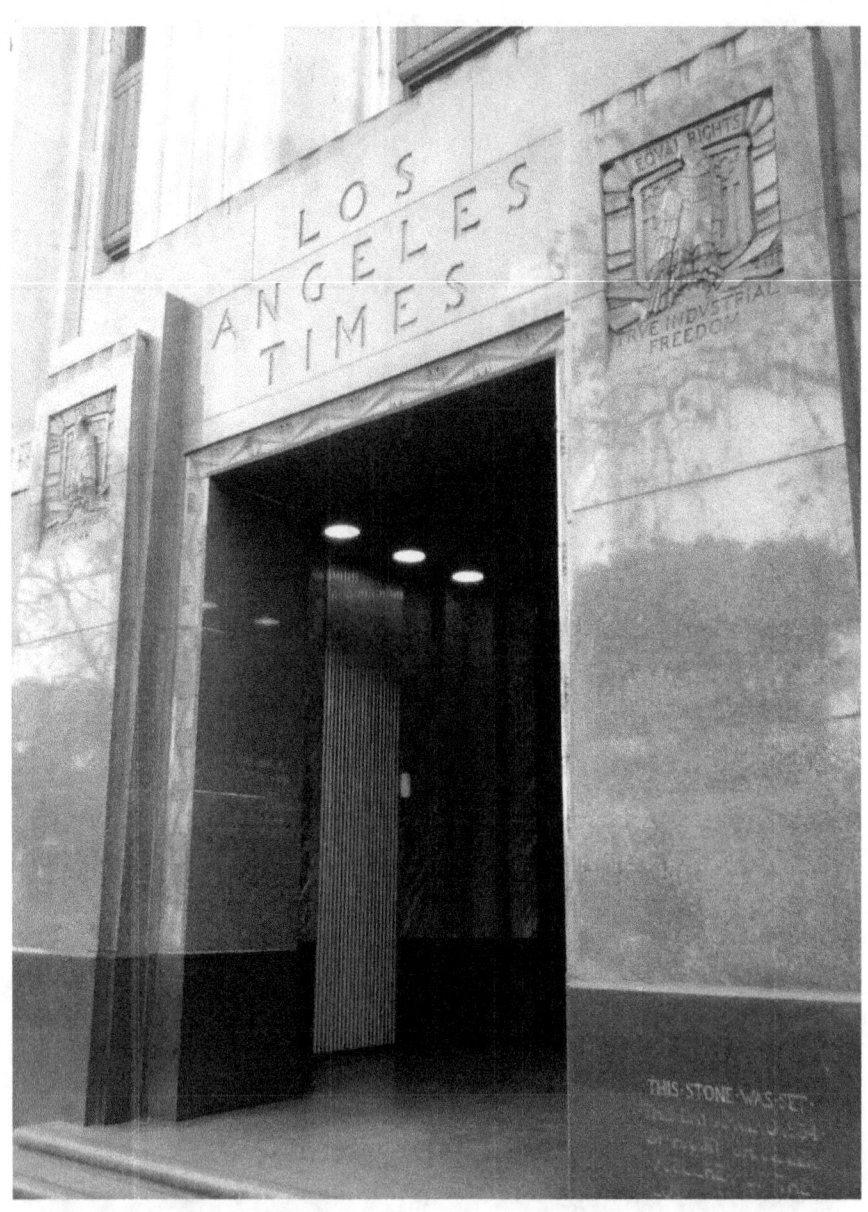

CIVIC CENTER

Broadway and First Street

Literally chiseled into the stone flanking the First Street entrance of the LA Times are these words: "This building is the fourth home of the Los Angeles Times and stands as a symbol of faith in California". The Chandlers were legendary publishers and boosters who did indeed have tremendous faith in California. Early publisher Harrison Gray Otis kept the paper going even after union leaders bombed an earlier Times building in 1910, killing 21 people, and in the wake of the sensational trial that followed. Harry Chandler (Otis' son-in-law) succeeded Otis as publisher in 1917, and passed the torch to his son Norman in 1944. Norman Chandler handed the reins (or the reign) to son Otis in 1960. Between 1960 and 1980, Otis Chandler transformed the "LA Times" into a respected, world-class paper. In this new, highly digital millennium, the "LA Times" is working to find its footing—but still it stands.

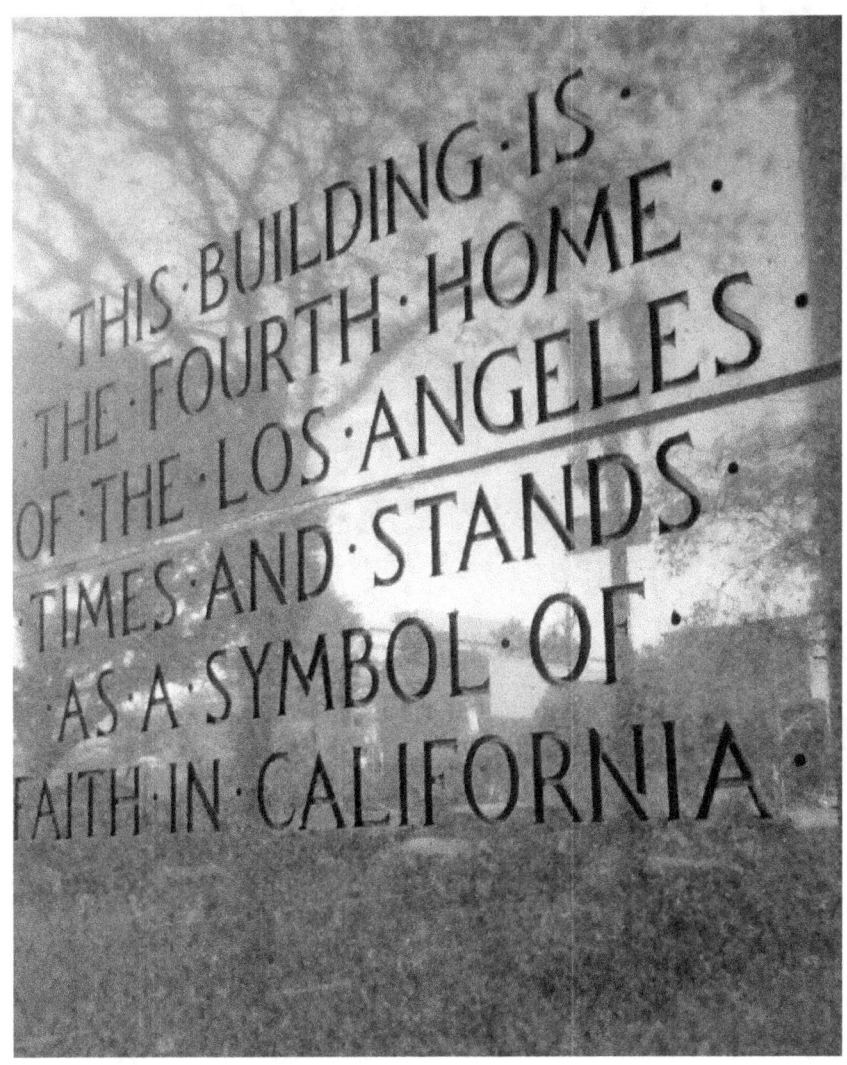

CIVIC CENTER

Broadway and First Street

From the northeast corner of Broadway and First Street one has an unobstructed view of Grand Park's Event Lawn and, to the east, LA City Hall, which anchors the 100 block of Spring Street. Standing 32 stories tall, LA City Hall opened in 1928. Its distinctive silhouette—capped by a ziggurat— is recognized worldwide, and remains one of LA's most enduring icons.

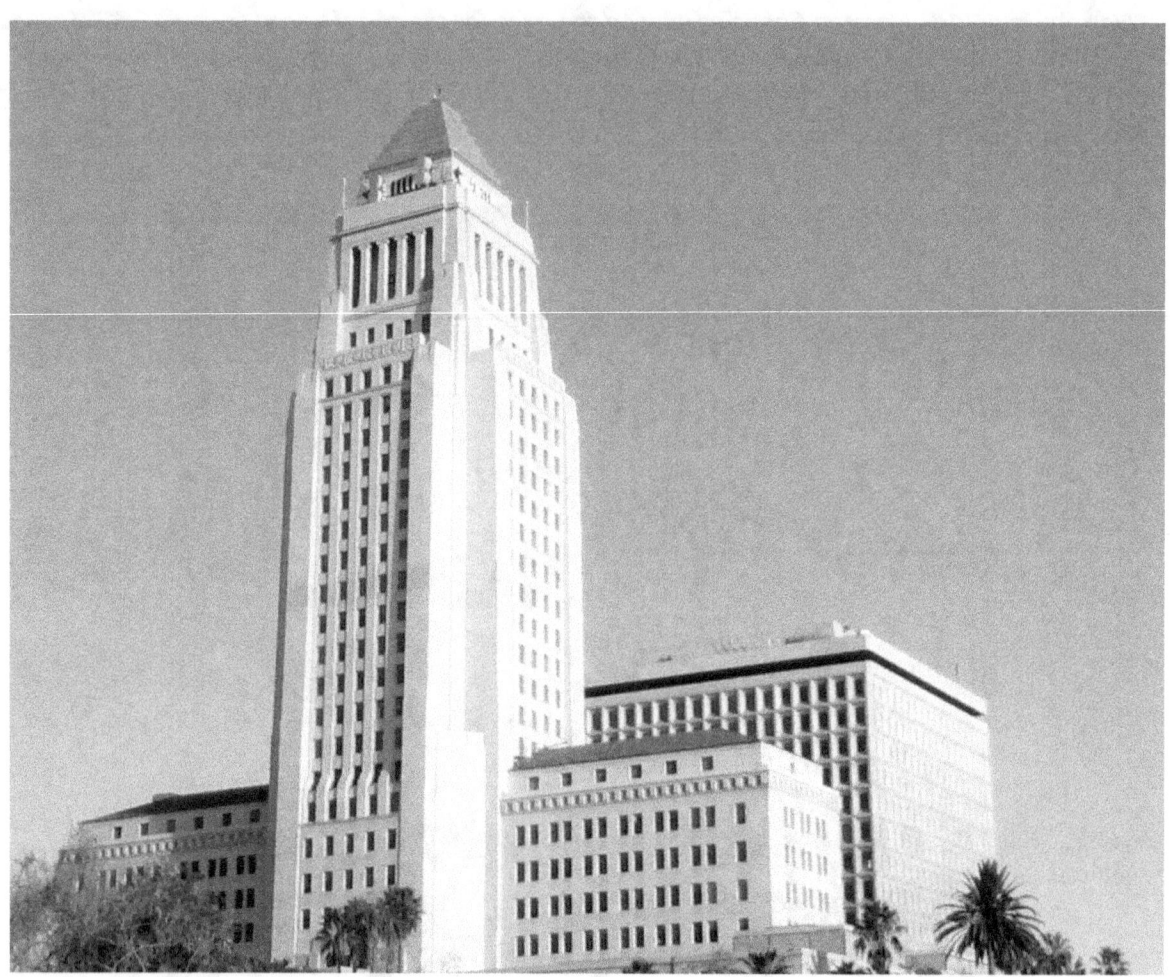

CIVIC CENTER

100 – 200 Blocks of S. Broadway

As one travels south along S. Broadway's initial blocks, the grand edifices of Downtown LA's civic center rapidly give way to construction sites, parking lots, and often-shabby low-rise buildings. A glance backward, to the northeast, gives a reassuring reminder of civic glory. Visible here are the LA Times' parking garage (bottom left), the top of LA City Hall (center left), and the LA Times building (right).

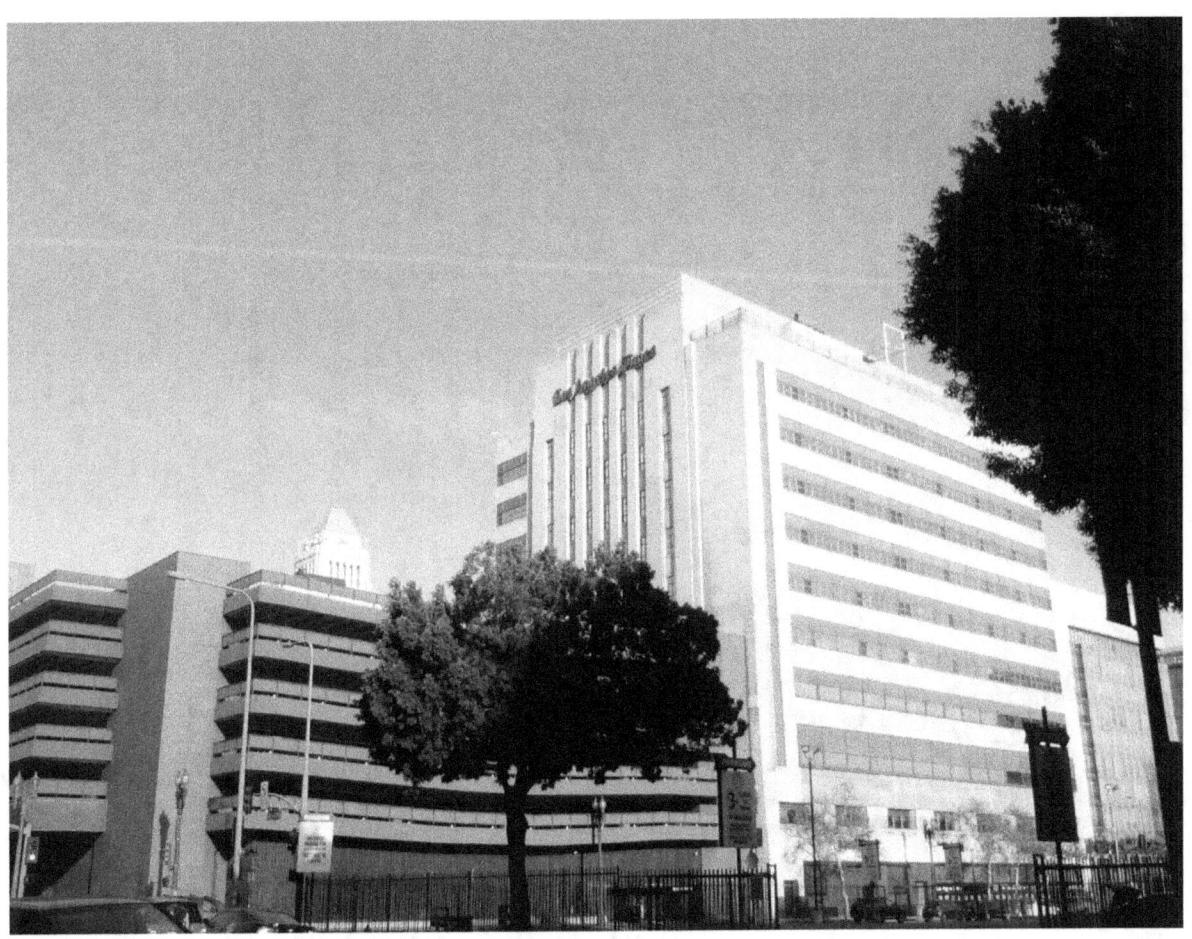

THEATRE DISTRICT

233 S. Broadway

In the very early 1900s, many theatres and music halls graced the 100 – 300 blocks of S. Broadway, easily accessible to the well-to-do patrons who lived in N. Broadway mansions. One such place of entertainment was the Blanchard Music Hall. It stood at 233 S. Broadway. At night, along this section of S. Broadway, carriages and early automobiles would have lined up, waiting under the gaslights for the performances to end and the theatre-goers to emerge. Now, where the Blanchard Music Hall would have stood, there is nothing but a parking lot (right).

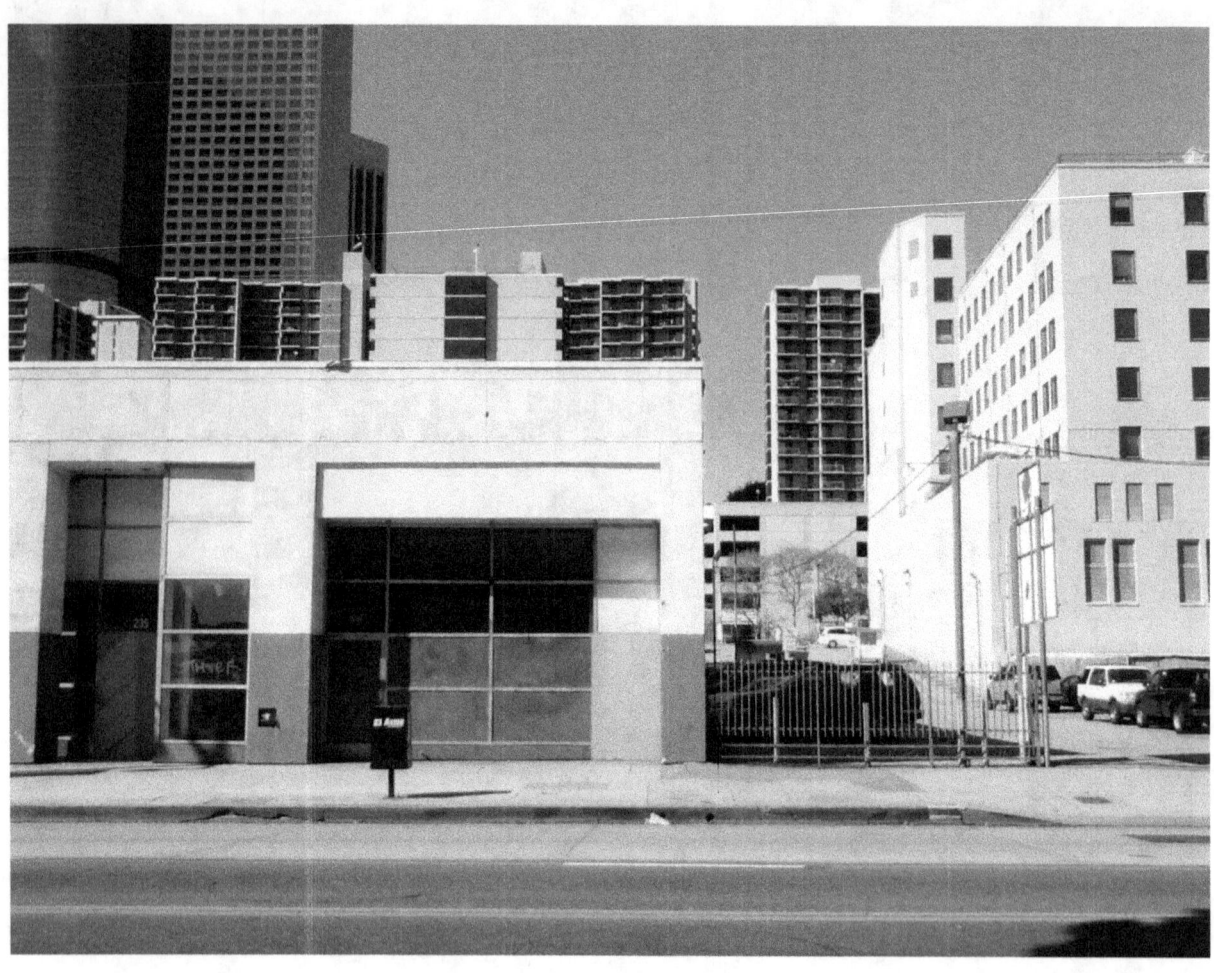

THEATRE DISTRICT

246 S. Broadway

Across from the Blanchard Music Hall, the Royal Theatre opened around 1908, just south of where the Hosfield Building rose in 1914. The Royal Theatre (briefly called the Cecil) would have been roughly where the flower shop at 244 S. Broadway and a bridal and tuxedo shop at 250 S. Broadway stand today. The Royal Theatre is gone, but the Hosfield Building still stands (see below).

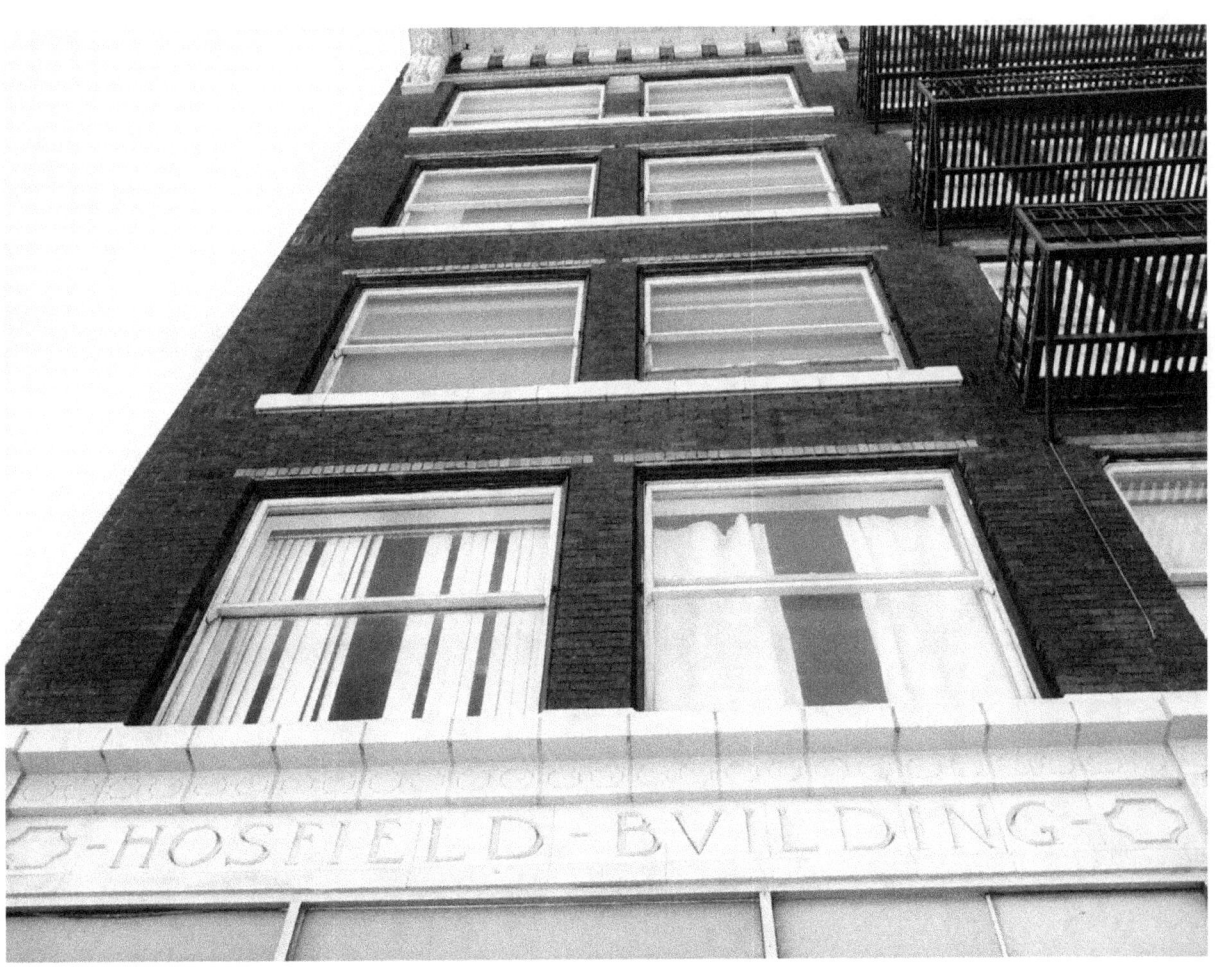

THEATRE DISTRICT

200 Block of S. Broadway

In this photograph: A colorful and intricate mural on the north face of the Hosfield Building. The view here is looking west toward the Financial District, which is certainly a towering contrast to the old buildings and low skyline of S. Broadway. The murals on the Hosfield building are among many public art projects in Downtown LA. Victory Clothing owner Paul Harter commissioned this particular mural (titled "El Nuevo Fuego" ("A New Fire")). It was executed by mural artists "East Los Streetscapers" (founded by David Botello and Wayne Healy) and celebrates LA's 1932 and 1984 Olympics, with images that reference Aztec traditions and local residents. (Ref: www.publicartinla.com.)

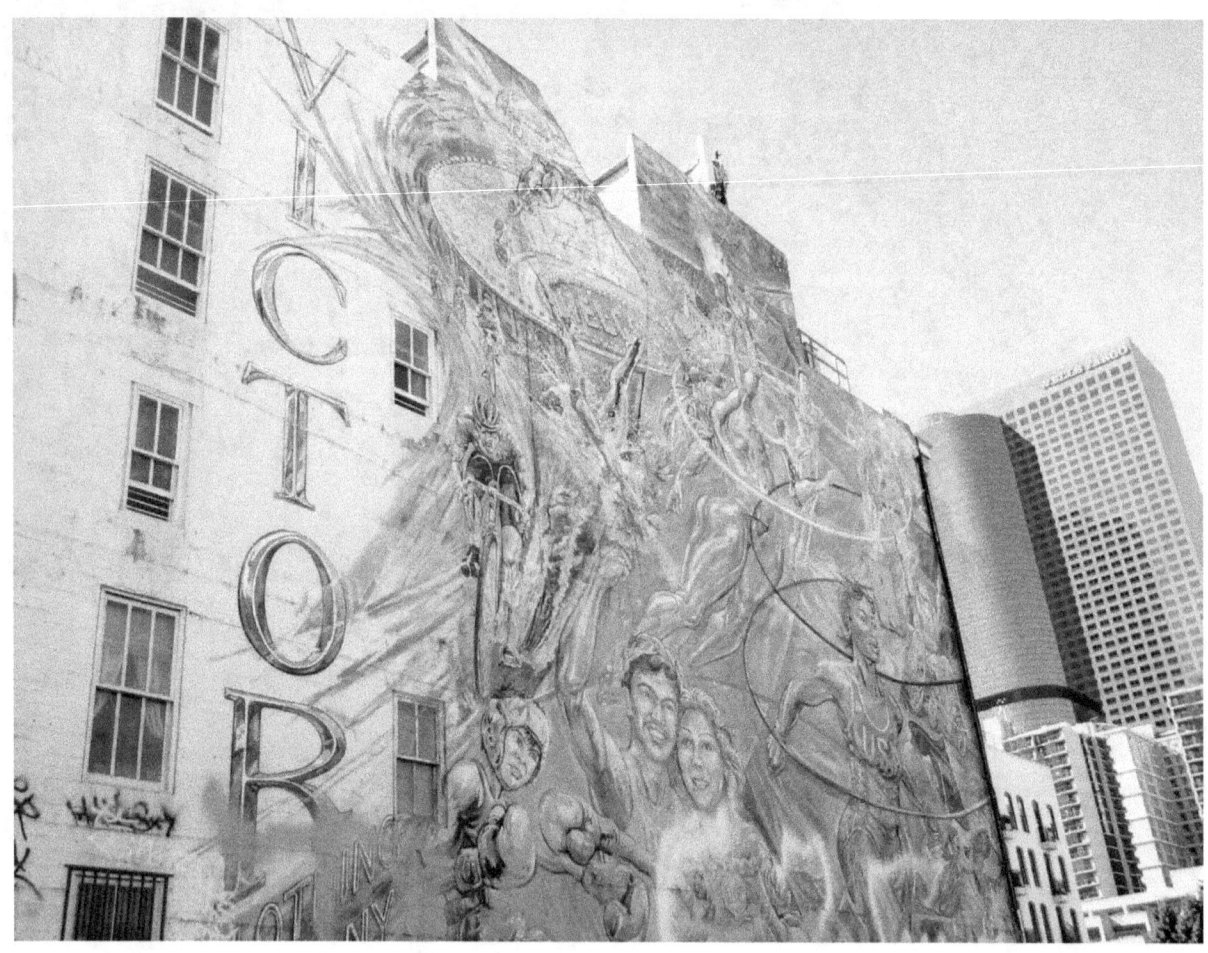

THEATRE DISTRICT

300 Block of S. Broadway

LA's existing Theatre District on S. Broadway begins in the 300 block. This is a view looking south on Broadway at S. Broadway and Third Street and shows not a theatre but, rather, a famous landmark across from LA's first "movie palace". The Bradbury Building (left) is a fanciful jewel box of a structure that opened in 1893. Designed by George Wyman because of a dream of his dead brother, its interior design is based on a science fiction novel of the day. The Bradbury Building's interior is truly unique in appearance (as any interior based on dreams and sci-fi should be) and is still in use as an office building and film location. On a grim note: Ross Cutlery stands just down the block (bottom center); it was established 1930, and is where OJ Simpson infamously purchased a knife.

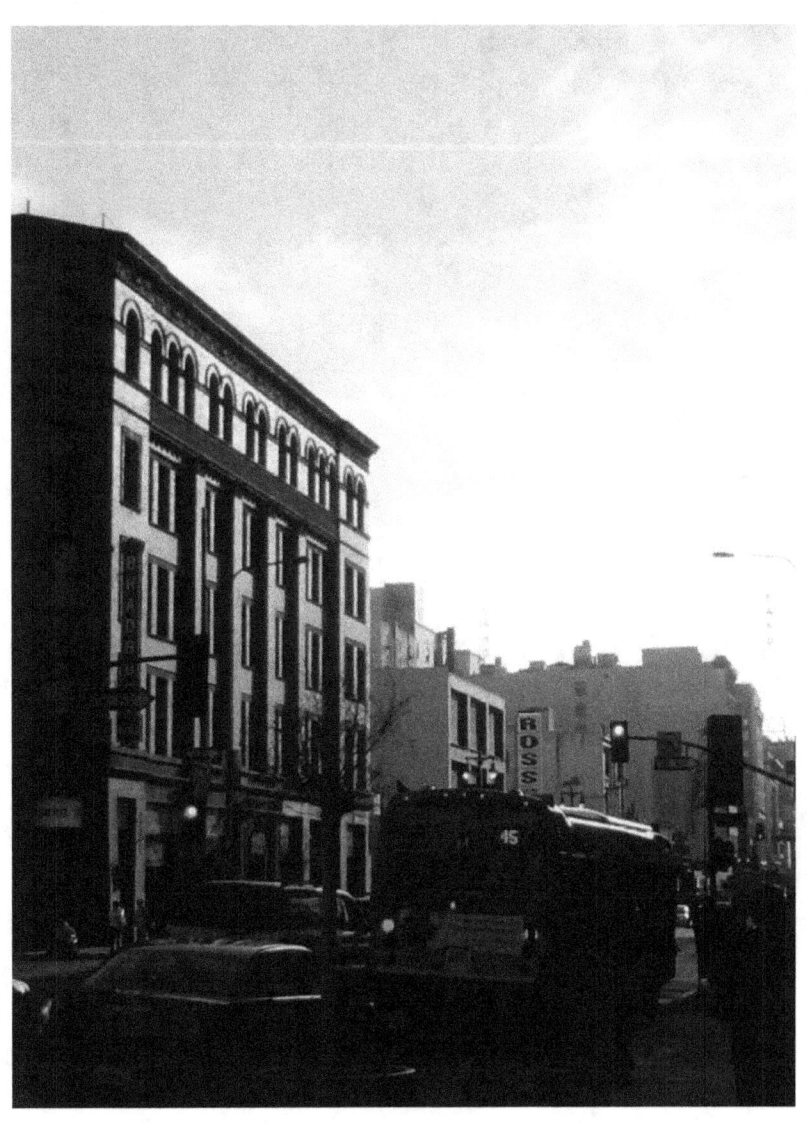

THEATRE DISTRICT

307 S. Broadway

Across the street from the Bradbury Building looms they Million Dollar Theatre, housed in the Metropolitan Water District Building. The ornate Churrigueresque exterior made it sufficiently striking to host entertainment impresario Sid Grauman's first "movie palace"—and the city's first movie palace as well. Note the heavily ornamental base and capital. Billed as "Sid Grauman's Million Dollar Theatre" it soon became simply the "Million Dollar Theatre". The building and the theatre opened in 1918.

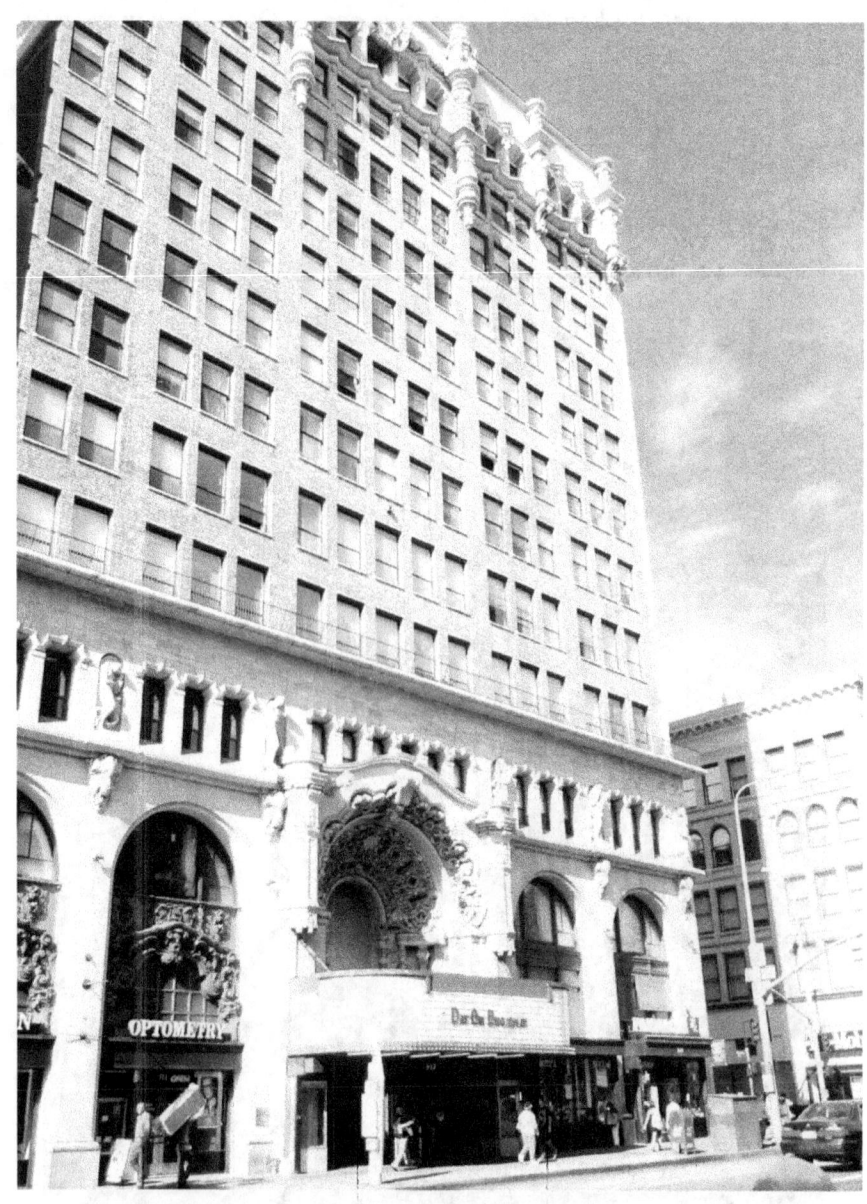

THEATRE DISTRICT

307 S. Broadway

In January 2014, the "Bringing Back Broadway" initiative (championed by LA Councilmember Jose Huizar) hosted "A Day on Broadway" and invited guests to visit grand old LA theatres such as the Million Dollar Theatre. The opportunity to explore the interiors of these privately owned movie palaces is a rare treat indeed. Note the "Day on Broadway" sign on the Million Dollar Theatre's marquee. Note also the elaborate decorative carvings over the theatre's main entrance, a hallmark of the busy Churrigueresque architectural style.

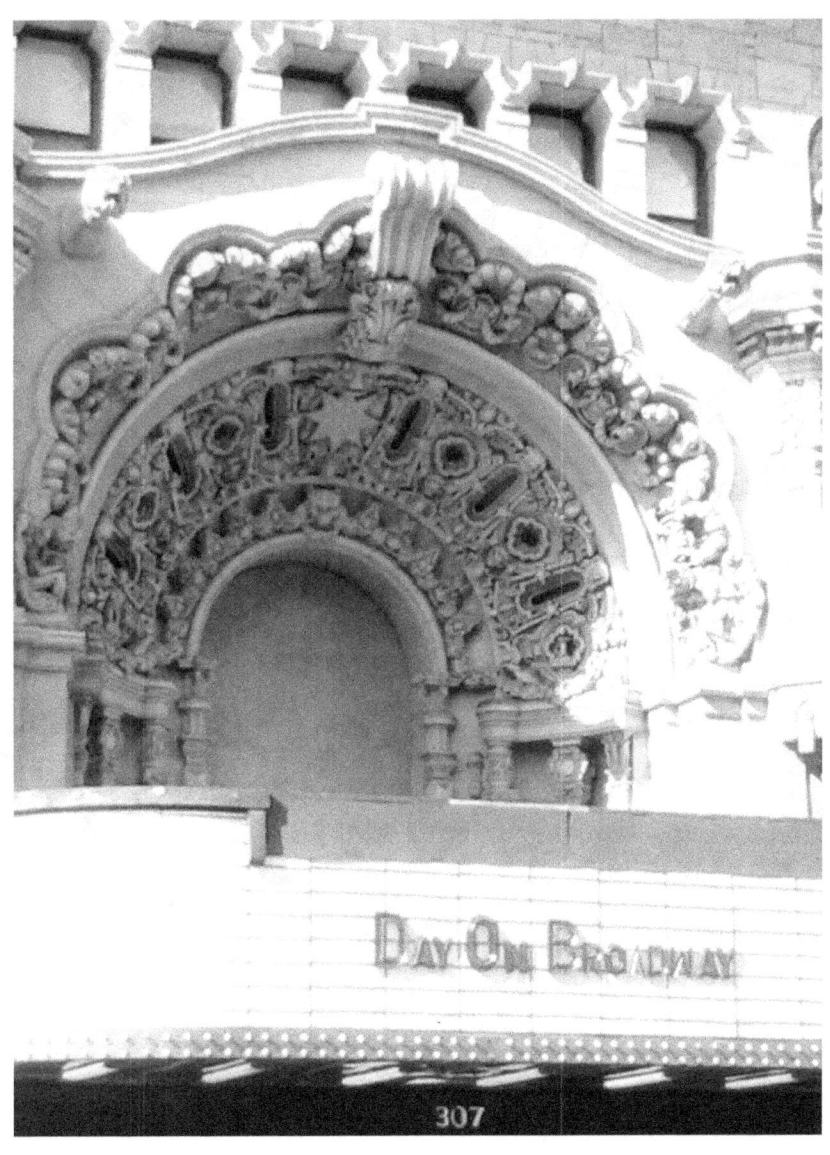

THEATRE DISTRICT

307 S. Broadway

In the lobby of the Million Dollar Theatre, the faux pressed-tin ceiling looks vintage, but it was installed by recent owners. (Some preservationists are not fans.) For a more authentic view of the original lobby, explorers should peek into the optometrist shop next door. Sid Grauman designed the Million Dollar Theatre to appeal to the wealthy Angelenos who lived nearby in the early 1900's—like the elite residents of Fort Moore Hill. They had not yet migrated westward, first along the Wilshire corridor, and then to the west side.

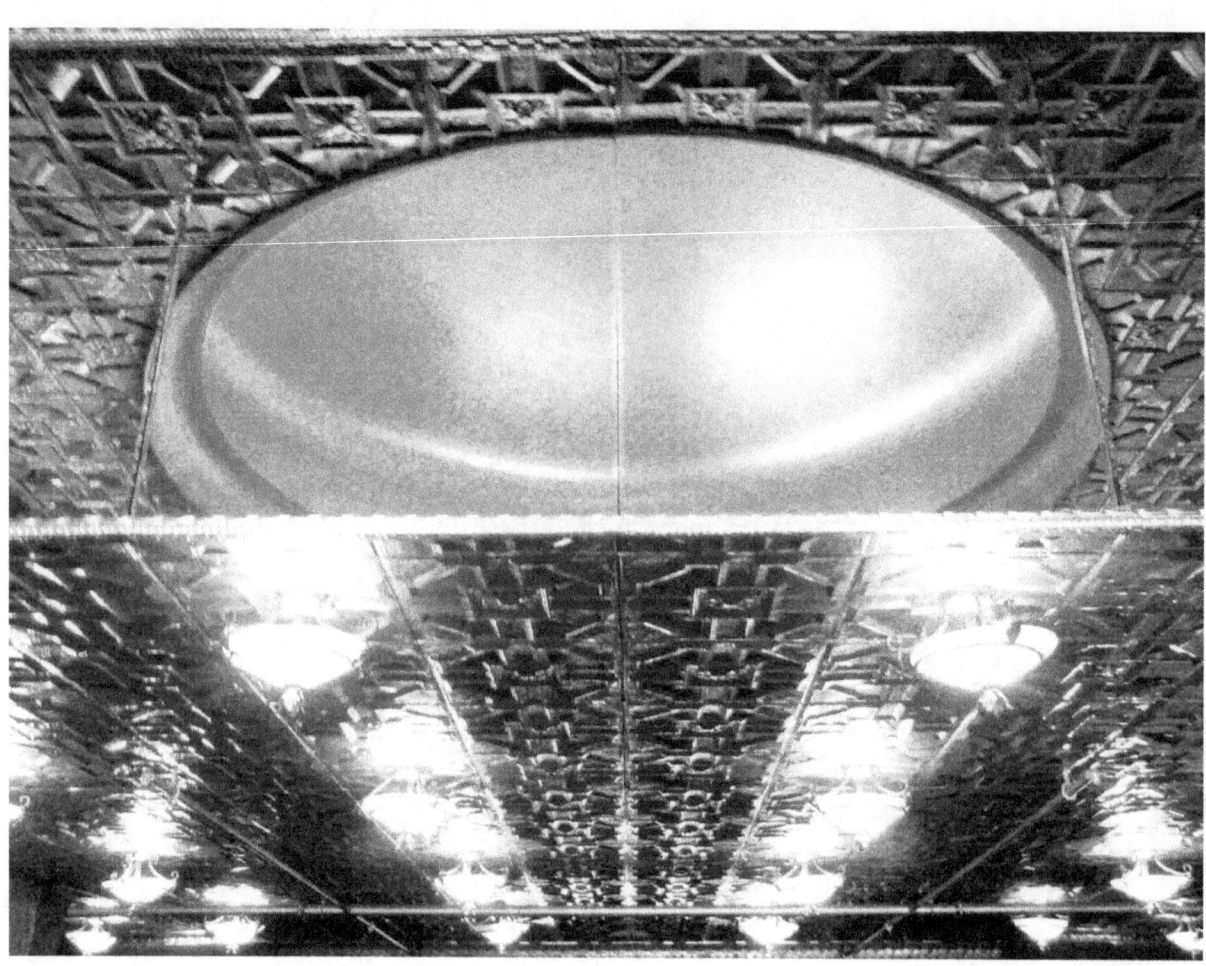

THEATRE DISTRICT

307 S. Broadway

The Million Dollar Theatre frequently changed hands, sometimes a movie palace, sometimes a venue for live performances, often a combination. Sid Grauman himself moved on not long after this theatre opened, soon launching his famous Egyptian and Chinese theatres in Hollywood. From the 1950's through the 1990's, the Million Dollar Theatre became an international hot spot for Spanish-language movies and live shows. The programs changed, but the theatre's interior remained largely unchanged, although the massive chandelier—the centerpiece of the theatre's dome—was a later addition.

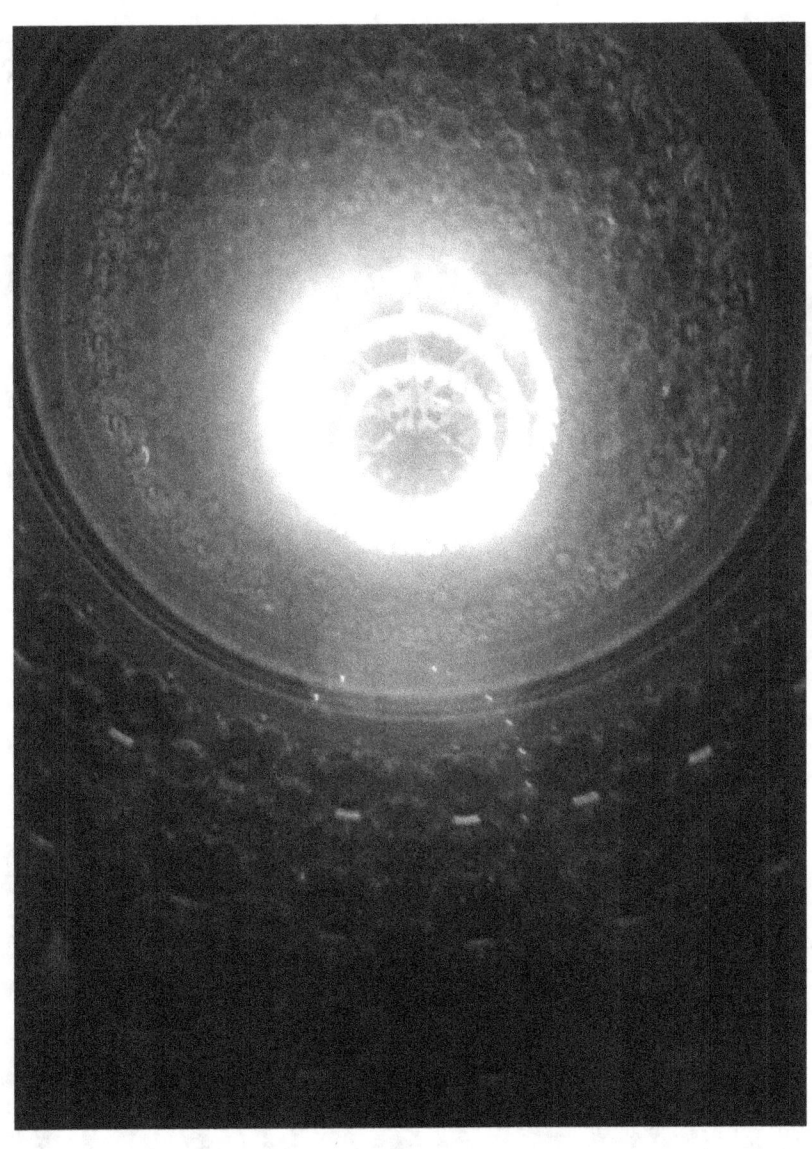

THEATRE DISTRICT

307 S. Broadway

The columns, the niches, the golden urns, the railings below the organ screen—all examples of décor essentially unchanged (although lovingly restored) since Sid Grauman opened his Million Dollar Theatre. Decorative influences were eclectic—to say the least—including everything from Shakespeare to ancient Greece to an obscure children's tale. The present owner has made substantial restoration efforts, but presently lacks the funding to make the necessary changes (e.g., installing elevators, modernizing the rest rooms) to make the theatre a going concern.

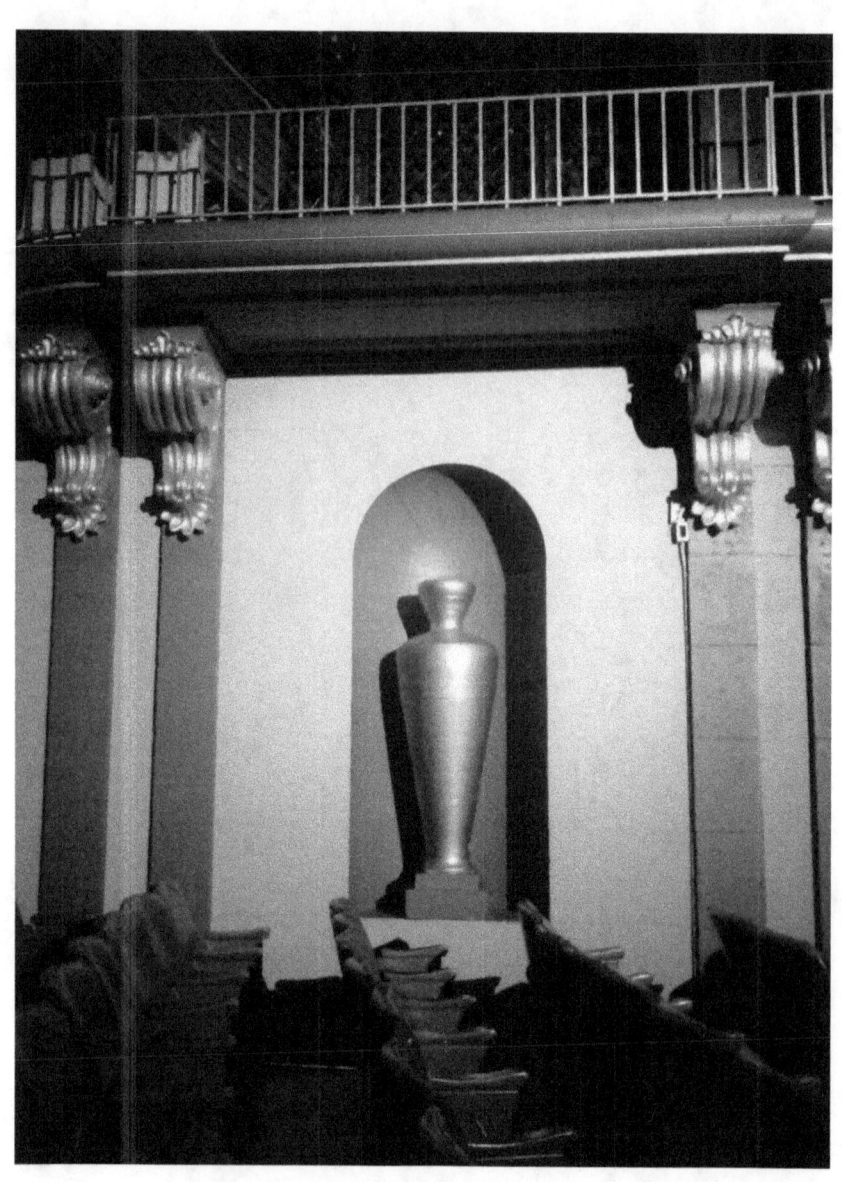

THEATRE DISTRICT

307 S. Broadway

A view of the Million Dollar Theatre's stage from the right side of the balcony ....

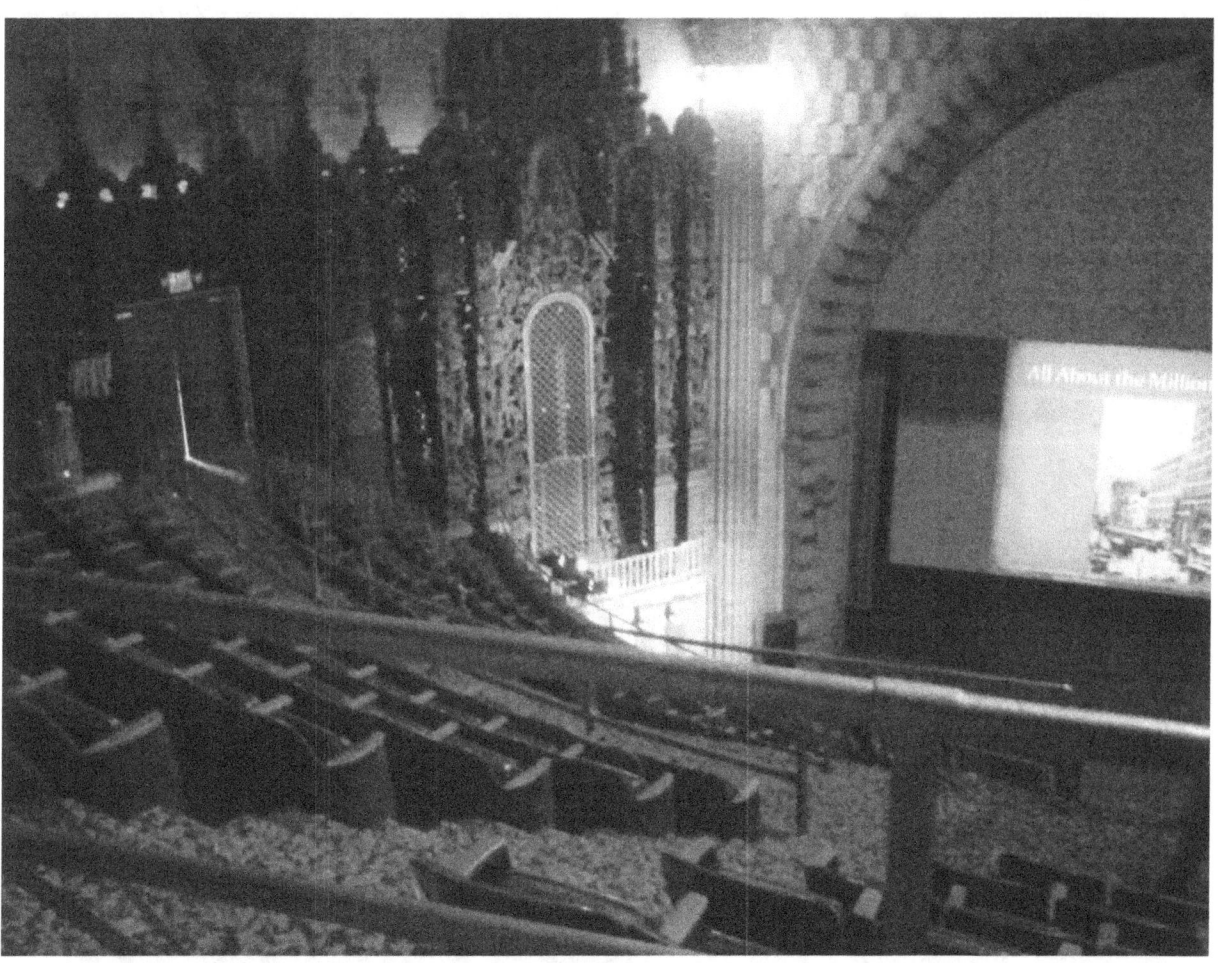

THEATRE DISTRICT

307 S. Broadway

... and from the left side of the balcony. Note the intricate organ screen (right top) above the urn. The screen is plaster, not wood. One significant early change to the theatre was the elimination of its rare "double orchestra pit" after a stage fire broke out in 1922. The original orchestra pit is gone, but the stage remains deep. The "All About the Million Dollar Theatre" presentation (bottom left) was delivered by Ed Kelsey, the official historian of the Los Angeles Historic Theatre Foundation (LAHTF).

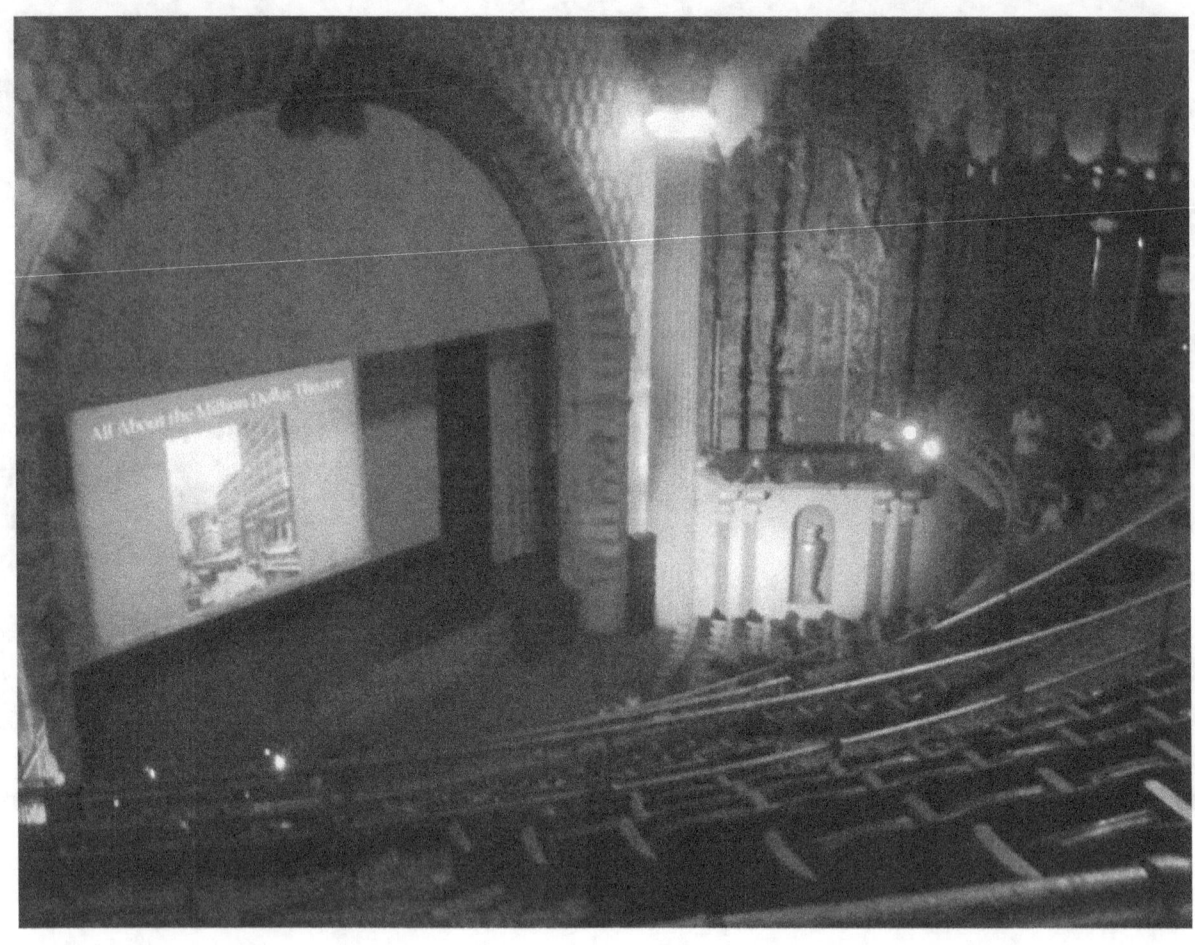

THEATRE DISTRICT

317 S. Broadway

The Grand Central Market, just south of the Million Dollar Theatre, is one of LA's beloved landmarks. Here locals and tourists rub elbows in the cavernous ground level of the Homer-Laughlin building. Fresh meats, fruits, produce, and pastry have been sold here since 1917.

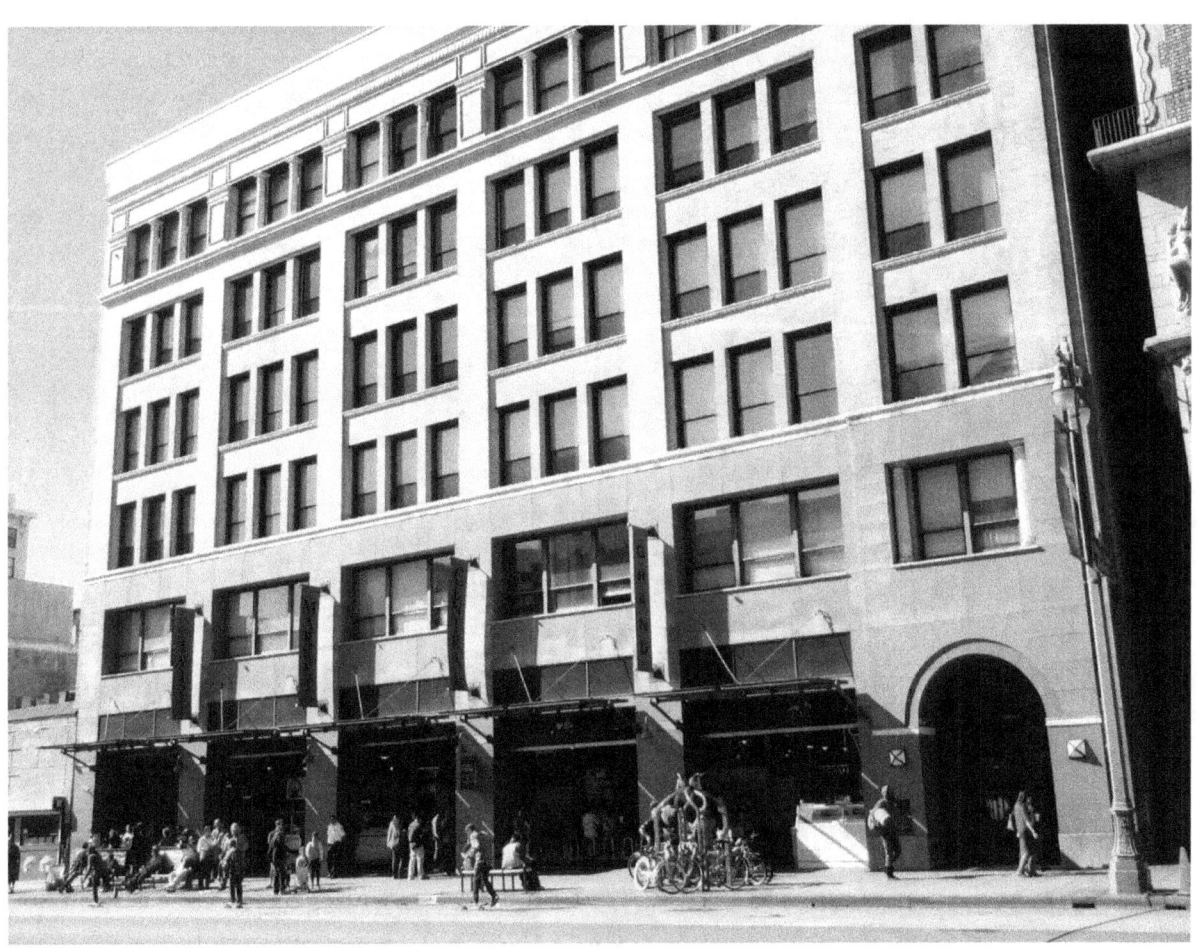

THEATRE DISTRICT

300 – 400 Blocks of S. Broadway

Between Third and Fifth Streets, most of the old theatres and music halls have been demolished for decades. Today's S. Broadway is an eclectic corridor of hole-in-the-wall shops and restaurants, fast food joints, bridal shops, leather goods stores, discount electronic stores—you name it, you seem to be able to buy it here. The scents of carne asada, hamburgers, and freshly cooked tortillas lace the air. How freshly cooked? A woman prepares tortillas on a stand just in front of her tiny eatery. Guitars and drum kits gleam in the front window of a music shop, while nearby an electronic shop pumps pounding House and Techno beats onto the street to entice passersby. Discount socks and hats and shoes and heavy metal T shirts are vended from narrow-slot storefronts. Between the buildings, alleys look so film-noirish one almost expects Dana Andrews or Robert Mitchum to step into view.

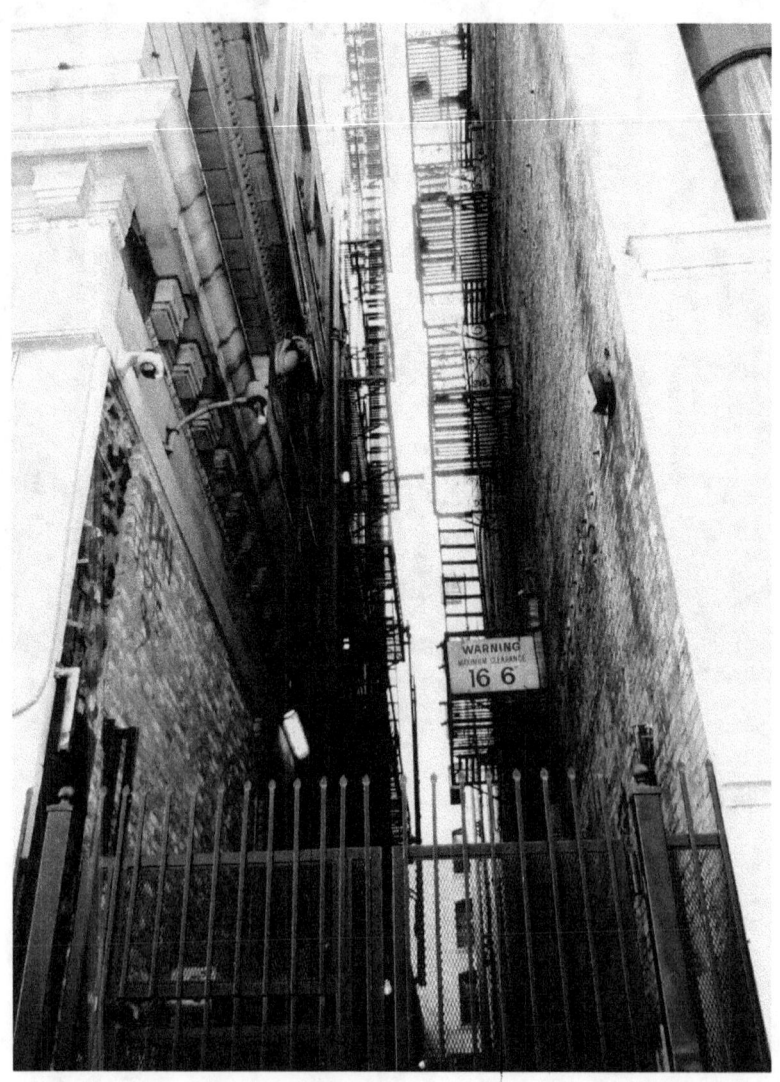

THEATRE DISTRICT

518 S. Broadway

Not all of the defunct theatres along S. Broadway have been demolished. Some were spared the wrecking ball, although they're no longer used as theatres. Three theatres in a row along the 500 block of S. Broadway have been converted to retail space, including the Roxie. The Roxie Theatre opened in 1932—making it the "youngest" of Broadway's movie palaces. (Quinn's Superba Theatre previously occupied the site.) The Roxie, known for its "Zigzag Moderne" design, is now a place to buy bargain bags and purses. Notice the KRKD radio tower on a nearby rooftop. Aimee Semple McPherson, a religious leader of bygone days, broadcast her services via KRKD (and owned KRKD).

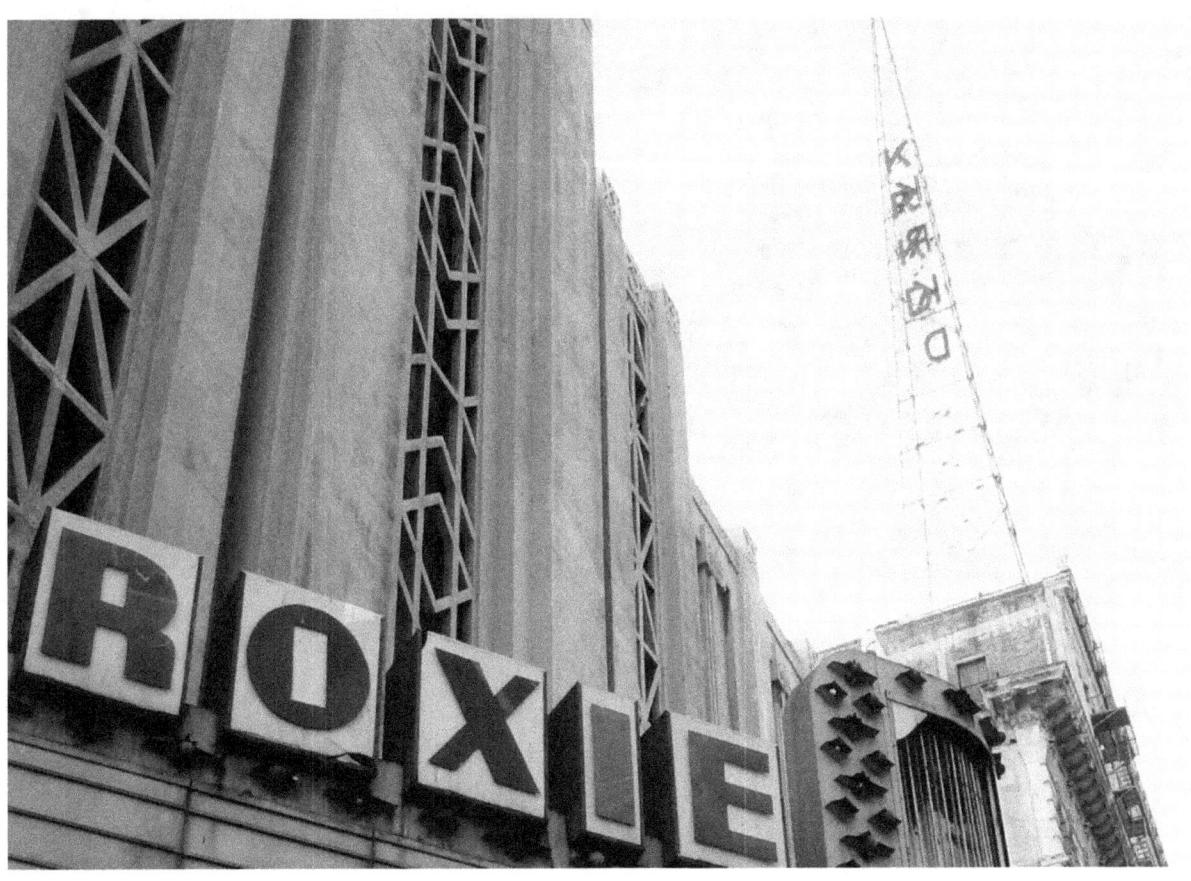

THEATRE DISTRICT

528 S. Broadway

These "lost" theatres retain their marquees, even though the shows are long over. Next door to the Roxie is the Cameo Theatre (originally Clunes Broadway). It launched in 1910, a relatively small (it held 900 seats) early movie theatre. As evident in the 2014 photograph below, the Cameo Theatre now houses jewelry stores. (South of Fifth Street, the Theatre and Jewelry Districts overlap.)

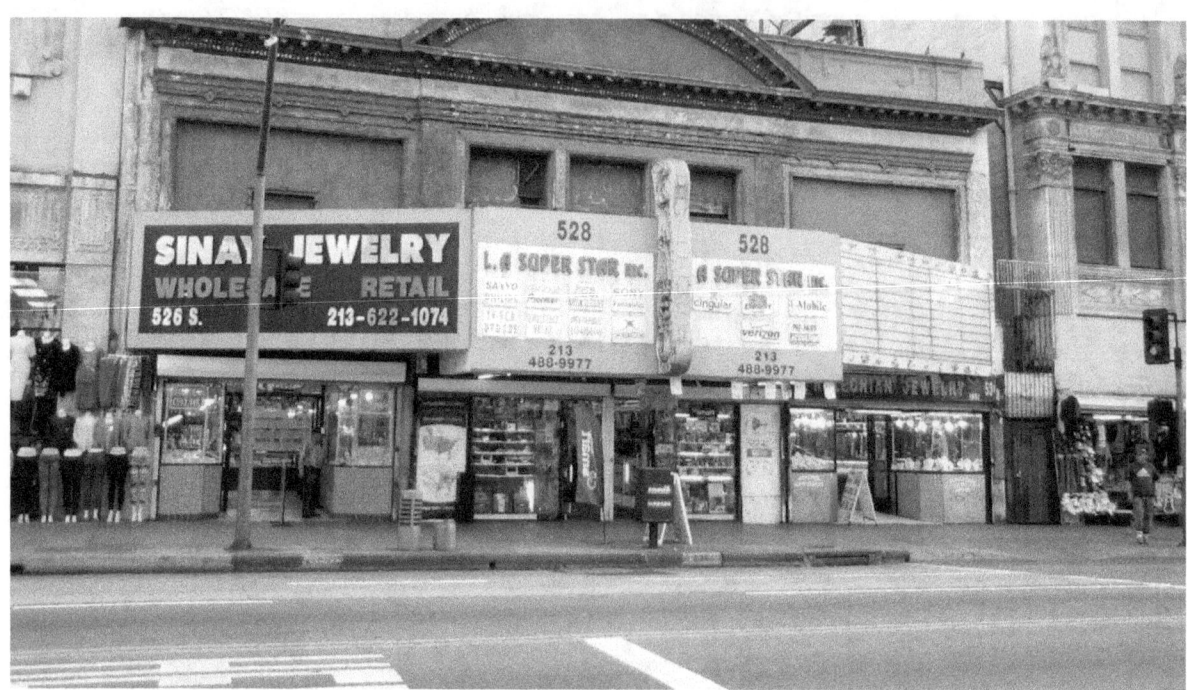

THEATRE DISTRICT

528 S. Broadway

A closer view of the Cameo's neon marquee sign. (Just to the left is the neon "Roxie" sign on the Roxie Theatre's tower.)

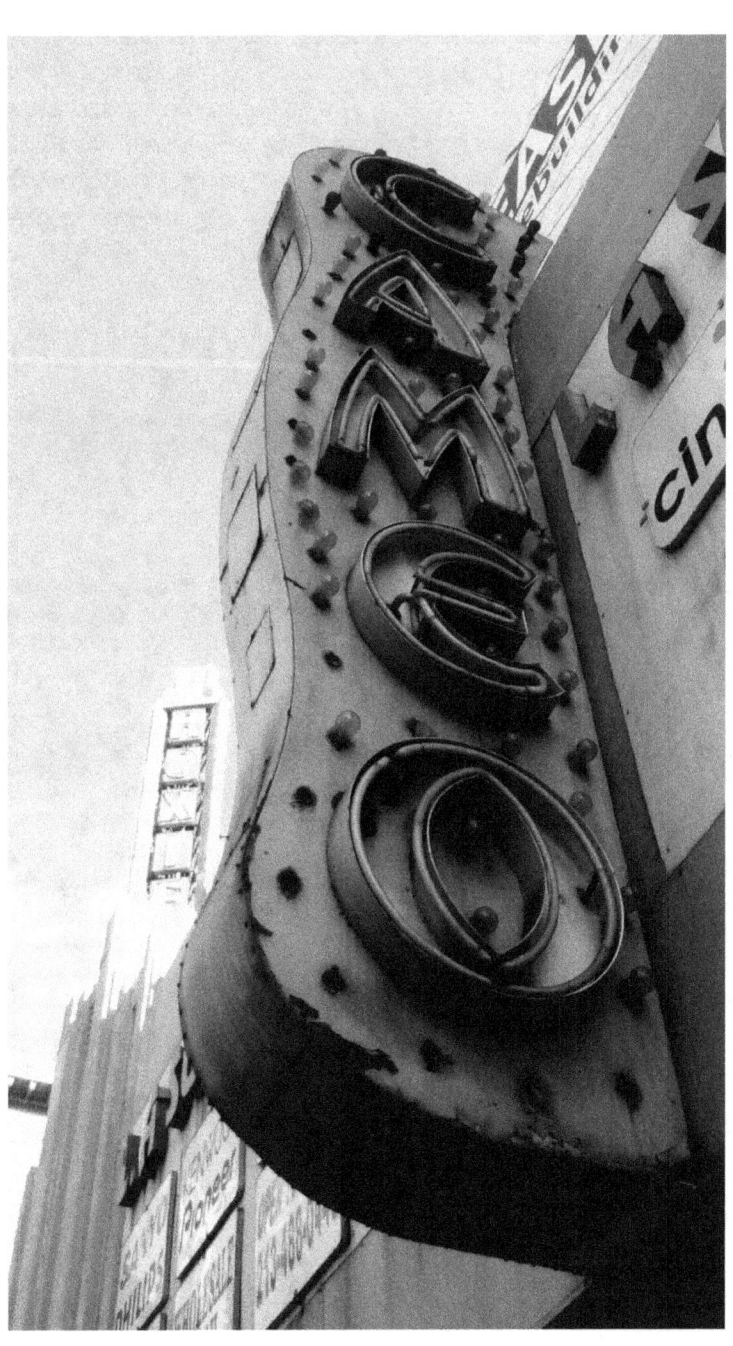

THEATRE DISTRICT

534 S. Broadway

The Arcade Theatre next door to the Cameo Theatre is presently the site of an "Audio Video Plaza". Discount electronic stores are a popular type of shop on Broadway, as well as discount fashion and jewelry stores. The Arcade Theatre, its building now defaced by graffiti, was designed by the same architects who designed LA's Mayan Theatre and Hollywood's El Capitan. The Arcade opened as a Pantages Theatre in 1910—you can still see the name "Pantages" carved over the marquee. Sophie Tucker sang here on opening night. Looking at a picture like the one below, it's difficult to believe the 500 block of S. Broadway was once a theatregoer's neon-lit paradise—but photos and postcards of the 1910's and 1920's reveal how elegant this neighborhood once was. The Roxie, Cameo, and Arcade Theatres currently belong to the same owner, who in recent years announced plans to build a high-rise behind the preserved theatre fronts.

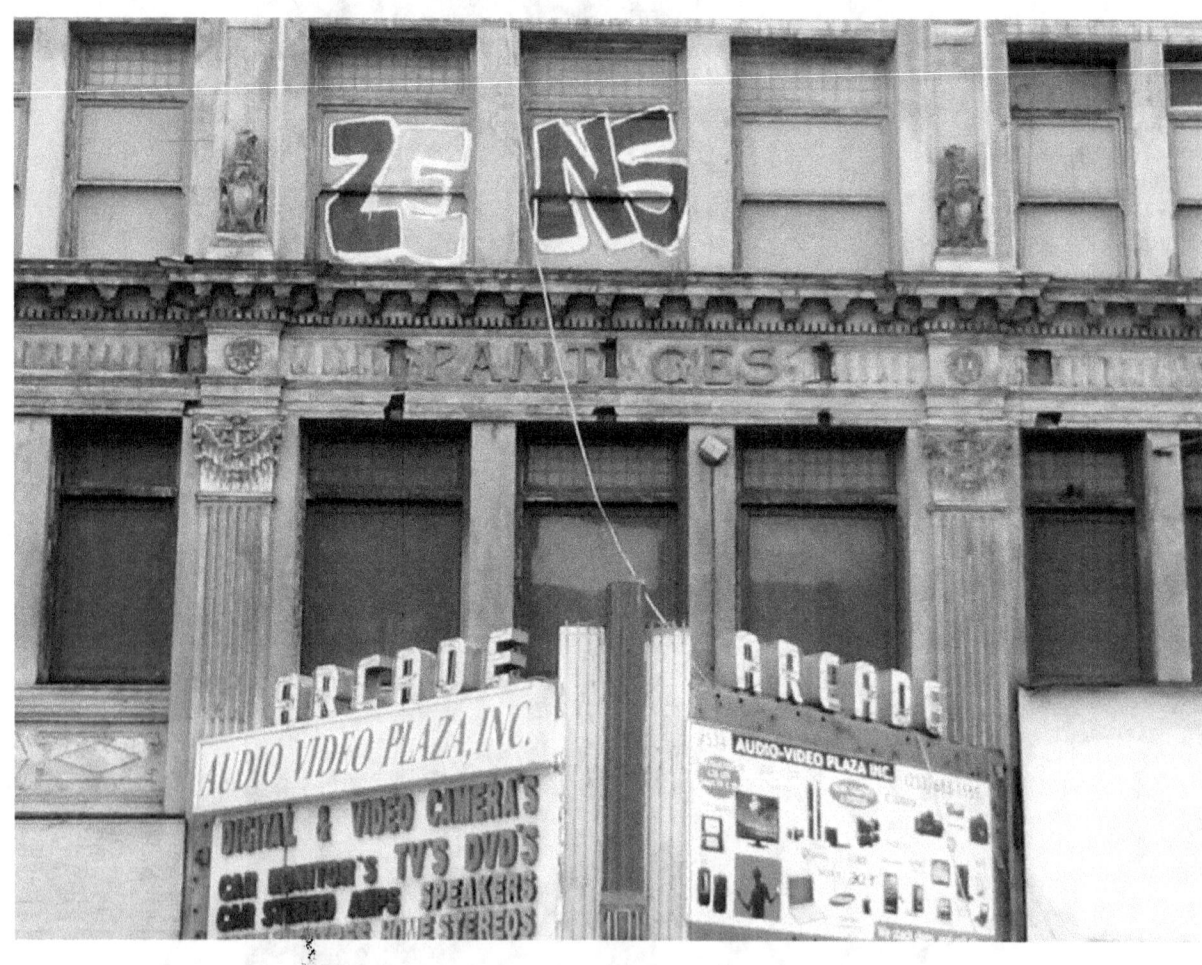

JEWELRY DISTRICT

556 S. Broadway

From Fifth Street to Ninth Street, along Spring Street, Broadway, and Hill, Los Angeles is densely packed with jewelry stores, everything from mom-and-pop shops to bazaar-like jewelry centers and jewelry marts. This is LA's Jewelry District, and along S. Broadway it overlaps with the Theatre District. Pictured below is the Broadway Jewelry Mart. Note the passing police car; LAPD patrols this district regularly, and many jewelry stores hire uniformed security staff to guard their shops.

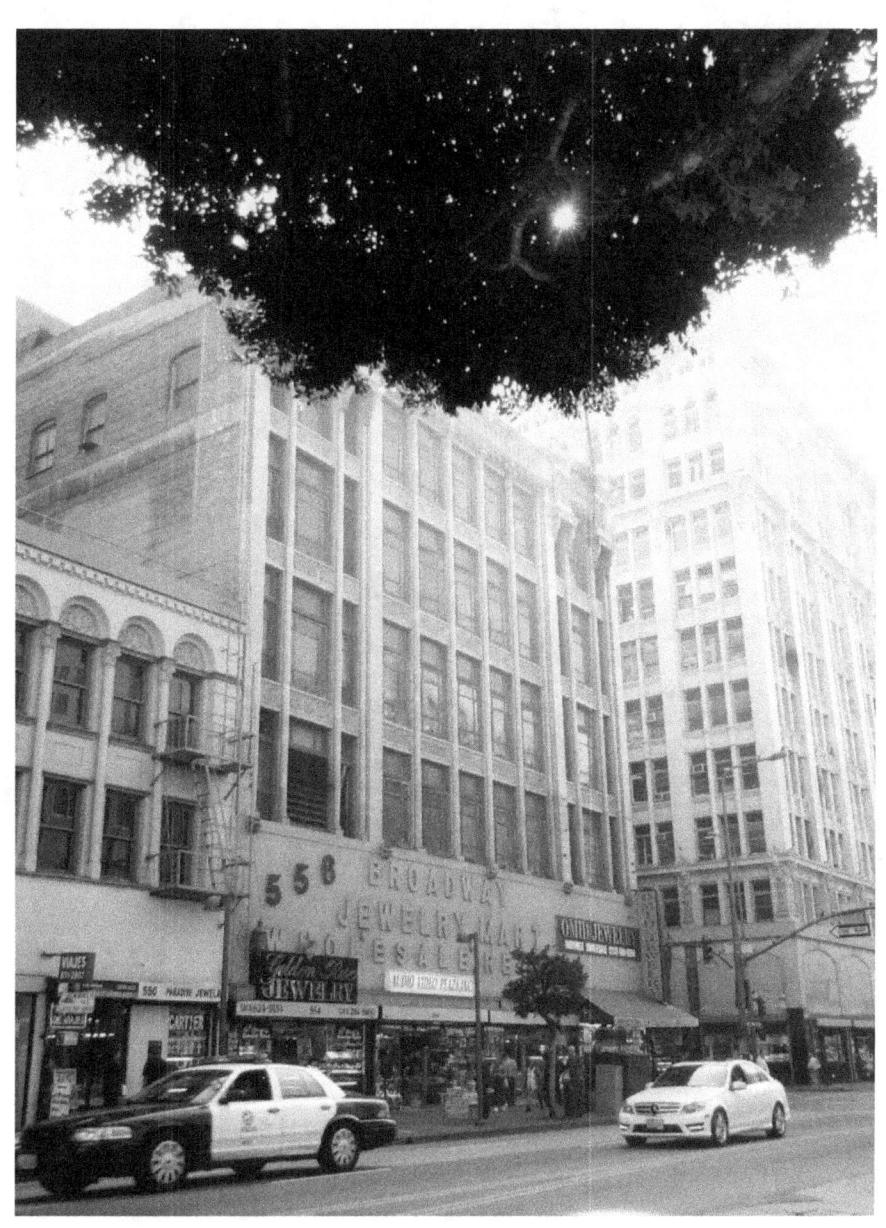

JEWELRY DISTRICT

600 Block of S. Broadway

Despite the rings, bracelets, and gems gleaming in their windows, the jewelry shops lining Broadway tend to have a bodega-like—rather than Tiffany-like—appearance due to neon signs and bright banners. Pictured below: A neon sign indicates that a store is "Open" for business, while signs in three different languages alert passersby that the shop buys gold.

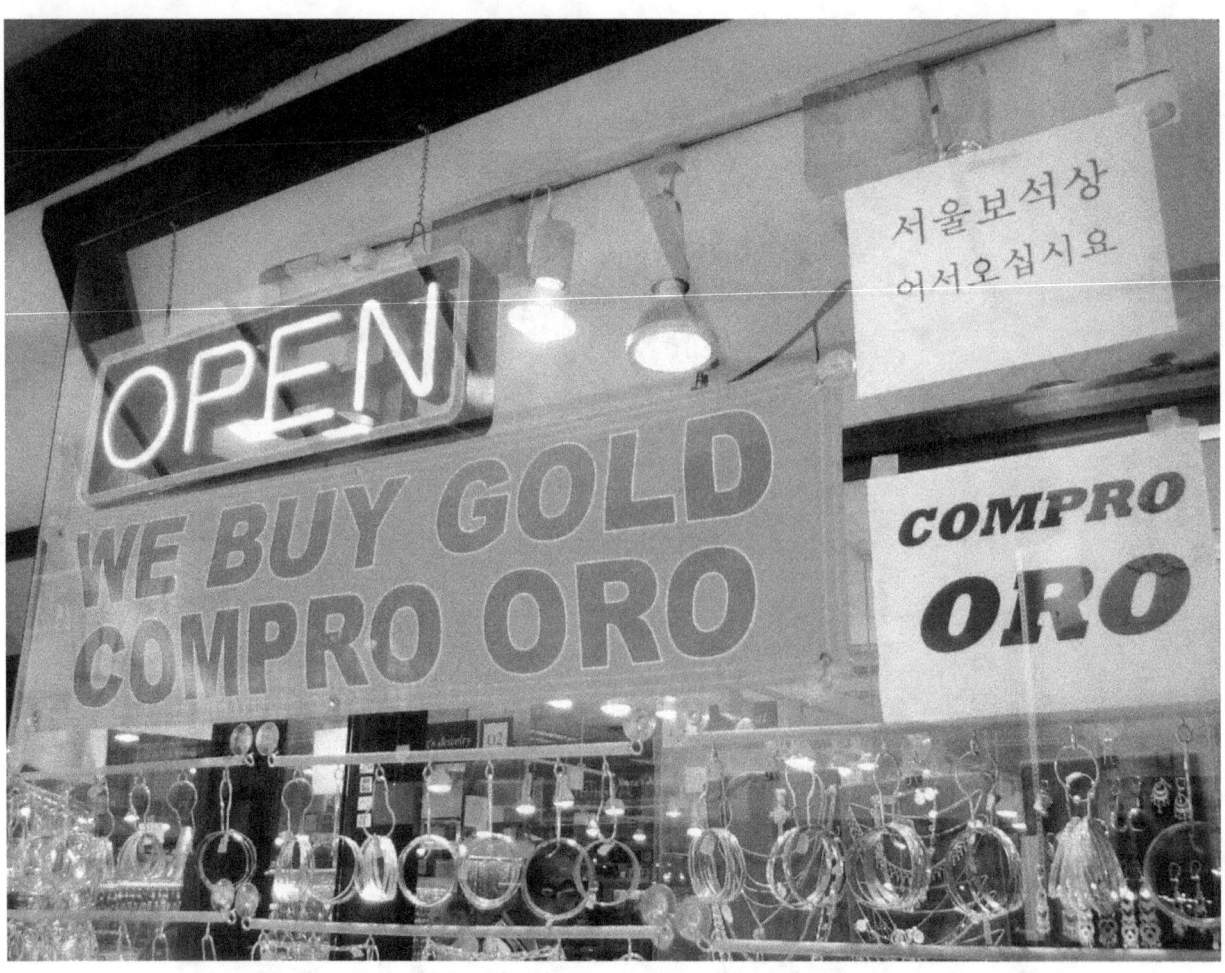

THEATRE DISTRICT

615 S. Broadway

Crossing Sixth Street, we reach the Los Angeles Theatre, with its ornate French Baroque façade. The Los Angeles Theatre opened in 1931 as one of the most glamorous movie palaces Broadway would ever see—not only in 1931, but today. The intricate exterior hints at the elegance within.

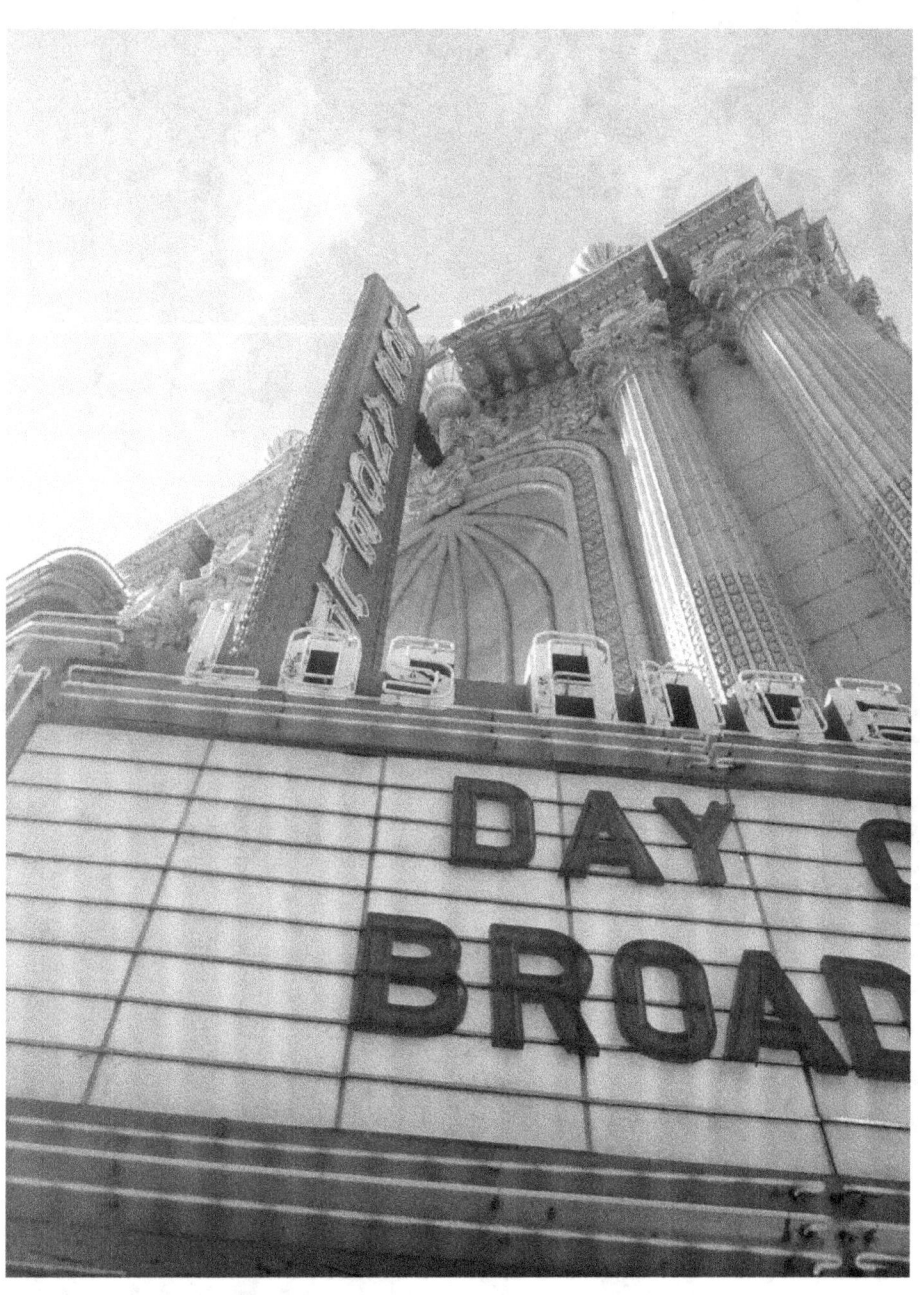

THEATRE DISTRICT

615 S. Broadway

Terrazzo detail on the pavement in front of the Los Angeles Theatre. Despite some cracks, the Los Angeles Theatre's terrazzo is quite well preserved—more so than much of S. Broadway.

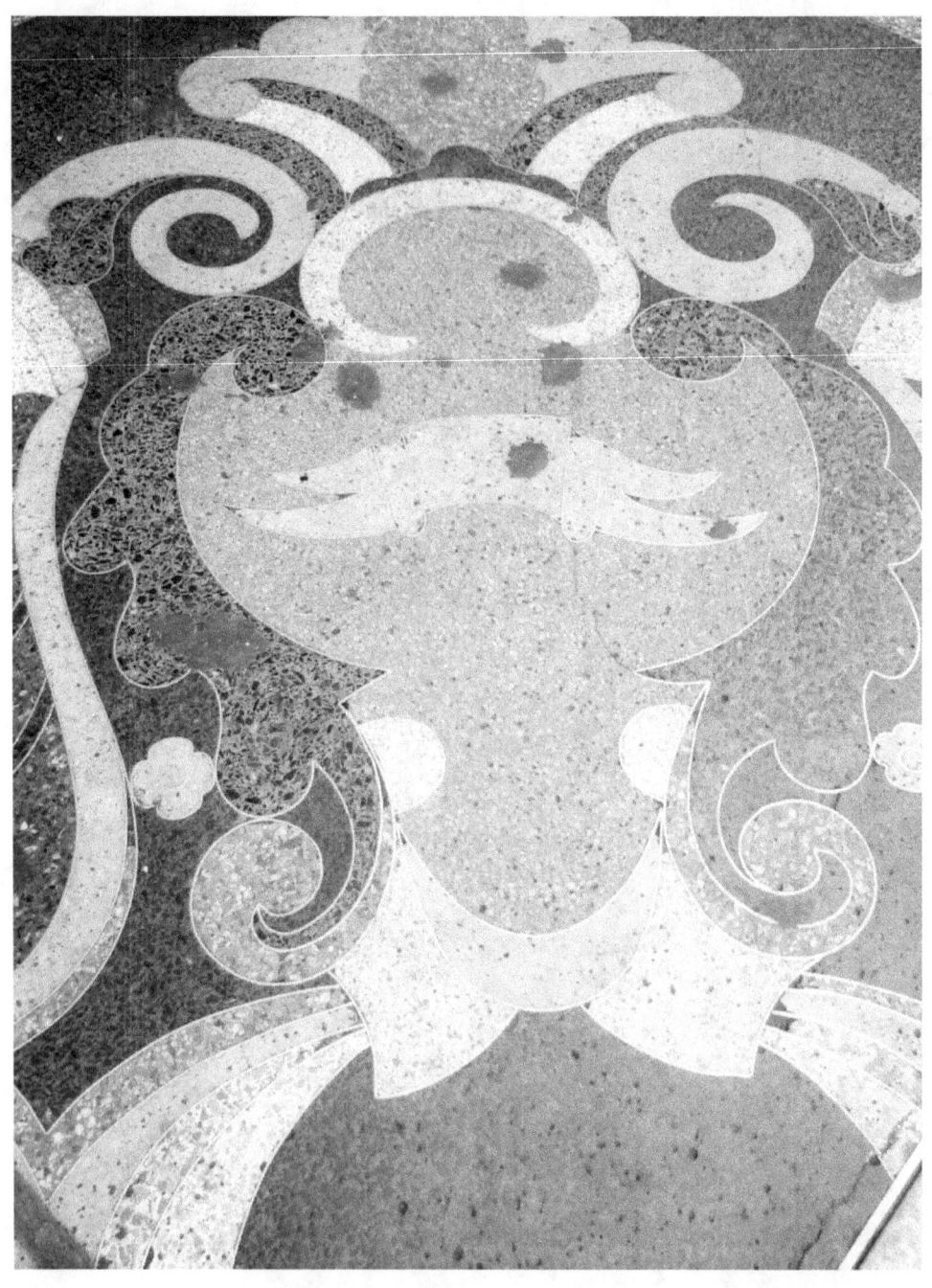

THEATRE DISTRICT

615 S. Broadway

Peering through the box office in front of the Los Angeles Theatre. From glass cubicles such as these, Broadway's theatre's sold tickets to movies, concerts, and vaudeville performances.

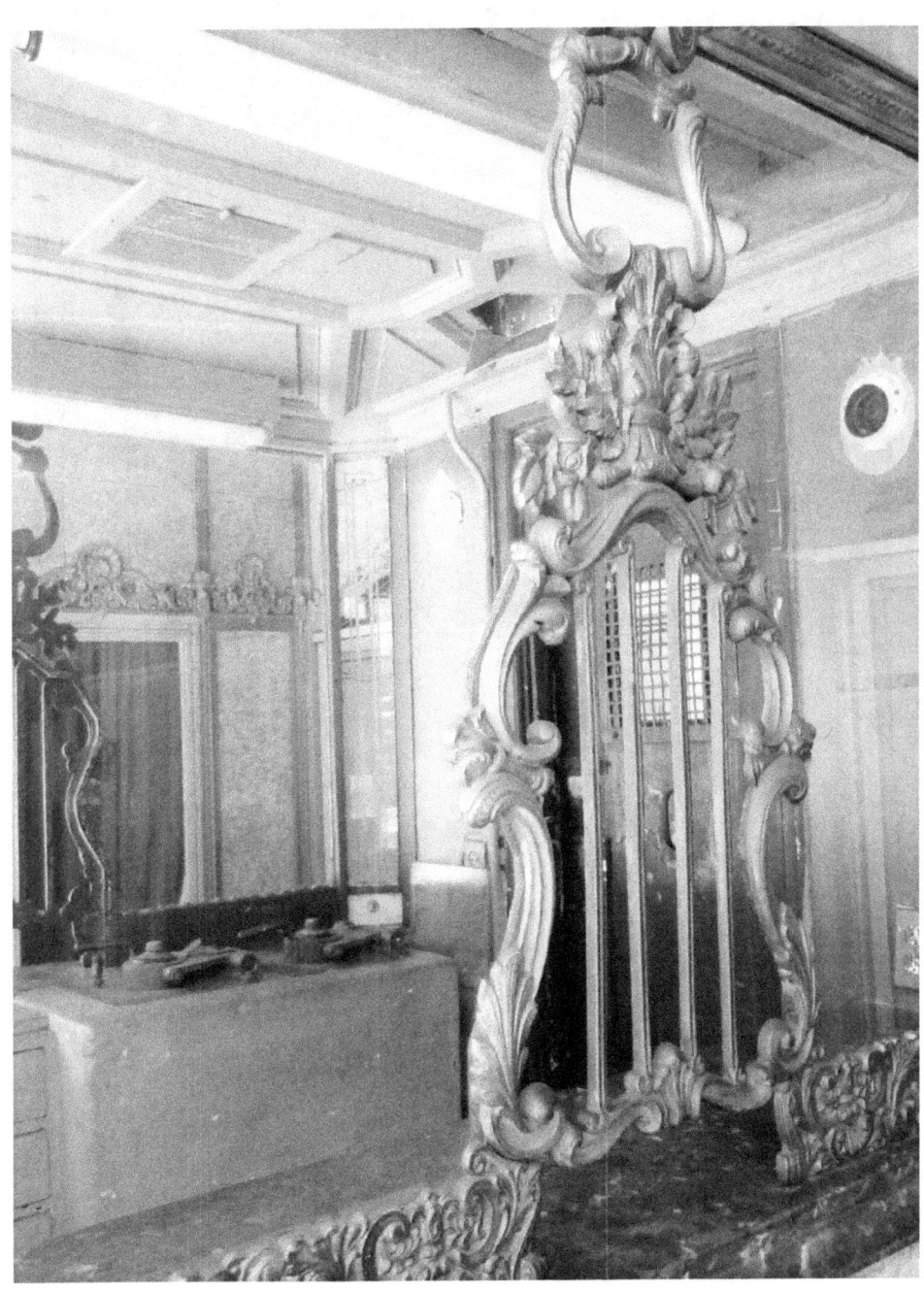

THEATRE DISTRICT

615 S. Broadway

The lobby ceiling at the Los Angeles Theatre—Baroque glamour painstakingly preserved.

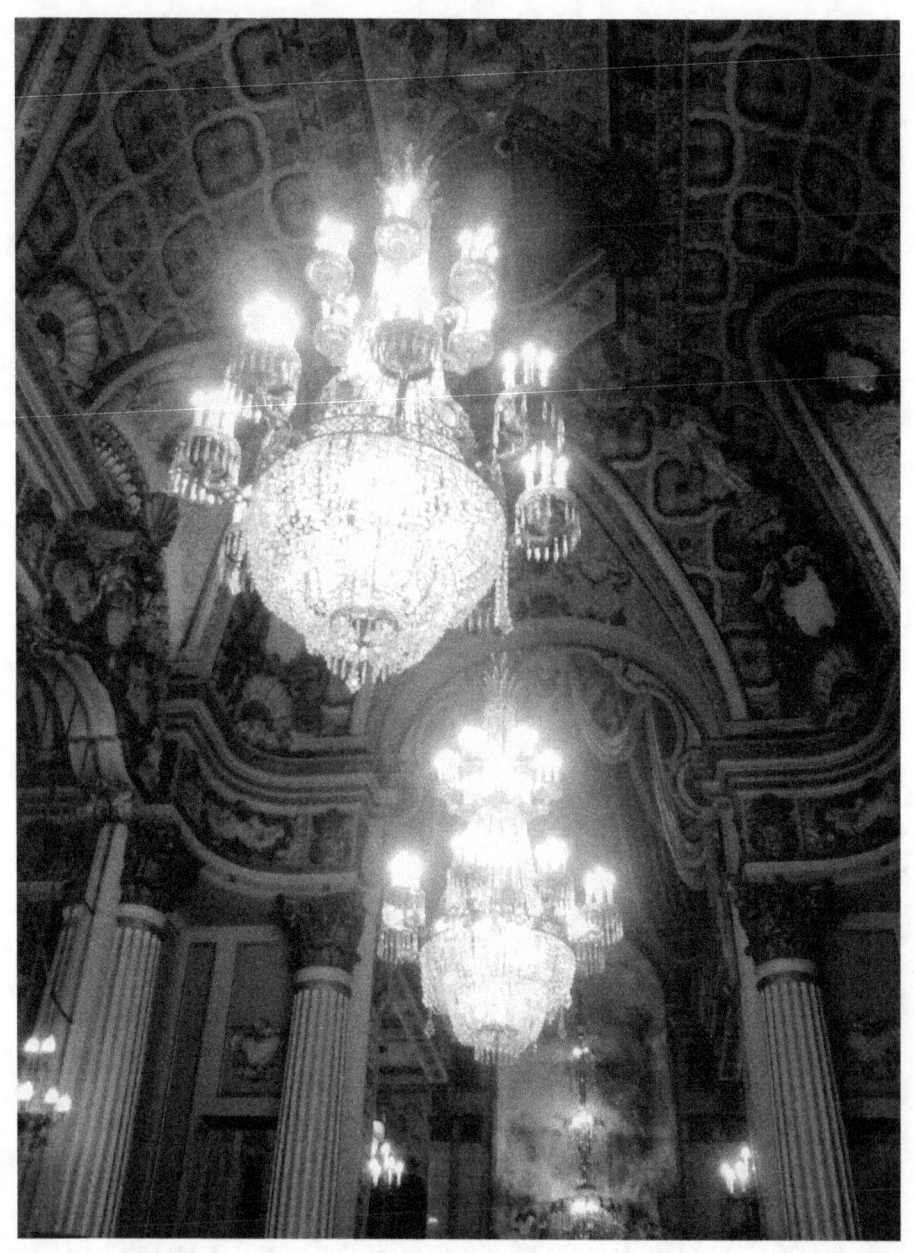

THEATRE DISTRICT

615 S. Broadway

Many pedestrians on S. Broadway have no idea that treasures like these chandeliers, columns, and sculptural elements even exist behind the closed doors of the Los Angeles Theatre. Pictured here: A view of the lobby from the mezzanine.

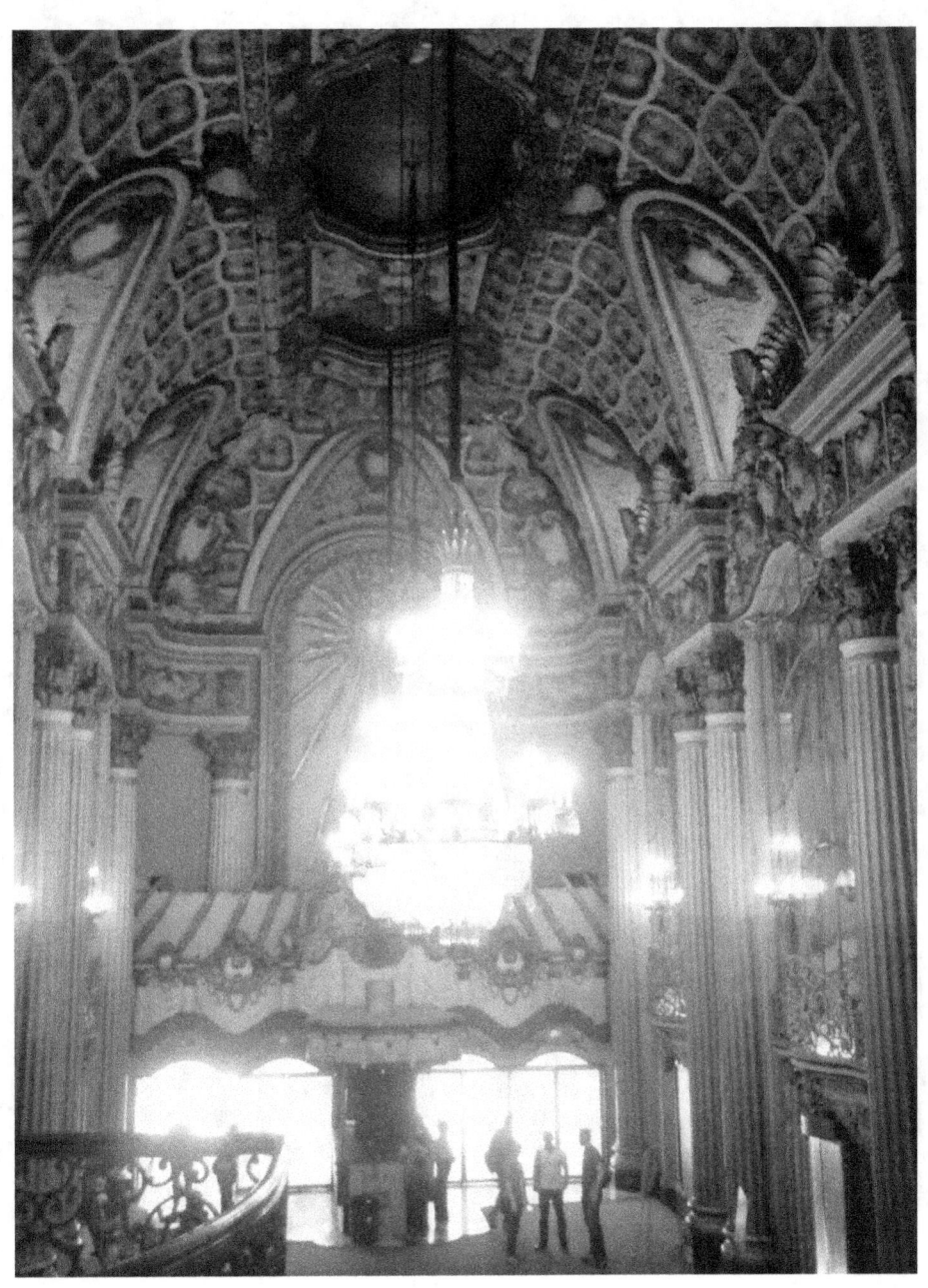

THEATRE DISTRICT

615 S. Broadway

A frozen waterfall of crystalline light illuminates a mural atop the mezzanine stairs.

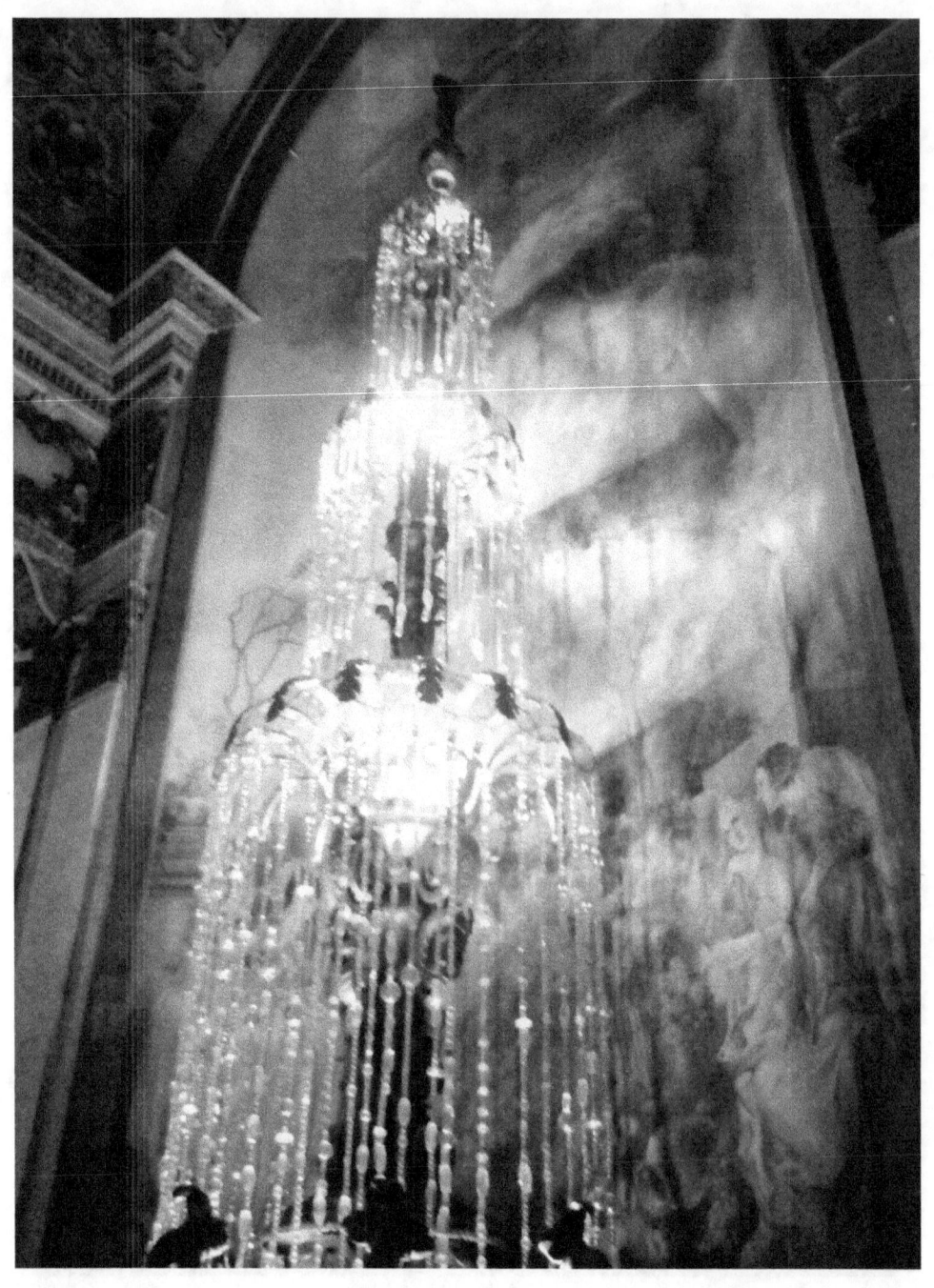

THEATRE DISTRICT

615 S. Broadway

Although the stage and auditorium at the 2,000-seat Los Angeles Theatre are lovely...

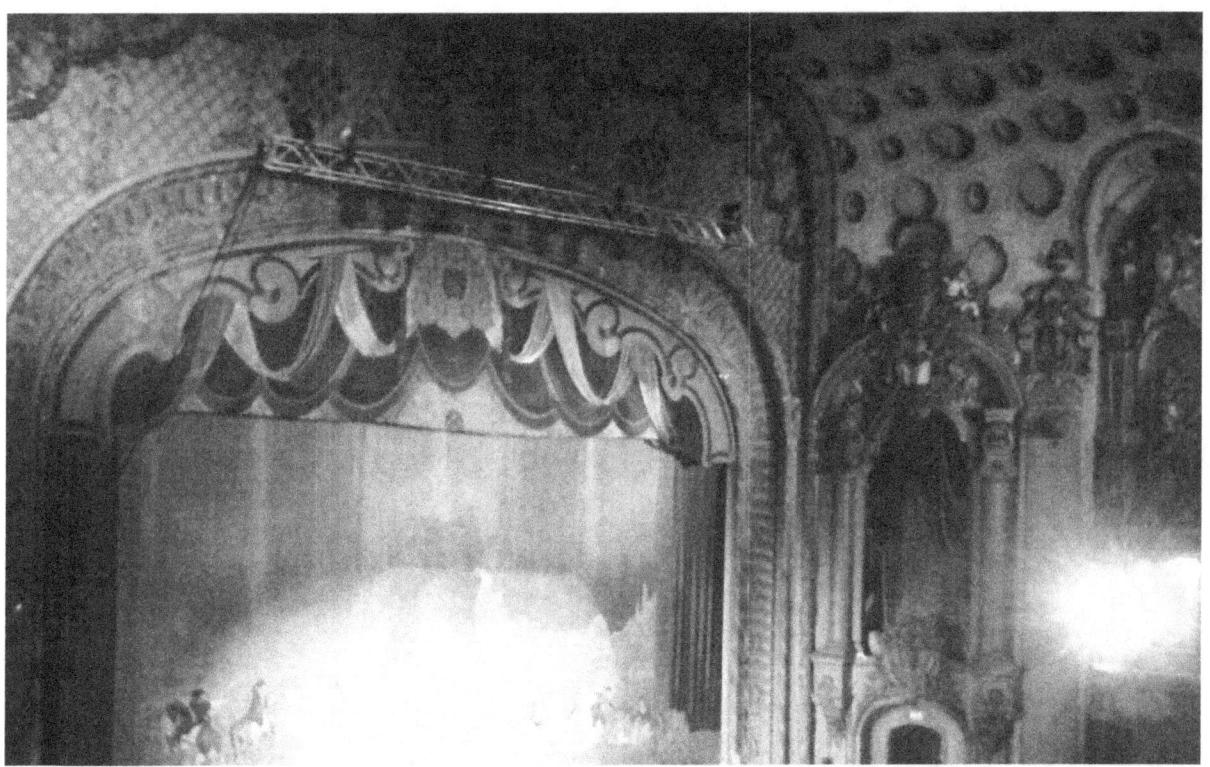

THEATRE DISTRICT
615 S. Broadway

... and well worth exploring should one have the opportunity ...

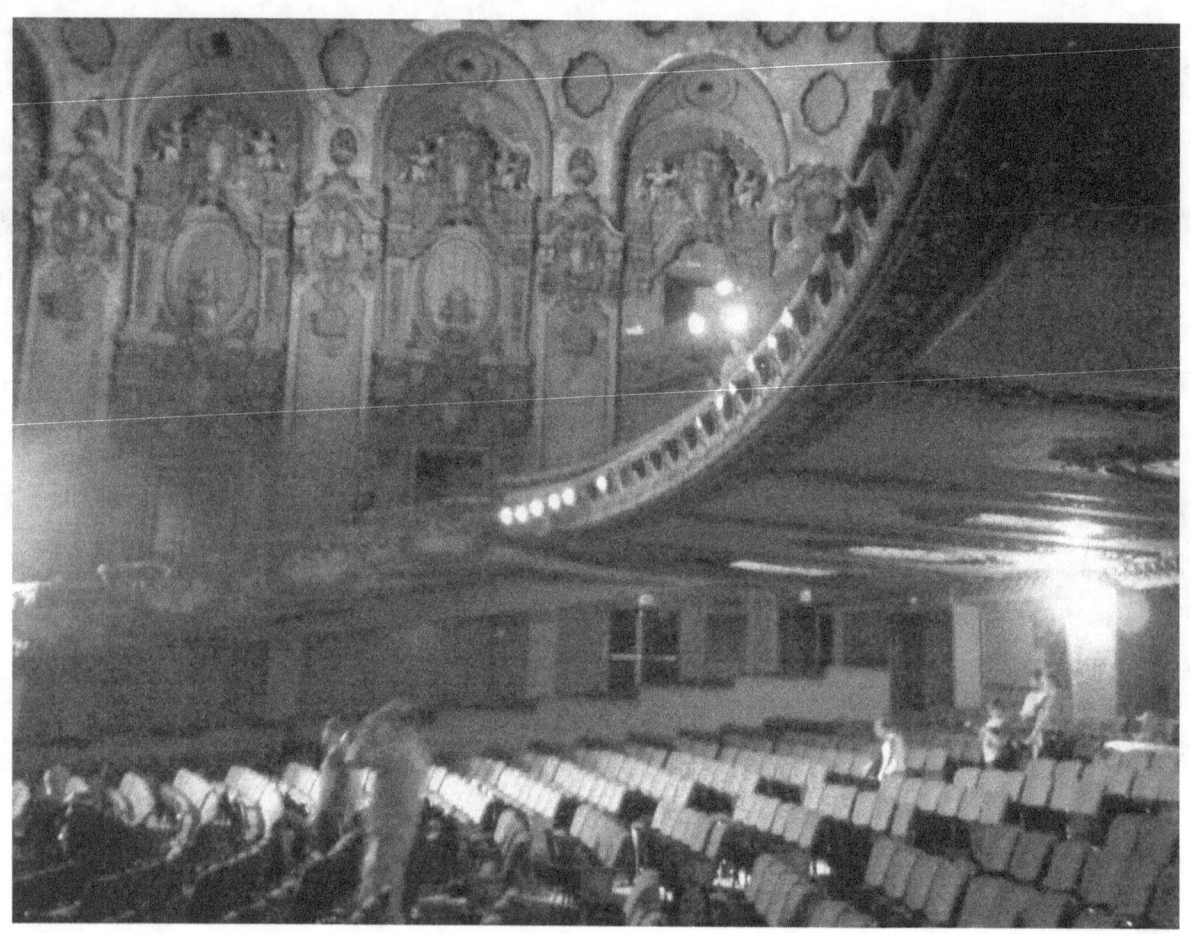

THEATRE DISTRICT

615 S. Broadway

... the real treasures at the Los Angeles Theatre are concealed well below street level. Upon descending this rather unassuming—if pretty—staircase, visitors discover ...

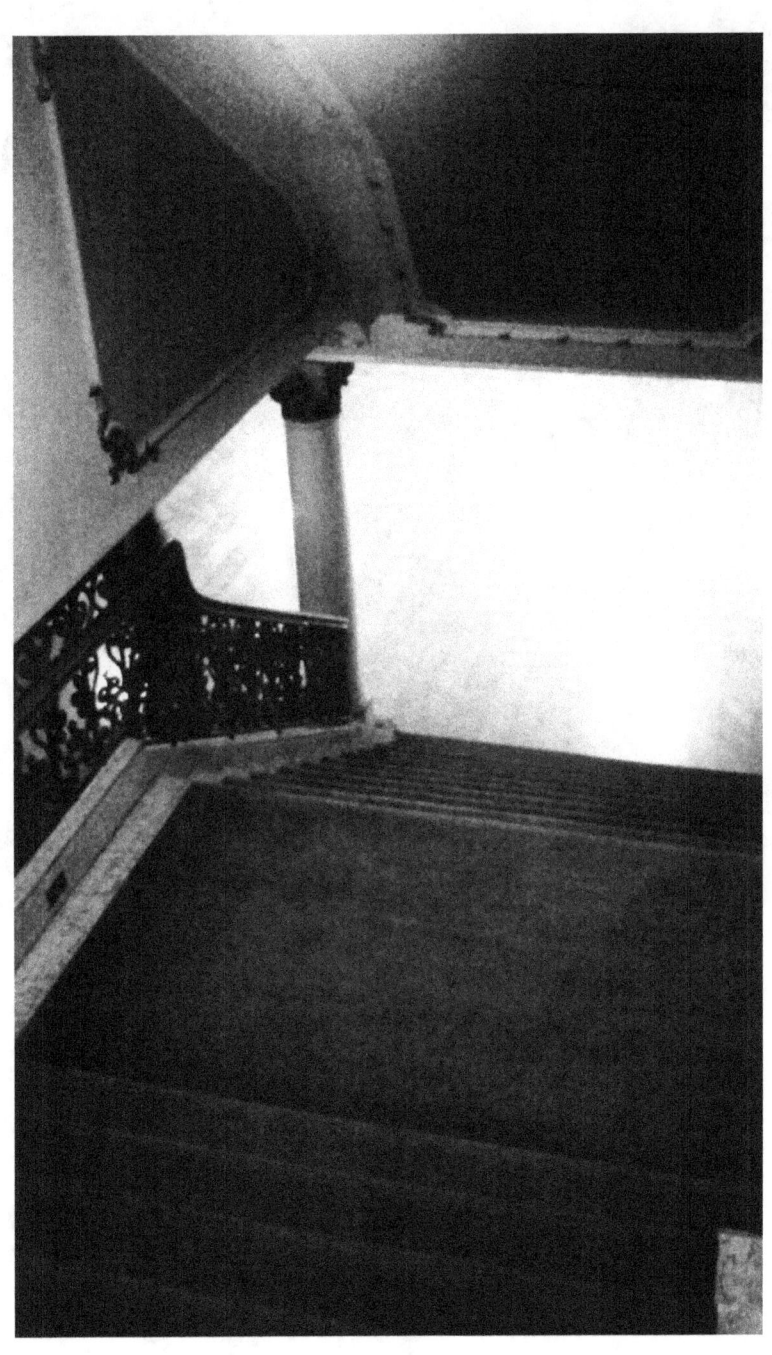

THEATRE DISTRICT

615 S. Broadway

... a grand, mirrored chamber with a polished hardwood floor, and intriguing anterooms.

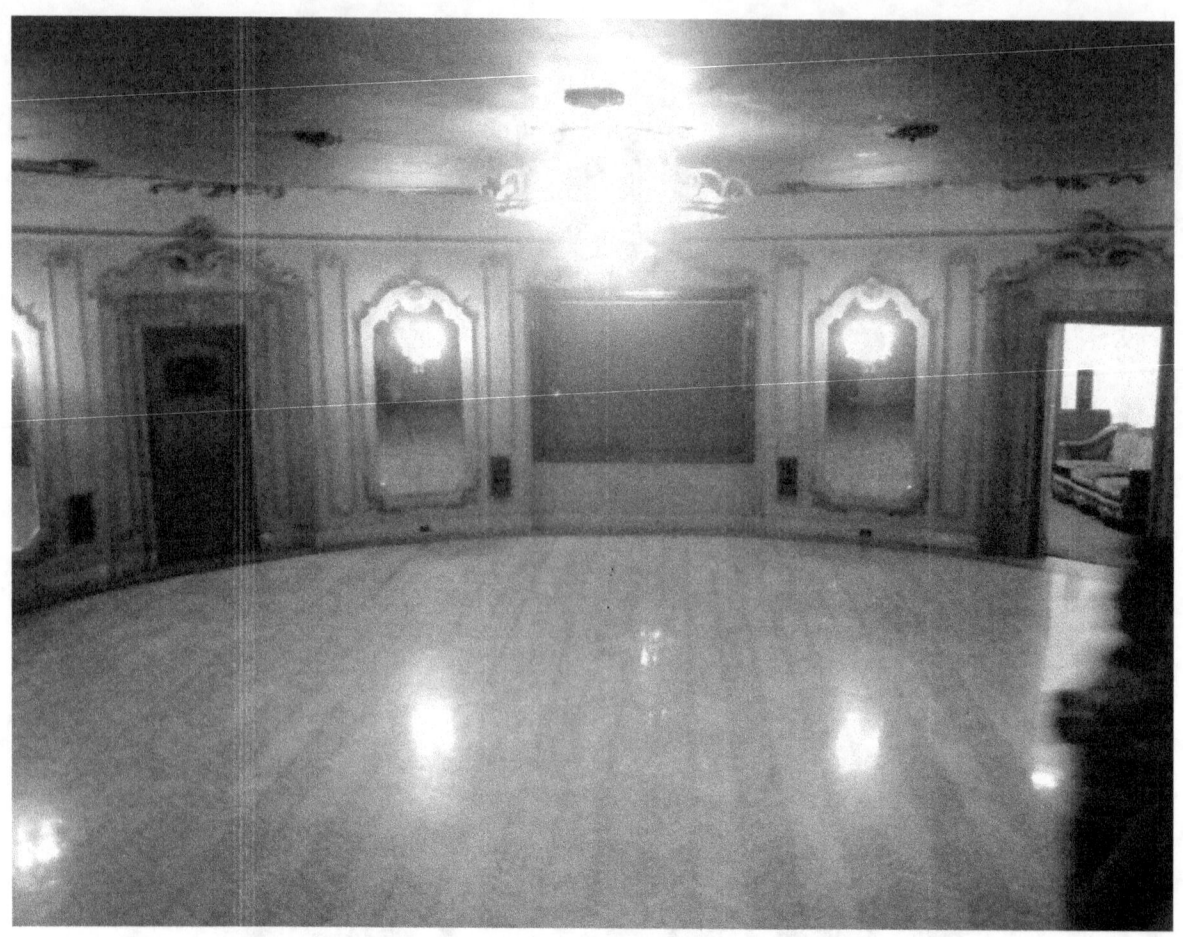

THEATRE DISTRICT

615 S. Broadway

Twin staircases sweep visitors down to a lower level for yet more of the Los Angeles Theatre's architectural riches ...

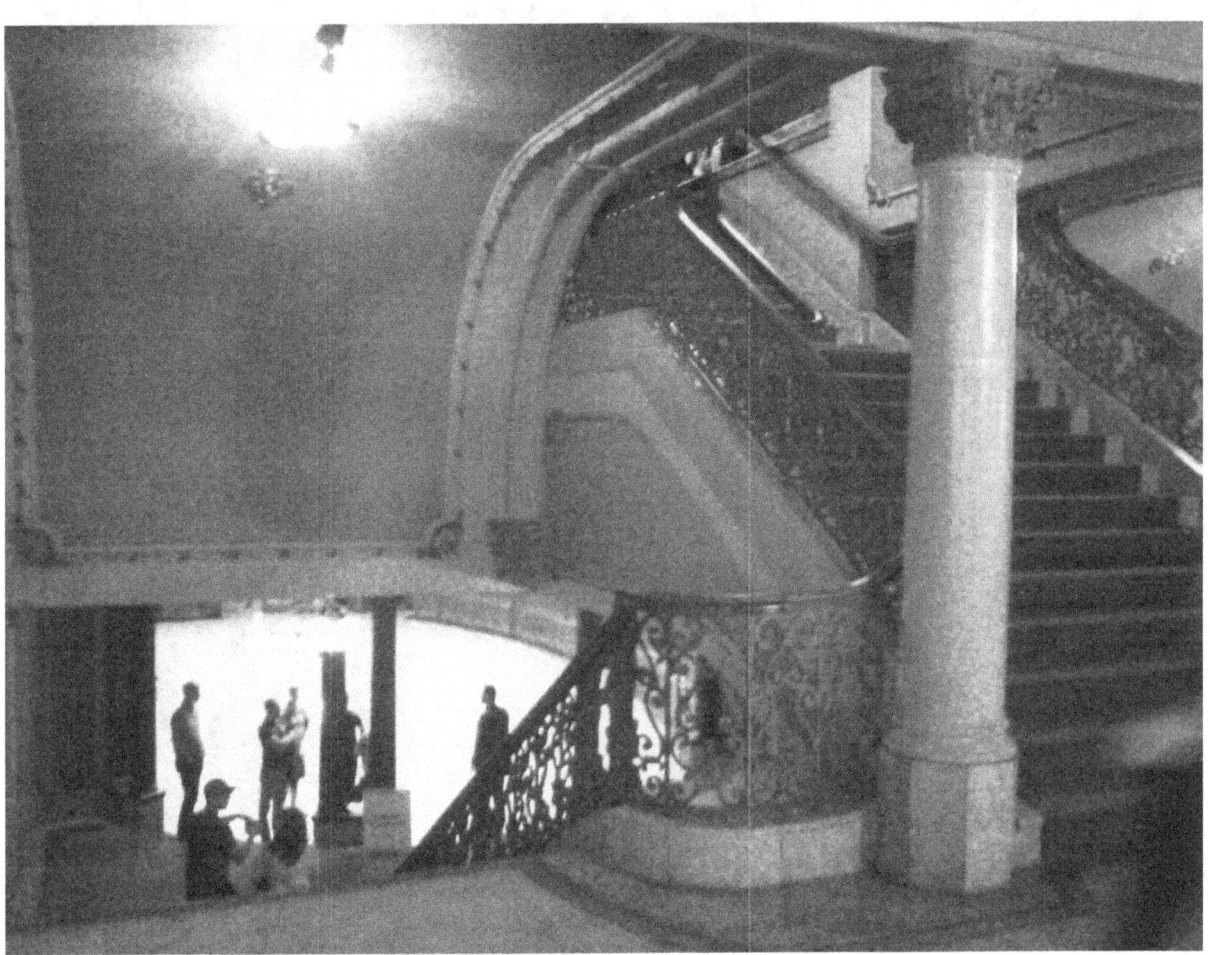

THEATRE DISTRICT

615 S. Broadway

... such as this grand ballroom, with its dark wood paneling and posts ...

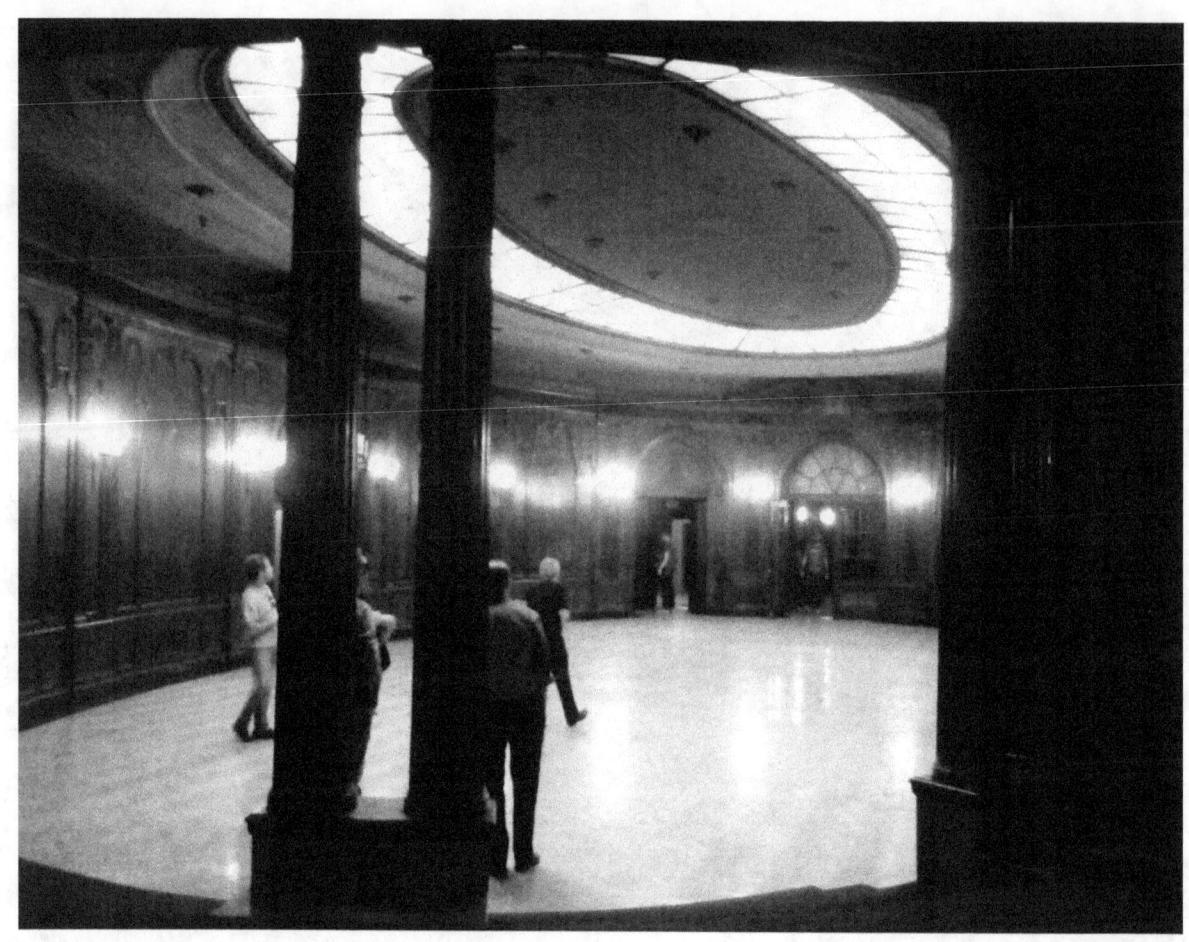

THEATRE DISTRICT

615 S. Broadway

... *lit by brilliant overhead light panels.*

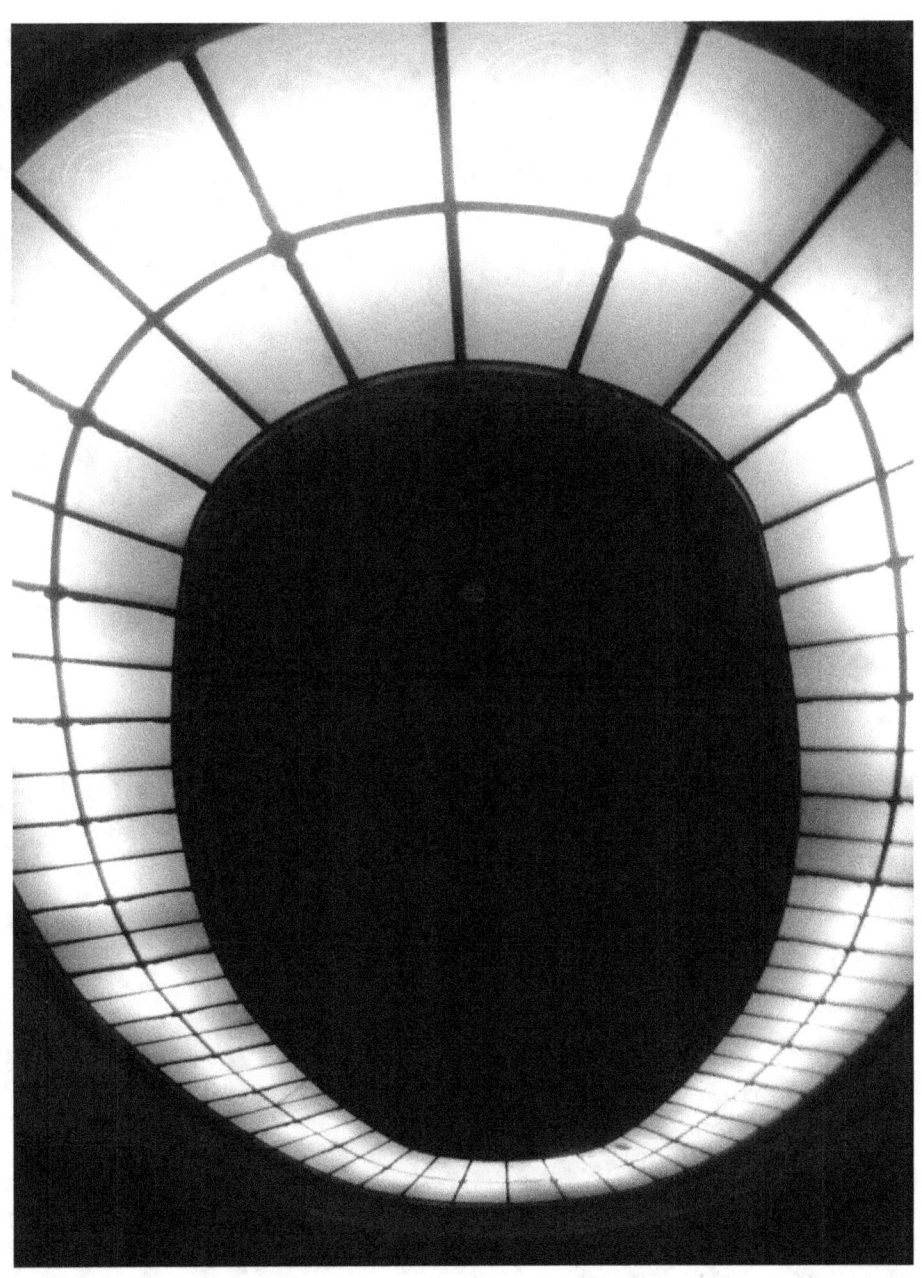

THEATRE DISTRICT

615 S. Broadway

The ballroom leads to other elegant chambers, like a Refreshment room ...

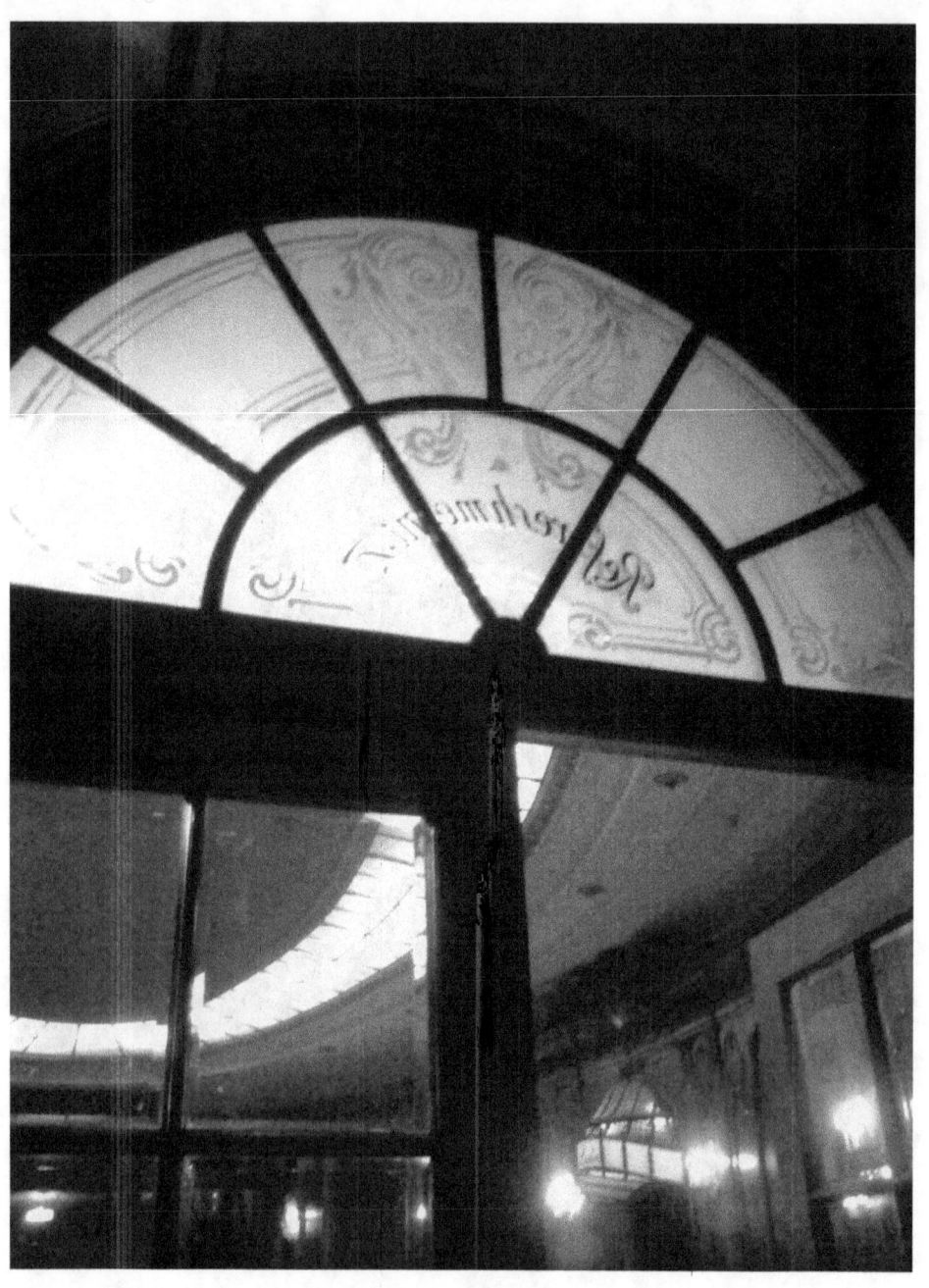

THEATRE DISTRICT

615 S. Broadway

... and a powder room that was the last word in glamour.

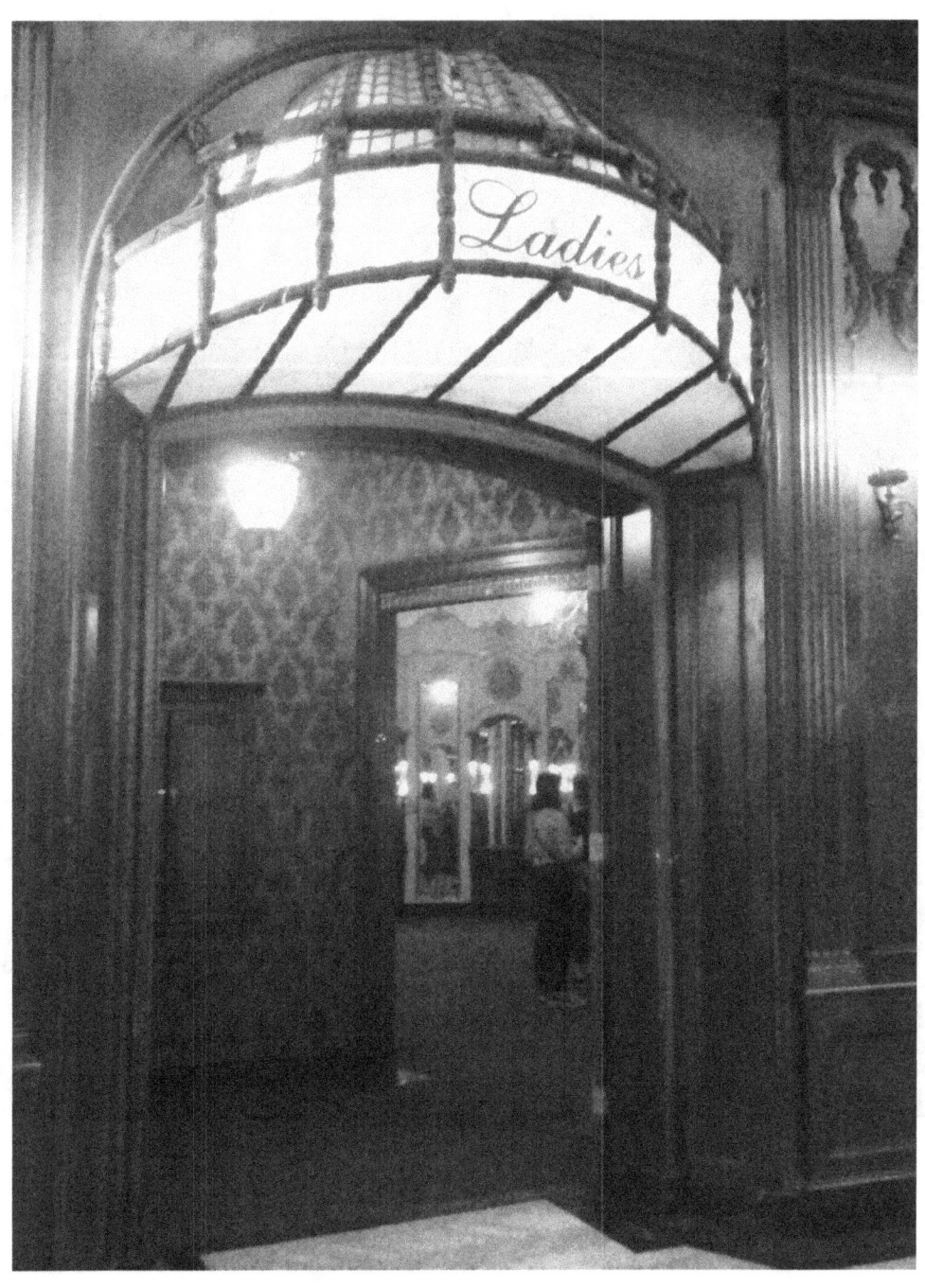

THEATRE DISTRICT

615 S. Broadway

The Ladies Lounge is a Versailles-like mirrored chamber where women visiting the Los Angeles Theatre could adjust their lipstick. Just beyond the lounge is a vast complex of pastel-painted commodes, each one tinted a different complementary color for a luxurious effect.

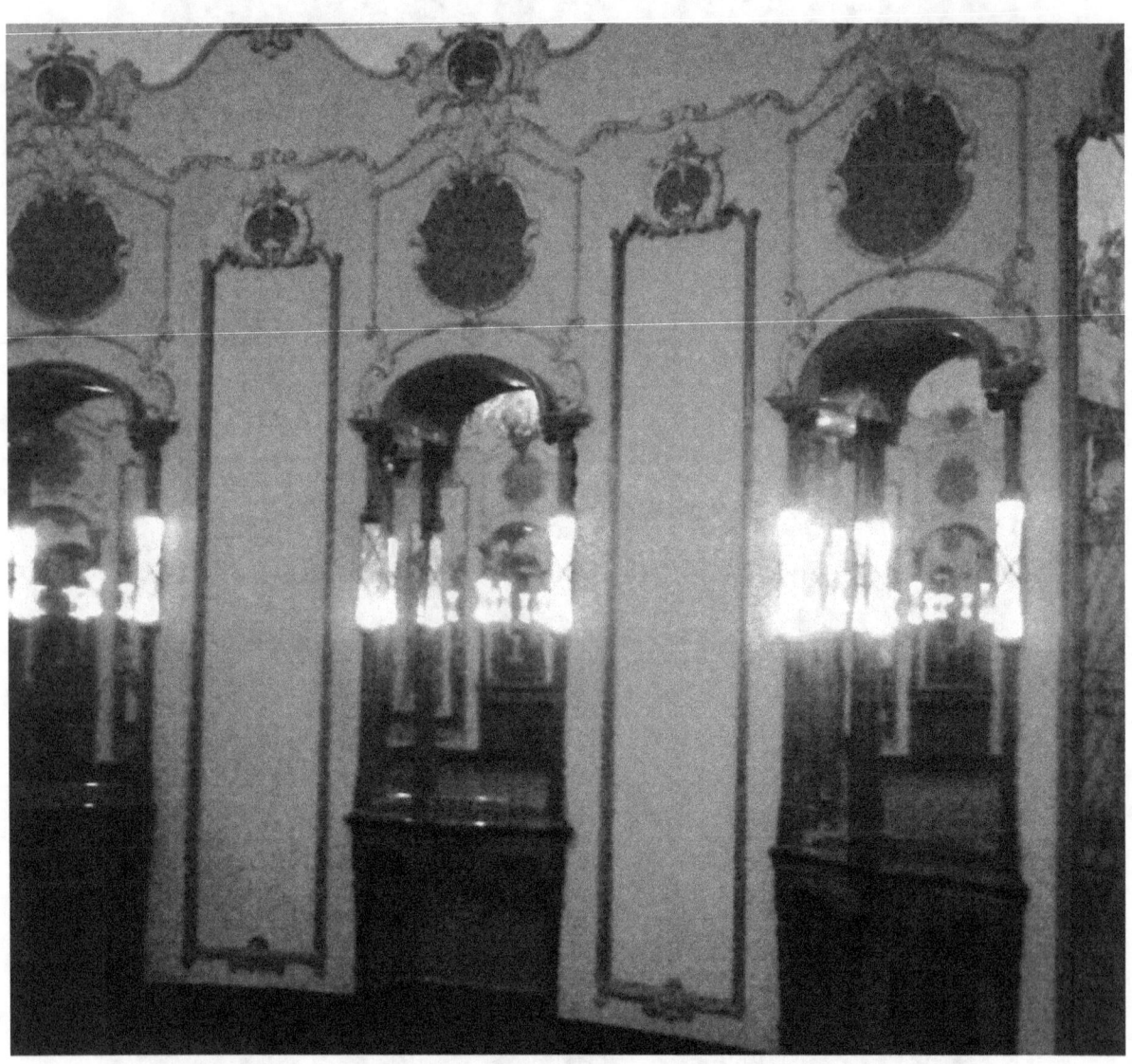

THEATRE DISTRICT

615 S. Broadway

A maze of unfinished rooms deep beneath the Los Angeles Theatre await further restoration.

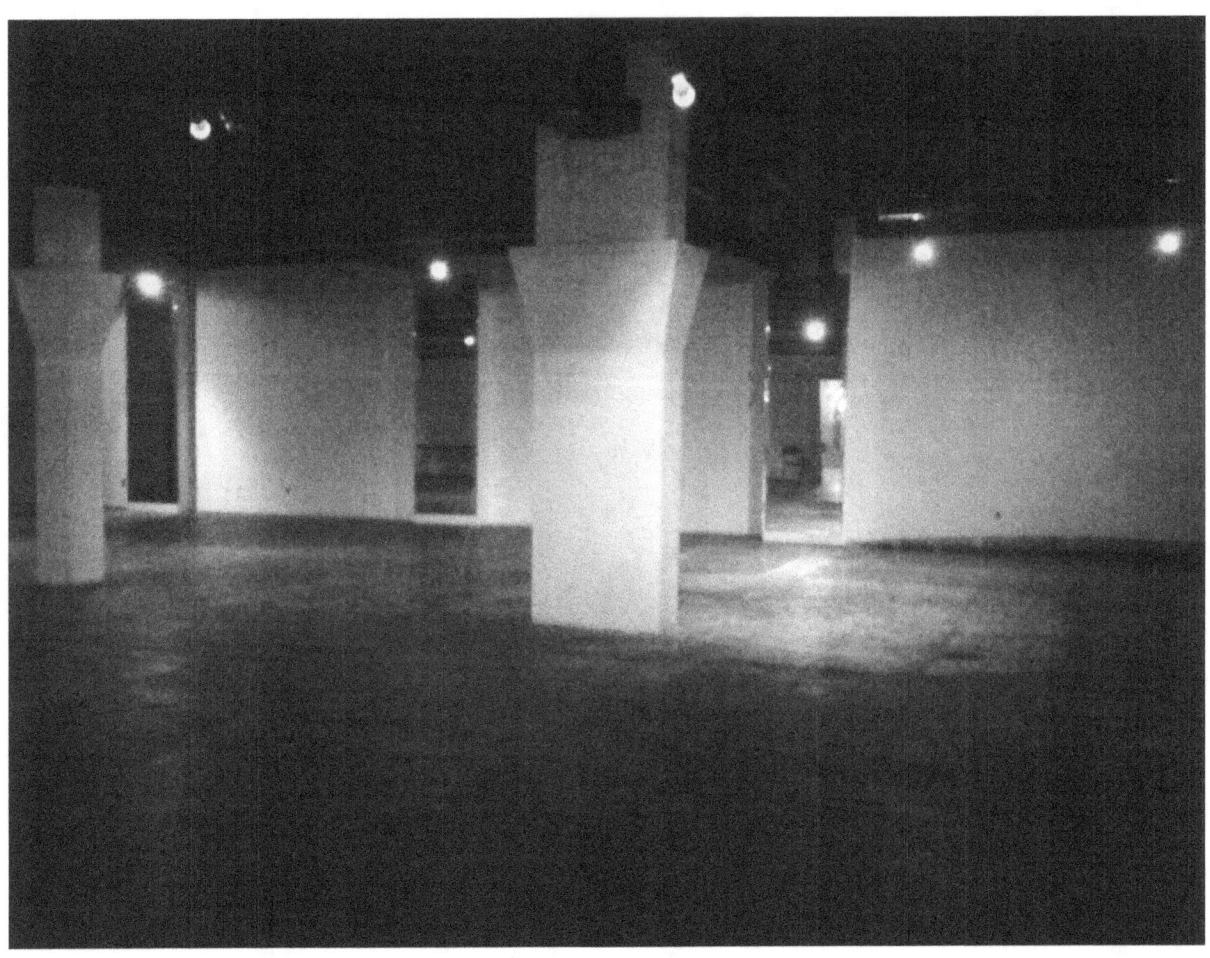

THEATRE DISTRICT

615 S. Broadway

This is one of the best-preserved theatres on S. Broadway. Readers are encouraged to visit if the opportunity arises.

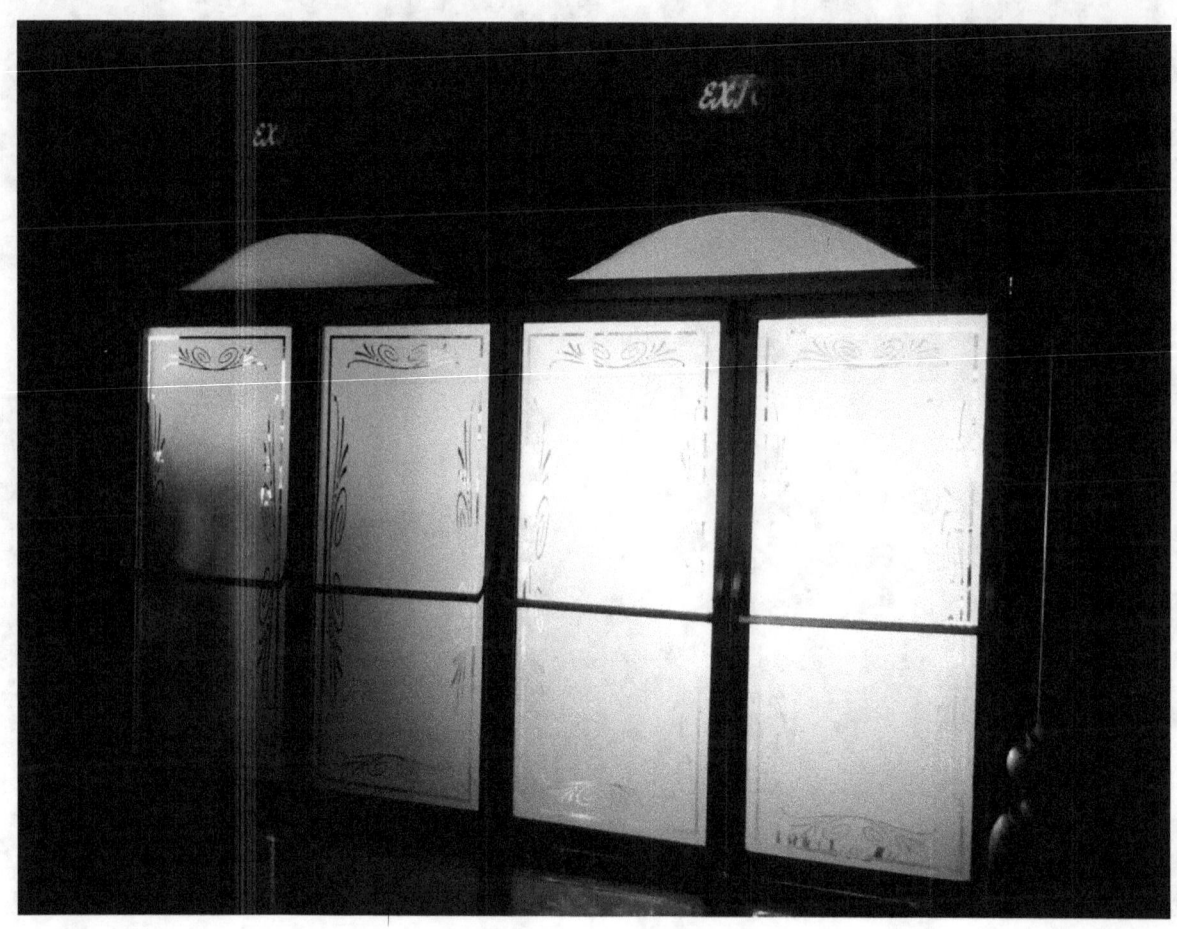

THEATRE DISTRICT

630 S. Broadway

Across the street from the Los Angeles Theatre is the Palace Theatre. Launched in 1911, it's presently sandwiched between a jewelry store—since this is a section of S. Broadway where the Jewelry District and Theatre District overlap—and a discount electronic shop.

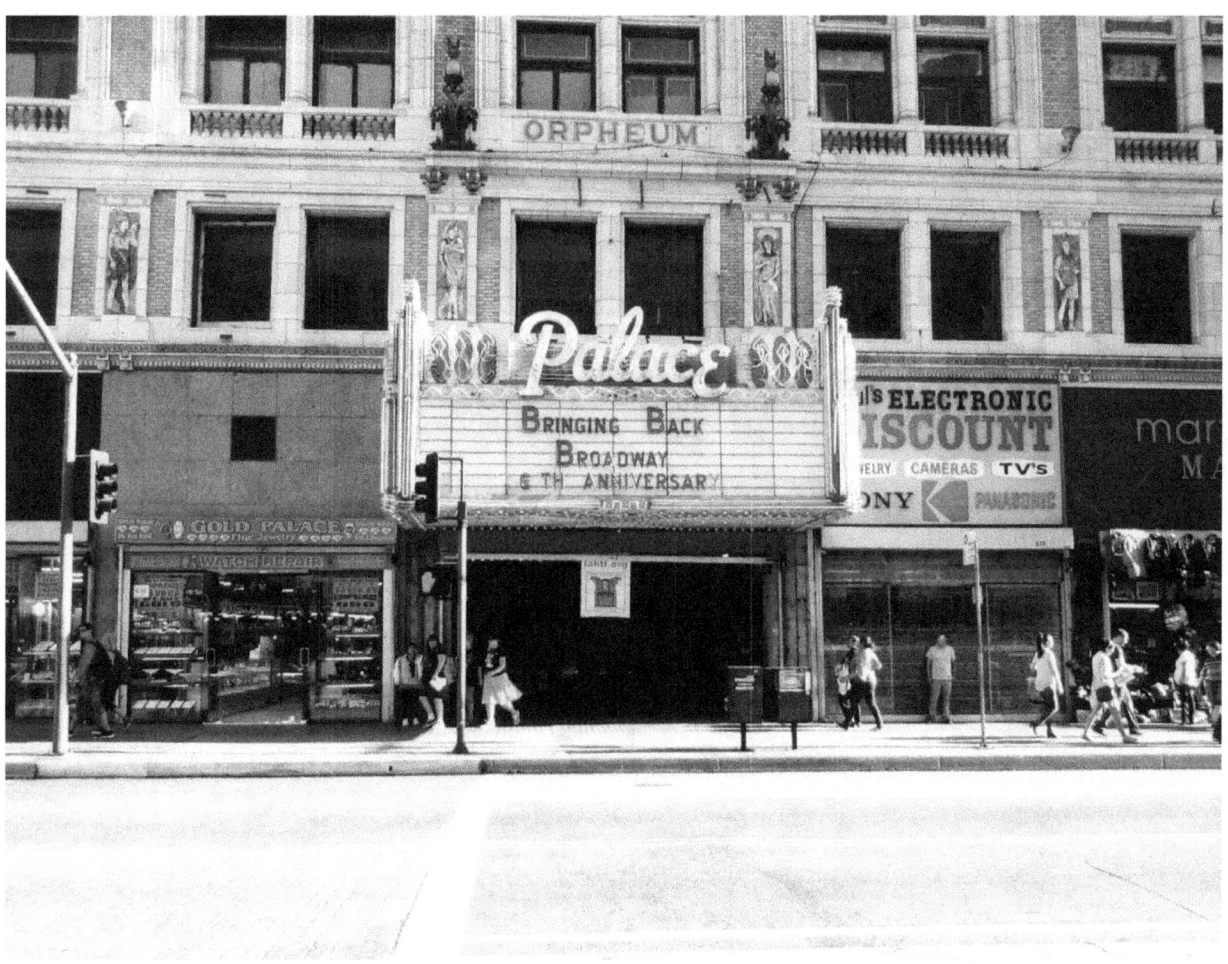

THEATRE DISTRICT

630 S. Broadway

The Palace Theatre was originally part of the Orpheum chain (as indicated by the name above the marquee). From its opening in 1911 until 1926 the theatre was a vaudeville house. No surprise, then, that the figures above the marquee depict the "muses of vaudeville".

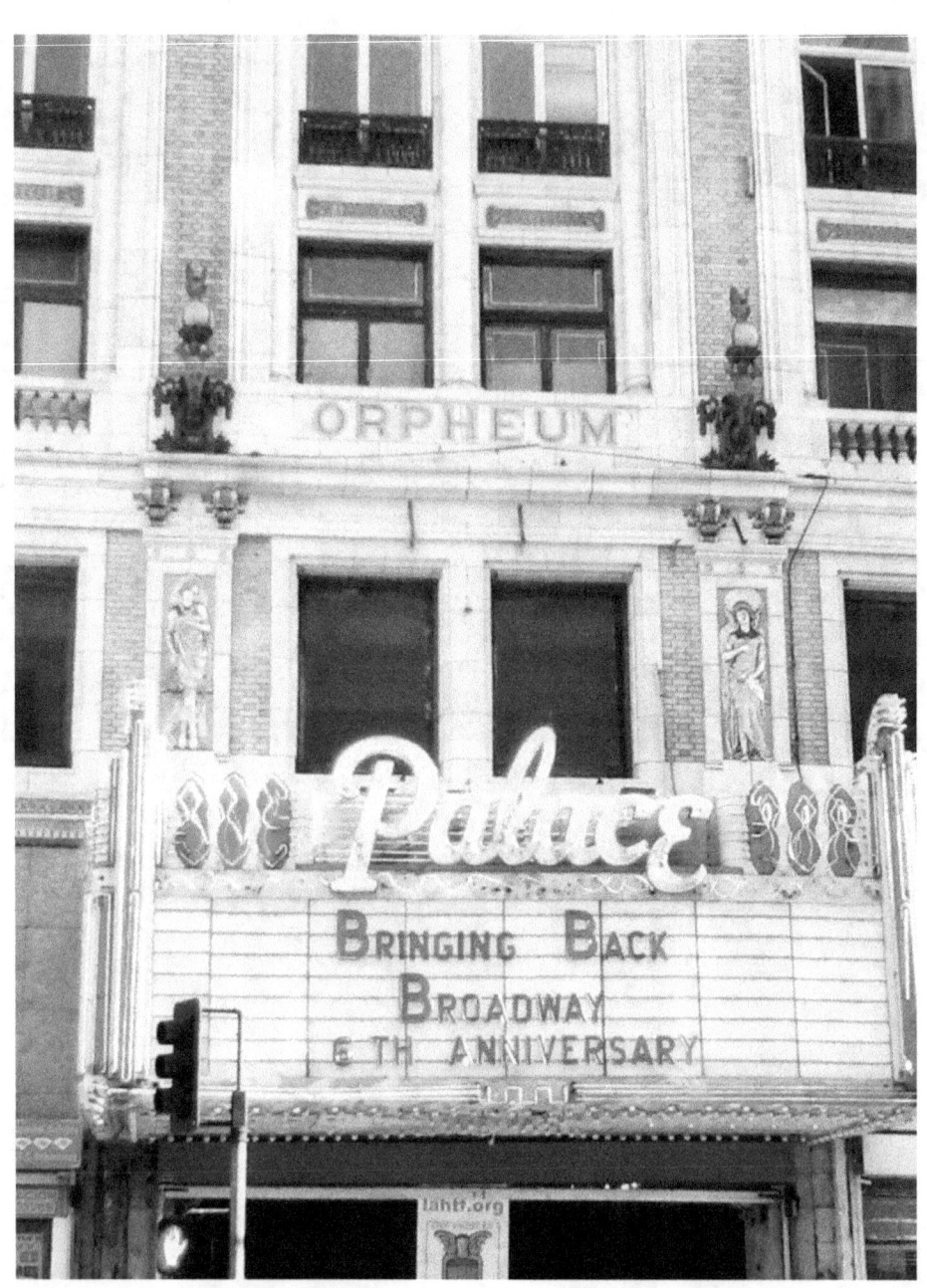

THEATRE DISTRICT

630 S. Broadway

Colorful floral and botanically themed stencils decorate the ceiling of the Palace Theatre's foyer. Even the chandelier (top center) has a "leaf" motif.

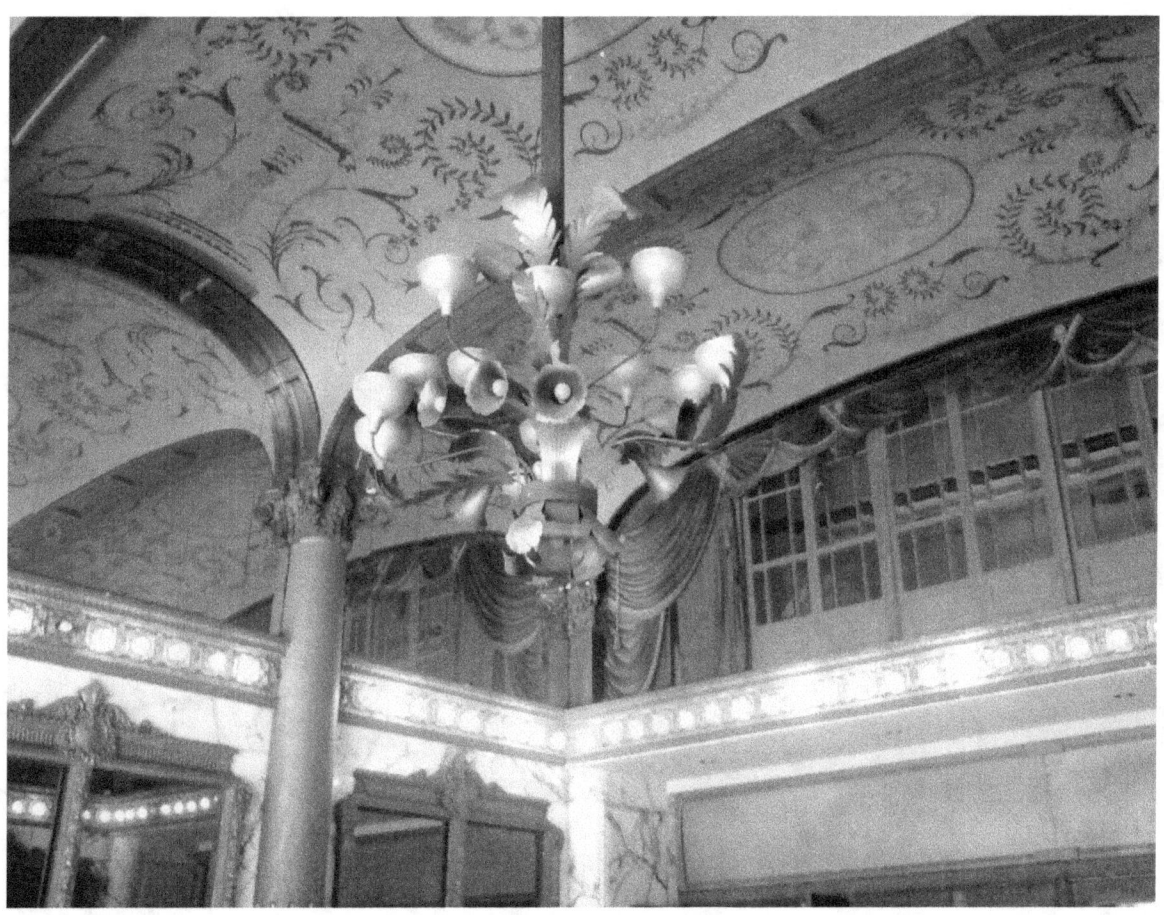

THEATRE DISTRICT

630 S. Broadway

When the Orpheum vaudeville theatre opened in 1911, it had 2,200 seats. Today's Palace Theatre feels much smaller—smaller, for example, than the 2,000-seat Los Angeles Theatre across the street. And despite touches like the moldings and the two enormous paintings flanking the stage, the Palace Theatre lacks the sumptuousness of its sibling across the street.

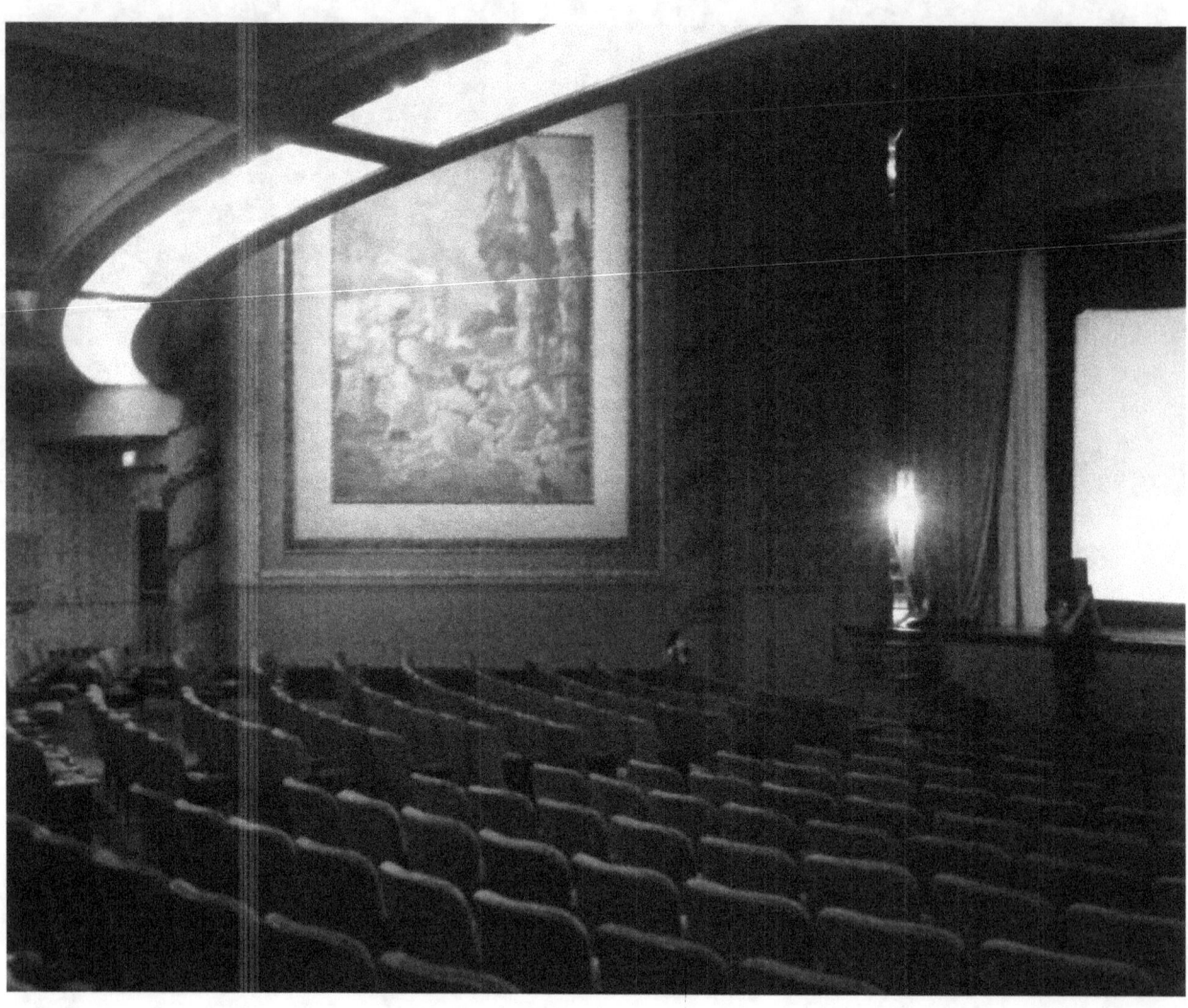

THEATRE DISTRICT

630 S. Broadway

Even so, the Palace Theatre has charm, particular since its recent million-dollar renovations by Ed Kelsey's team. Slowly, painstakingly, features that had been hidden away behind concrete, plaster, and layers of varnish and paint were rediscovered and restored for new generations to enjoy.

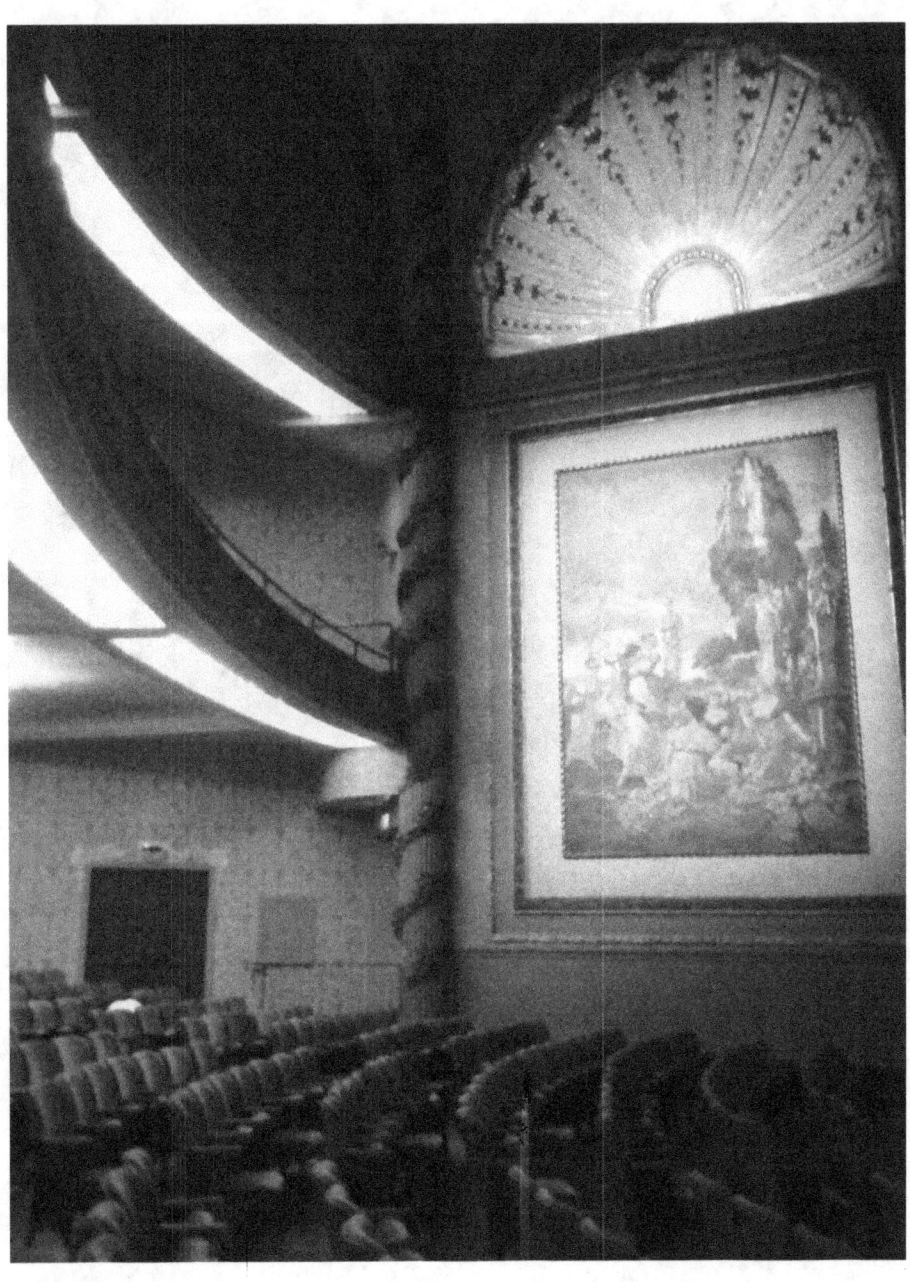

THEATRE DISTRICT

630 S. Broadway

A view of the Palace's lower-level balcony.

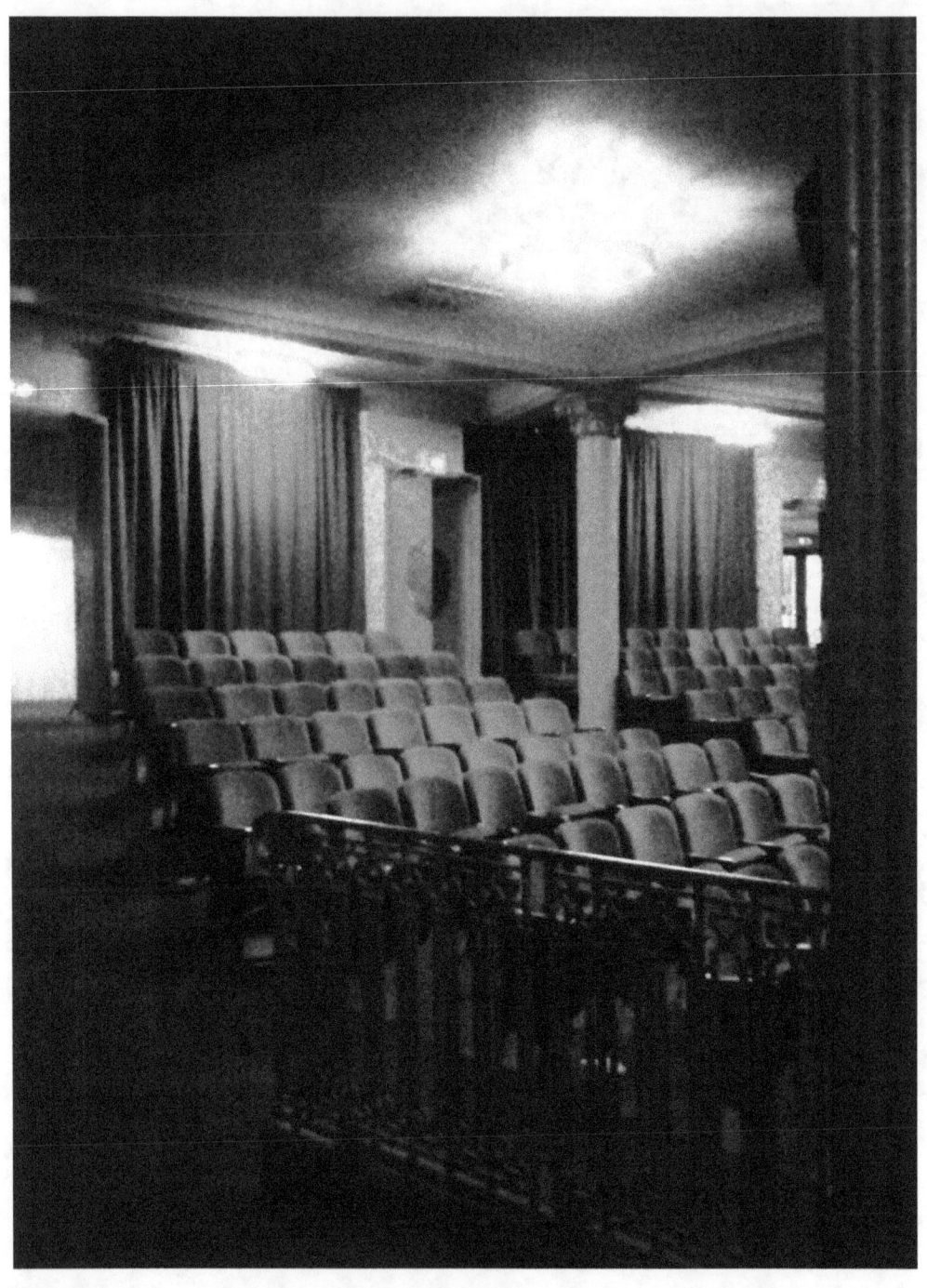

THEATRE DISTRICT

630 S. Broadway

The Palace Theatre was once segregated, as were other theatres along S. Broadway. Outside stairs led to balconies where segregated patrons were required to sit.

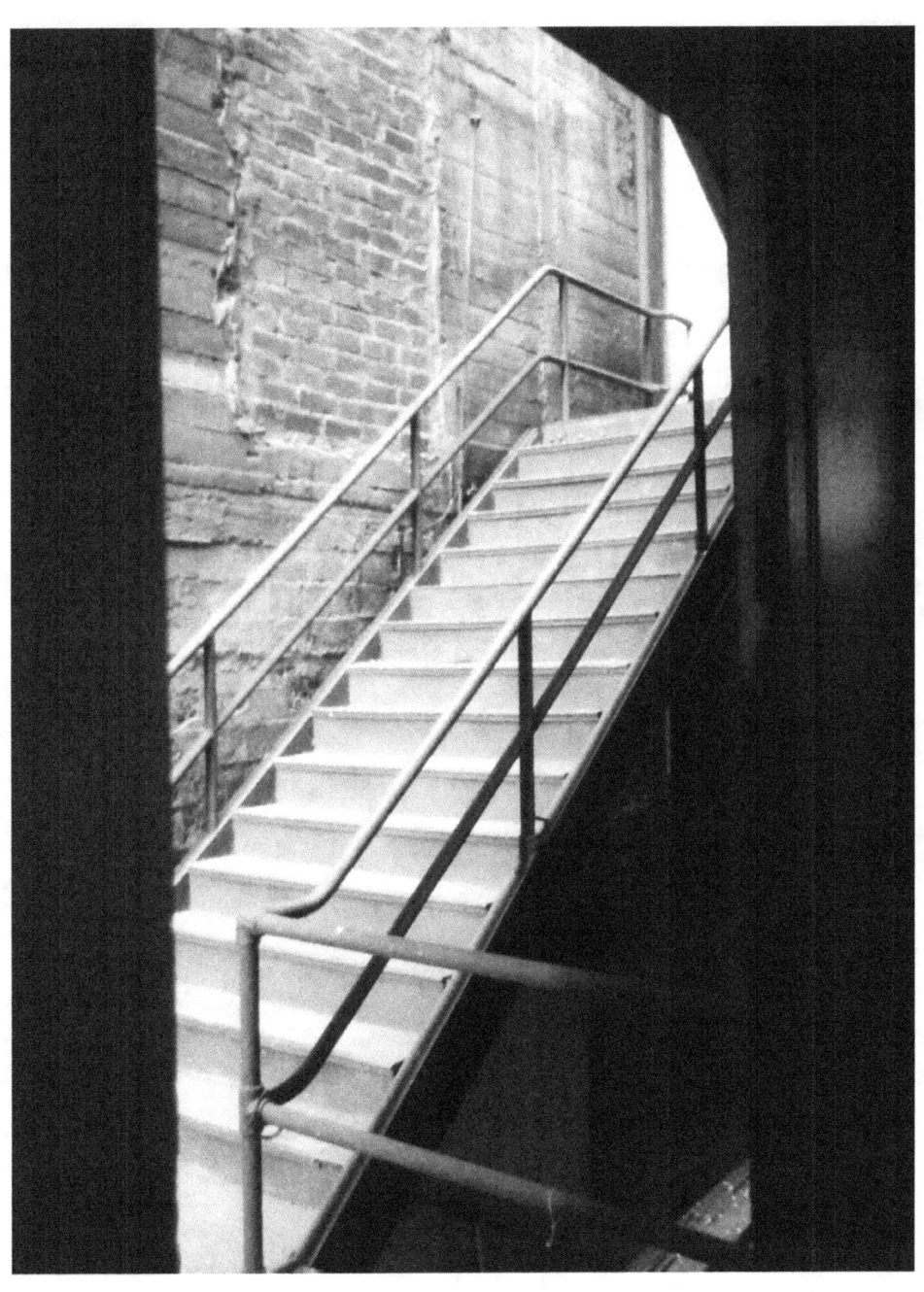

JEWELRY DISTRICT

640 S. Broadway

At this Pavo Real ("Royal Peacock") jewelry plaza just south of the Palace Theatre, jewelers sell their wares on the ground level, but the building is for lease. This is an example of how S. Broadway is in transition in 2014, a hodgepodge of beautifully restored properties, new businesses, and under-utilized, neglected or vacant structures. The building presently for lease is the Frank L. Forrester Building, which was completed in 1907. The neon sign attached to the façade reads "Bond" as a Bond Clothing Store (the chain is now defunct) once sold men's apparel here.

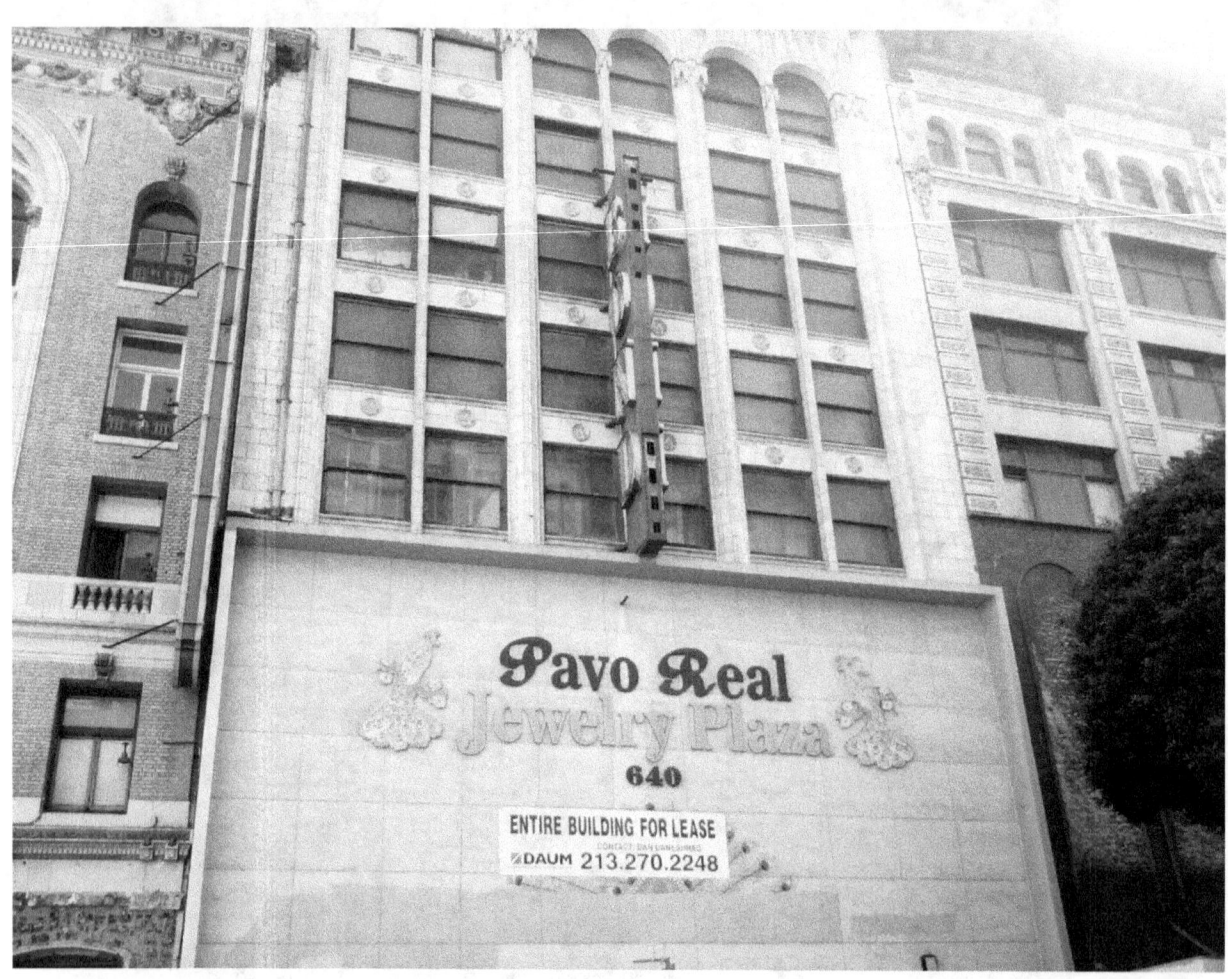

JEWELRY DISTRICT

S. Broadway and Seventh Street

Standing at the corner of Broadway and Seventh Street, looking west along Seventh, visitors are in the heart of the Jewelry District. Note the St. Vincent jewelry sign (left) at the corner of Seventh and Hill. In the bottom right of this photo, just left of the pizzeria, is an unprepossessing "Dead End" tunnel that leads to historic (and lovely) St. Vincent Court. Sometimes gems are hidden in unlikely places.

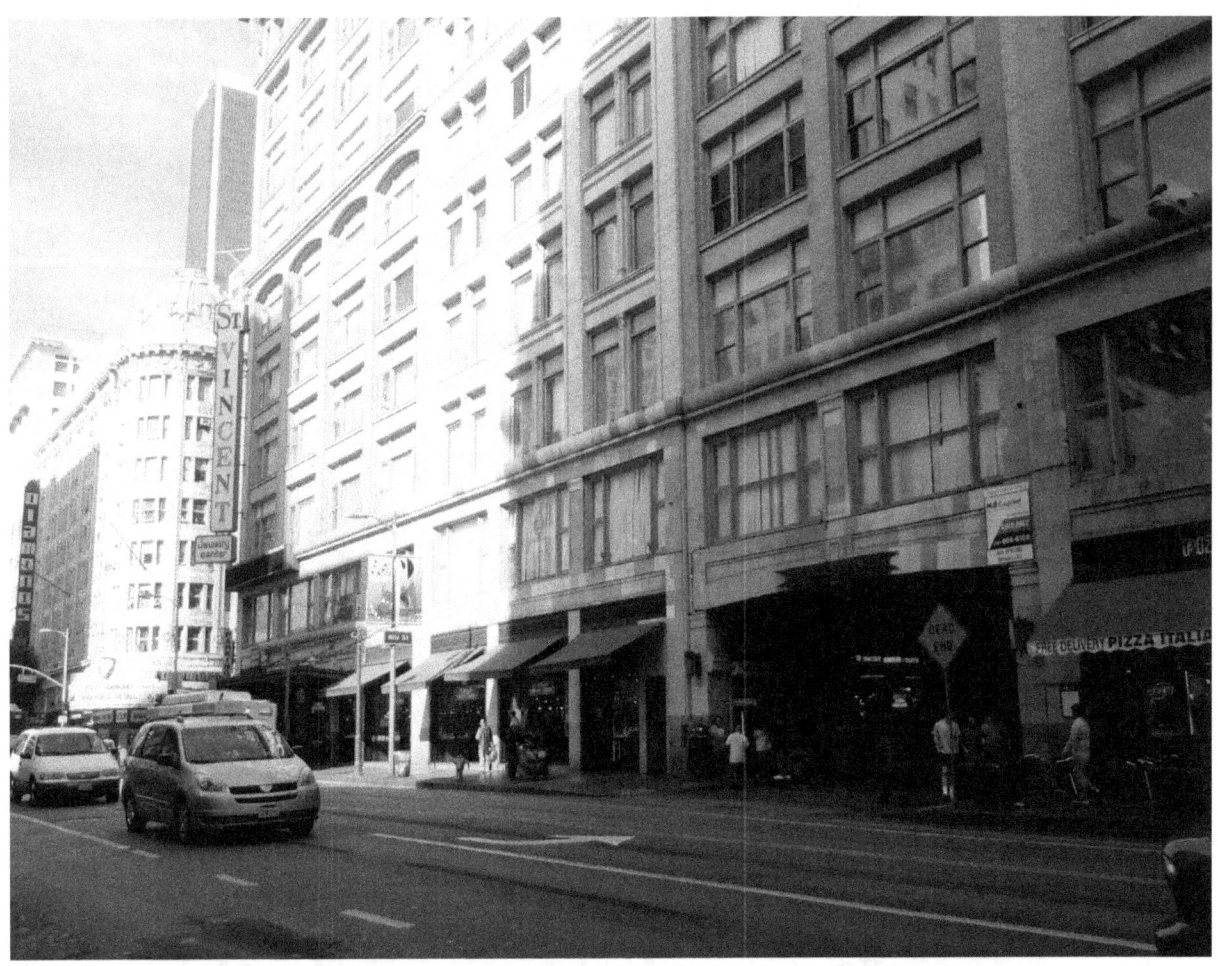

JEWELRY DISTRICT

S. Broadway and Seventh Street

In this quaint courtyard at the heart of the St. Vincent Block, between Broadway and Hill Street, tourists, workers, and those shopping for jewelry take a break to grab a bite or beverage at one of the courtyard's many cafés and delis.

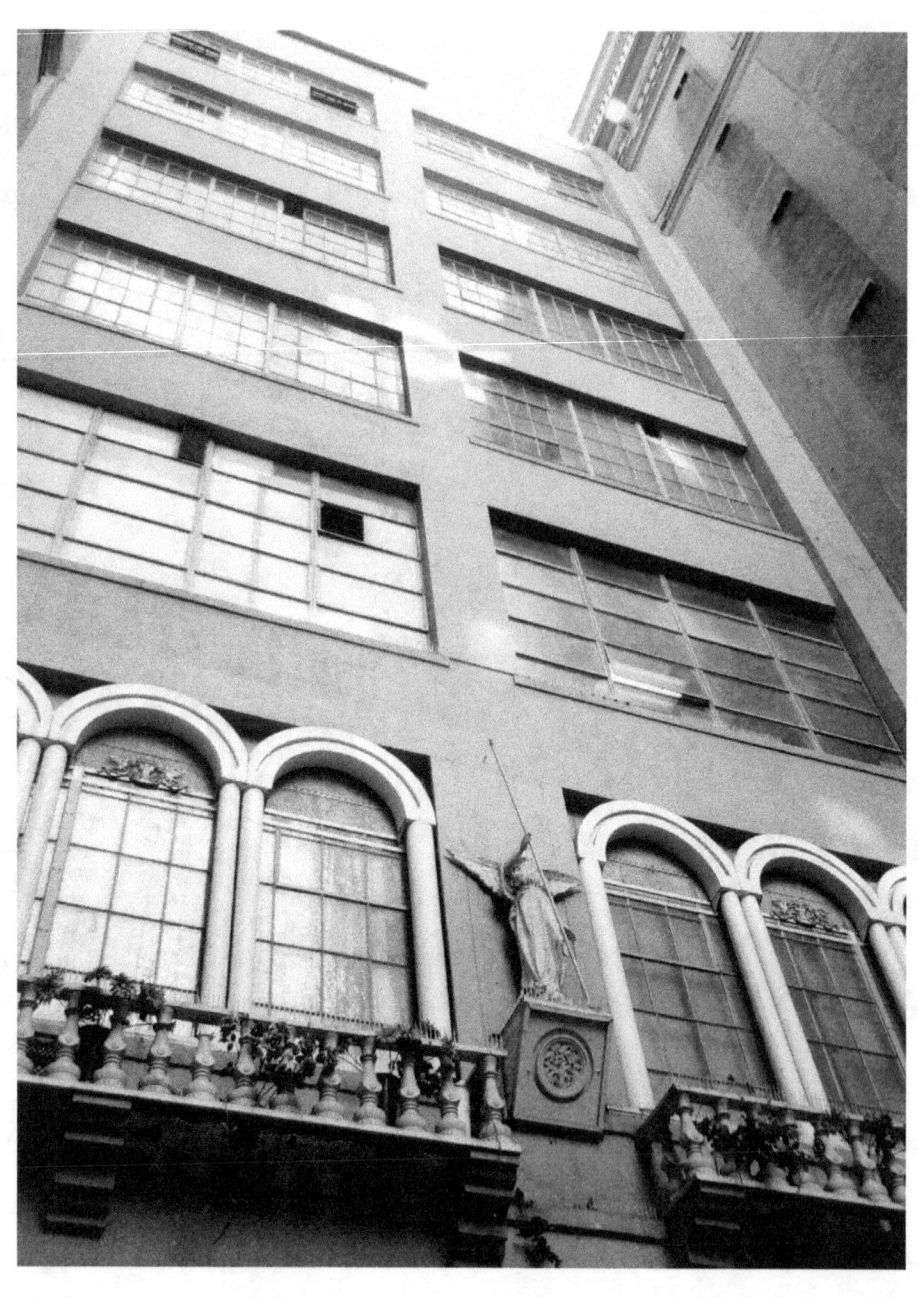

JEWELRY DISTRICT

S. Broadway and Seventh Street

St. Vincent's Court is fragrant with tempting foods from around the world—one of the "best smelling" places in Los Angeles. Note the predominance of "old world" European architectural motifs.

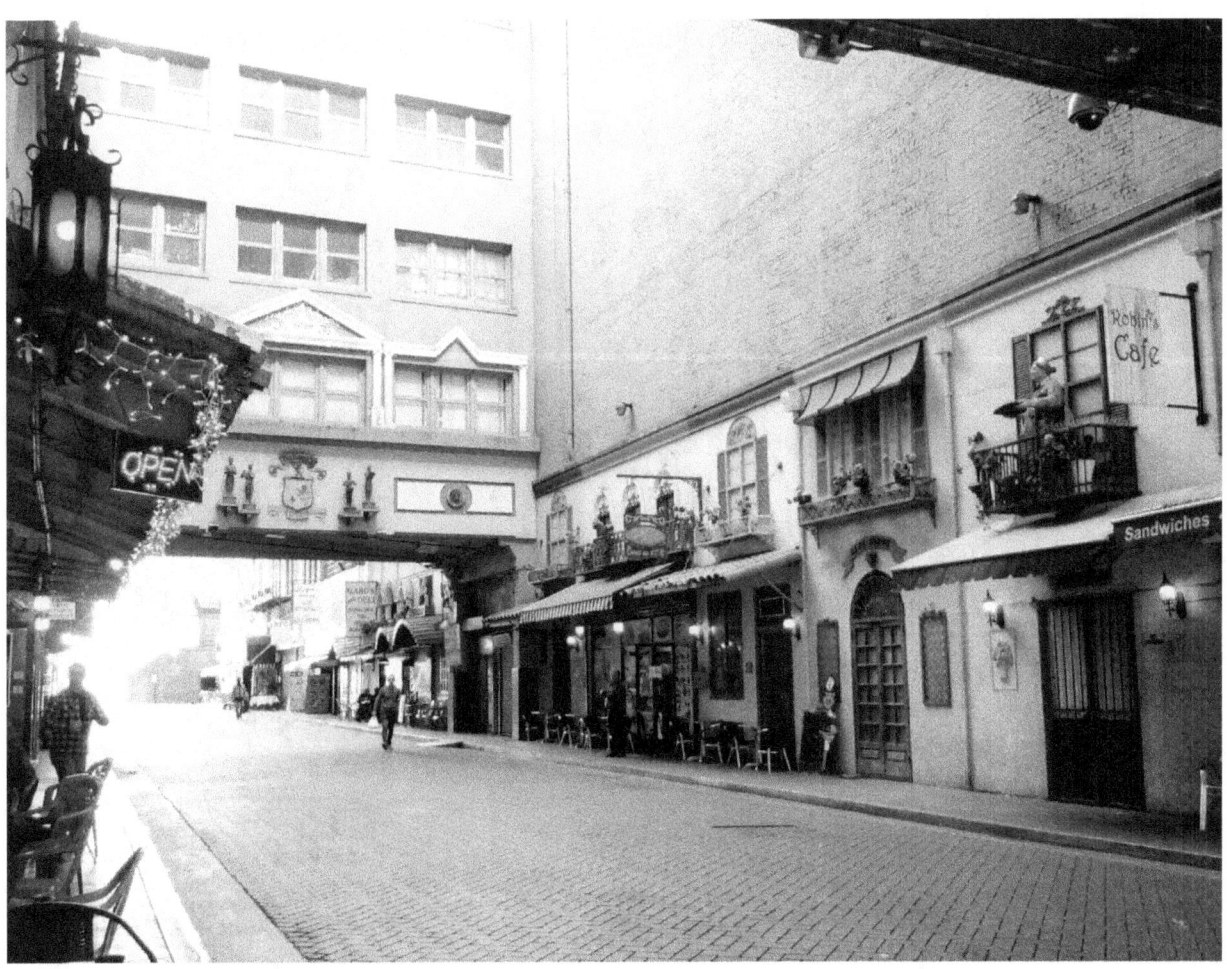

JEWELRY DISTRICT

S. Broadway and Seventh Street

In a quiet nook near the entrance to the courtyard, a plaque above a fountain relates the history and significance of St. Vincent's Court: Between 1868 and 1887, St. Vincent's College ("the first institution of higher learning in Southern California") stood on this site. St. Vincent's College subsequently became Loyola University.

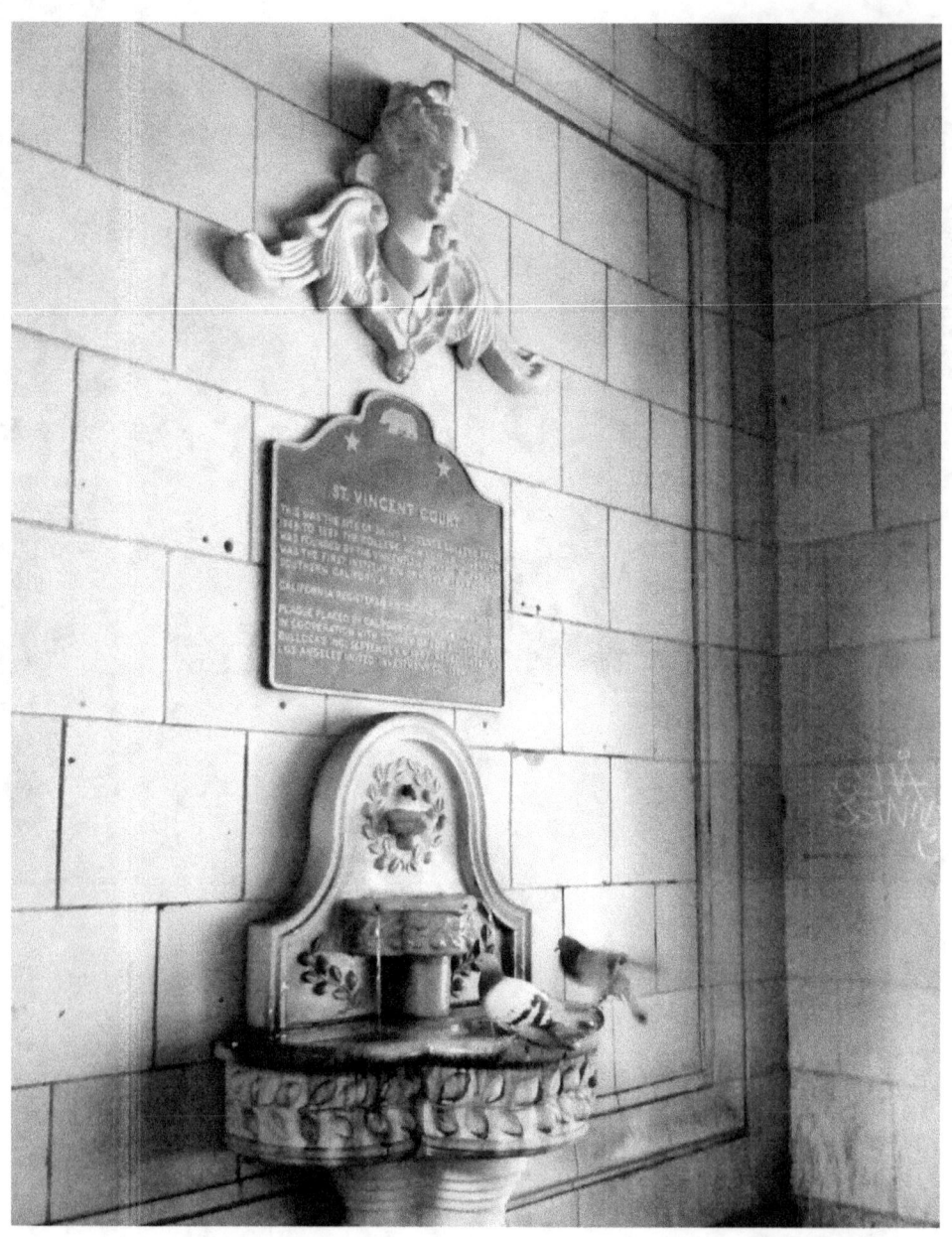

THEATRE DISTRICT

648 S. Broadway

On the northeast corner of S. Broadway and Seventh, in all its shabby glory, is the original face of Clifton's Cafeteria, revealed in 2012 when the "Mad Men"-era aluminum façade that had been in place since 1963 was removed. This was the second Clifton's Cafeteria, opening in 1935 (the first Clifton's, which opened in 1931, was on Olive Street). Diners paid what they could afford, and no one was refused a meal because they couldn't pay—a boon to those who had fallen on hard times during the Depression and in subsequent eras.

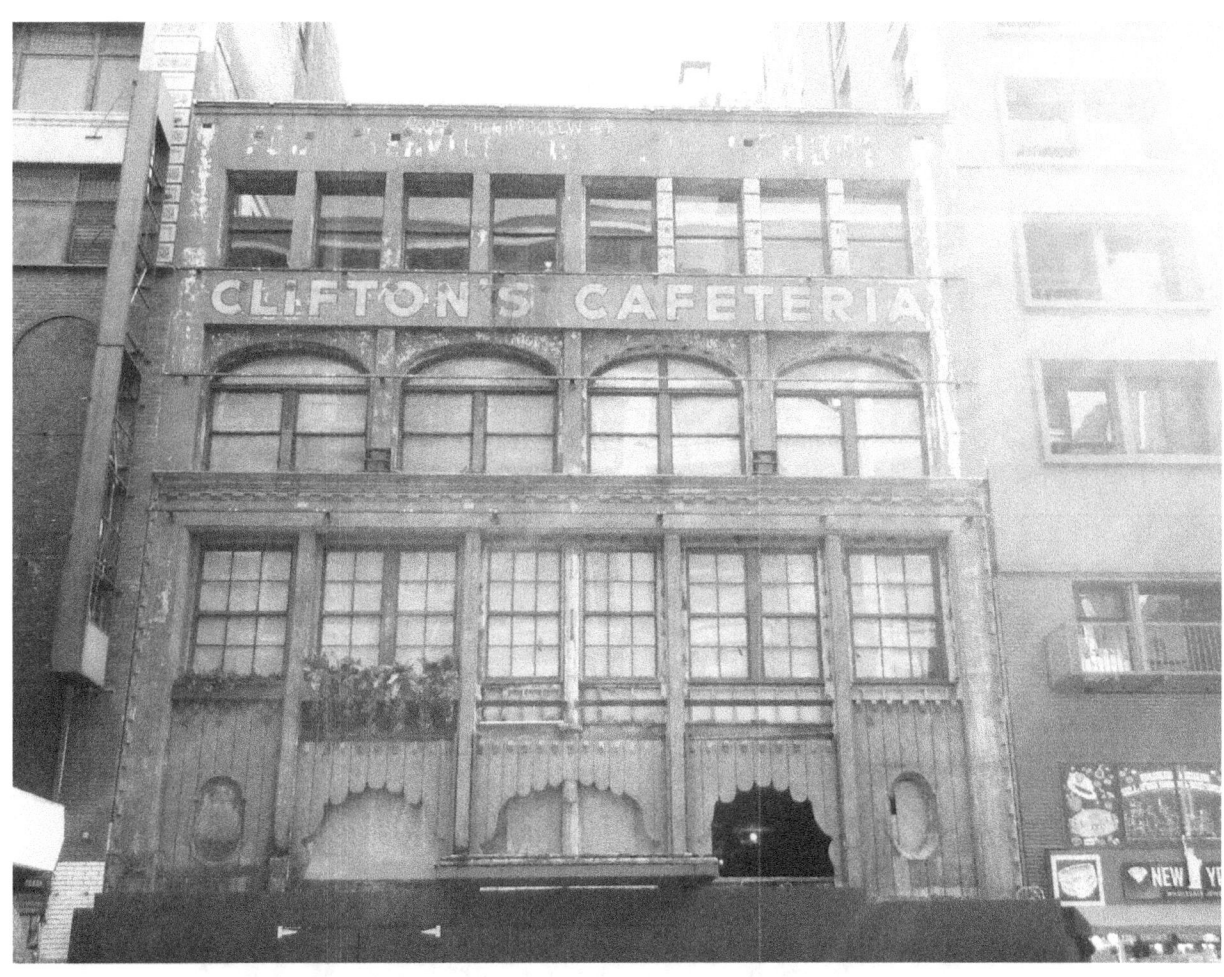

THEATRE DISTRICT

648 S. Broadway

Clifton's was famous not only for its kindness to the poor, but for its exotic interiors. Waterfalls and flowers and trees surrounded diners as if they were eating in lovely locales. The cuisine was stick-to-the-ribs, early-to-mid-20th-century American comfort food, including mac-and-cheese, mashed potatoes and gravy, and tasty desserts like Clifton's famous pies. You queued with your tray, selected your food, and paid what you could, then dined among beautiful trees. What could be better? Clifton's present owner closed the cafeteria in autumn 2011 for renovations that are slated to end in March 2014. Once again people who live, work, or stroll along Broadway will be able to eat at Clifton's.

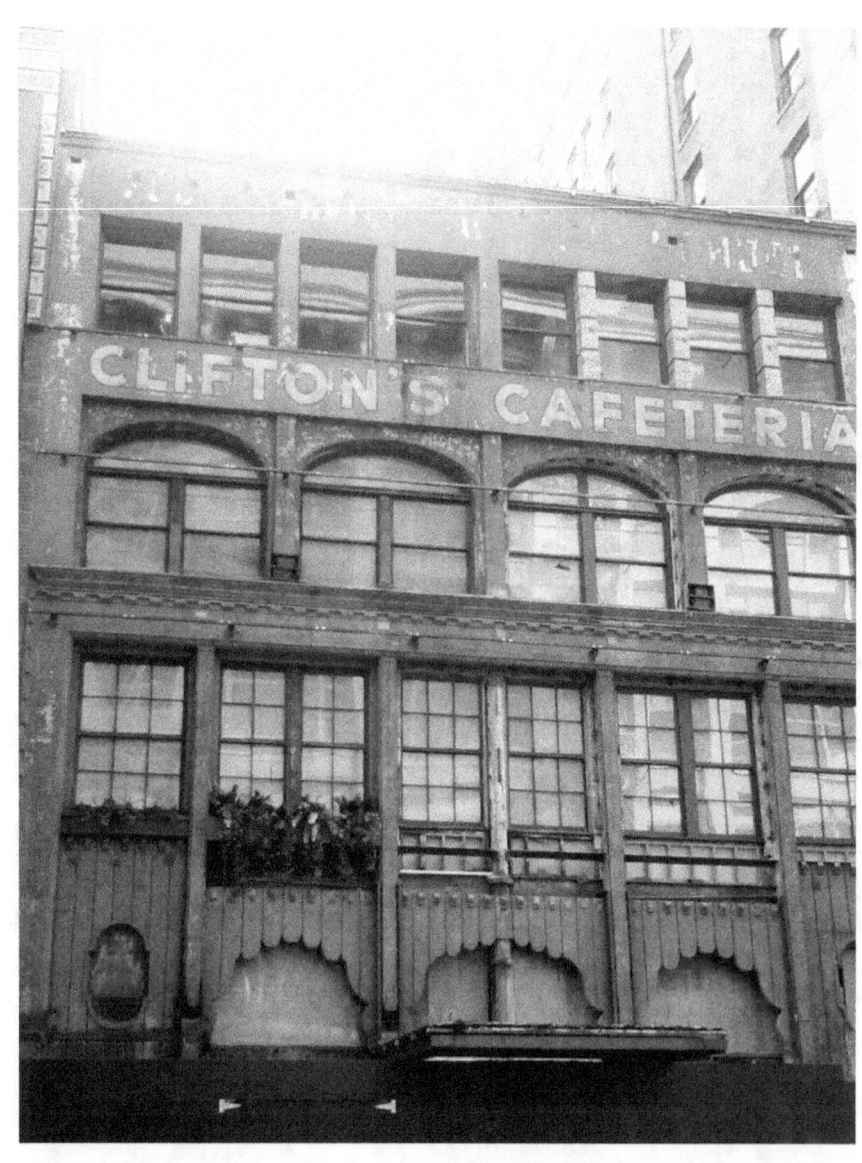

THEATRE DISTRICT

703 S. Broadway

Loew's State Theatre opened in 1921 on the southwest corner of S. Broadway and Seventh, a big theatre—even by S. Broadway standards—with 2,450 seats. From the beginning, it was both a movie theatre and a venue for live performances. Judy Garland entertained audiences here when she was a kid—before she was Judy Garland. The last movie at the State was shown in 1998.

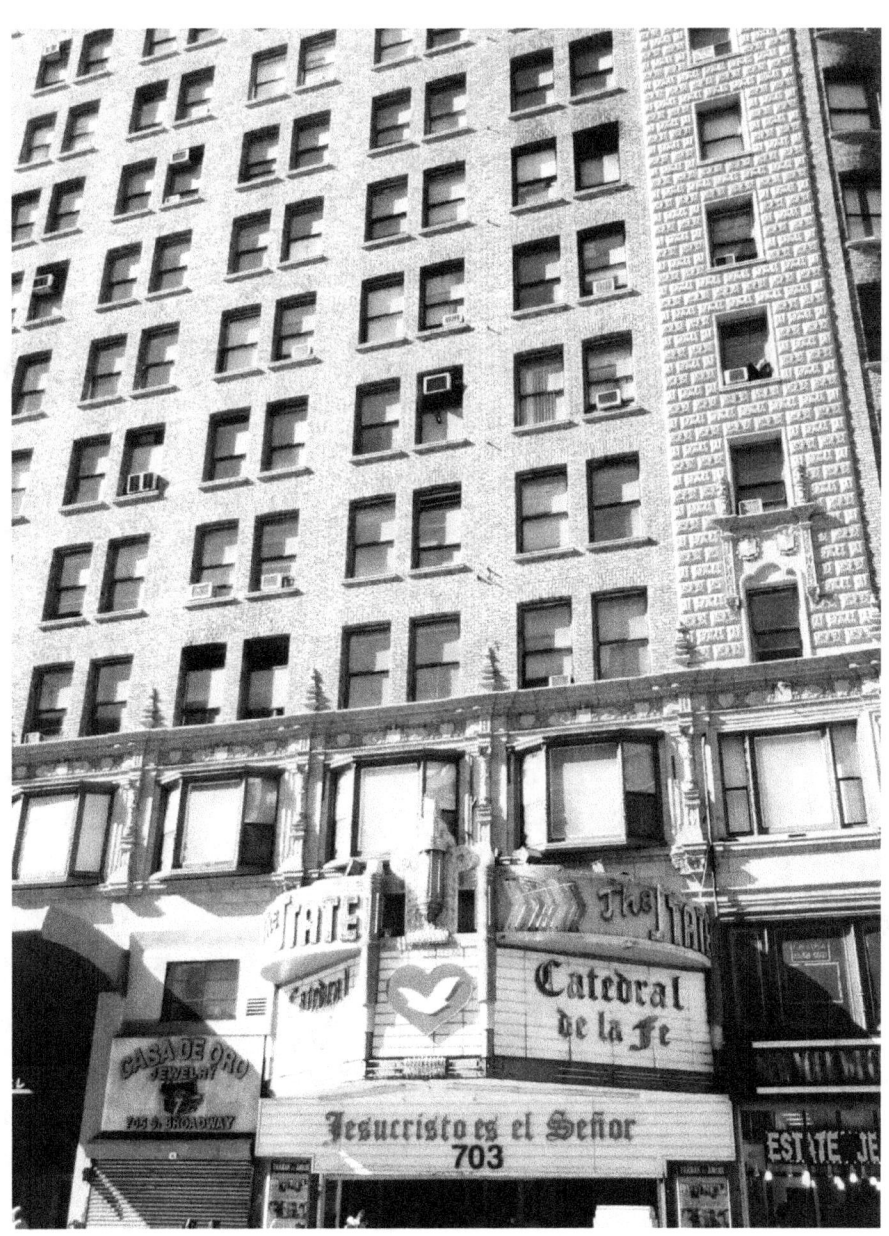

THEATRE DISTRICT

703 S. Broadway

The State Theatre's marquee remains intact. As it indicates, however, the theatre is now used as a cathedral ("Jesucristos es el Señor" means "Jesus Christ is the Lord" and "Catedral de la Fe" means "Cathedral of the Faith"). The high-capacity auditoriums and audio-visual technology of disused theatres make them perfect venues for religious services.

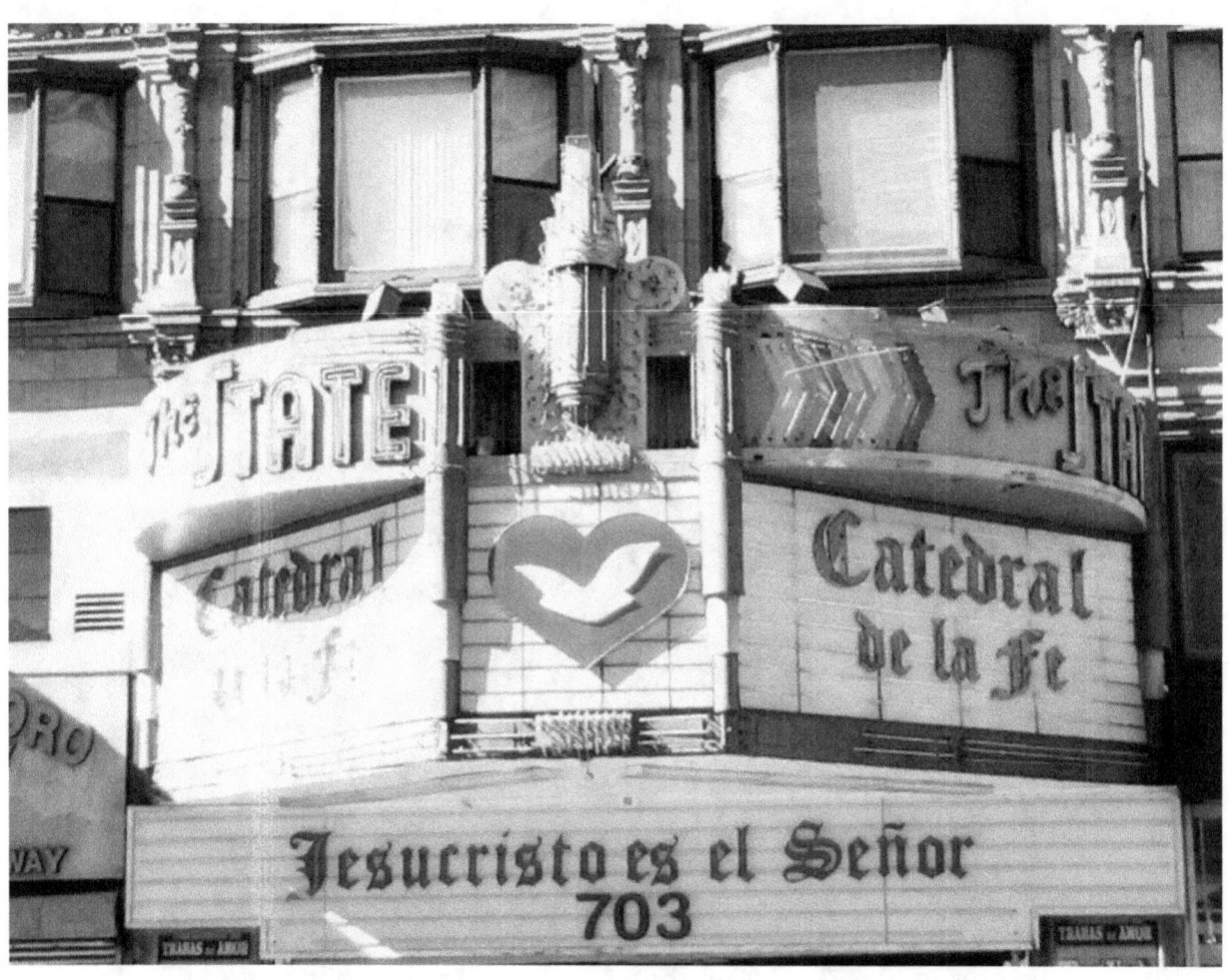

THEATRE DISTRICT

724 S. Broadway

One of the last real old-time game arcades in Los Angeles can be found on S. Broadway. The Sassony Arcade is still hanging in there. Variously described by patrons as dimly lit, dingy, grungy—even creepy—this hole-in-the-wall arcade has a lot of fans because it offers classic video games like Pac Man in the front, and pool tables in the back. Pinball machines? Sassony Arcade has got 'em. Pop culture note: The arcade scene in "Rocky III" was filmed here.

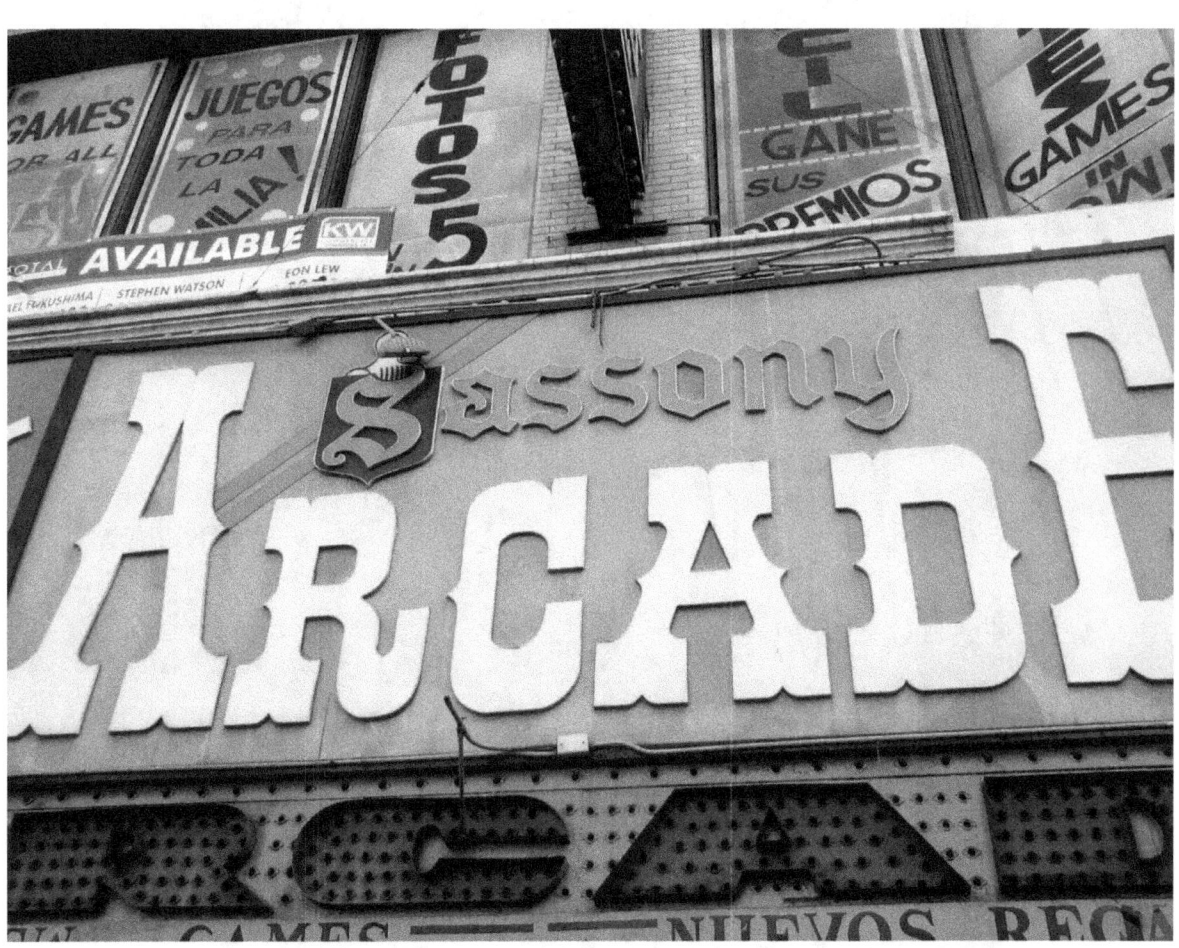

THEATRE DISTRICT

724 S. Broadway

As Broadway is revitalized and gentrified, some of its more colorful past remains, places like the Sassony Arcade. This arcade even has a Zoltar fortune-telling machine, like the one in Tom Hanks' 1980's hit "Big". (Visit www.zoltarmachine.com if you want to order your own Zoltar machine.) Why not step into Sassony Arcade for a moment to soak in the simple pleasures of LA's past?

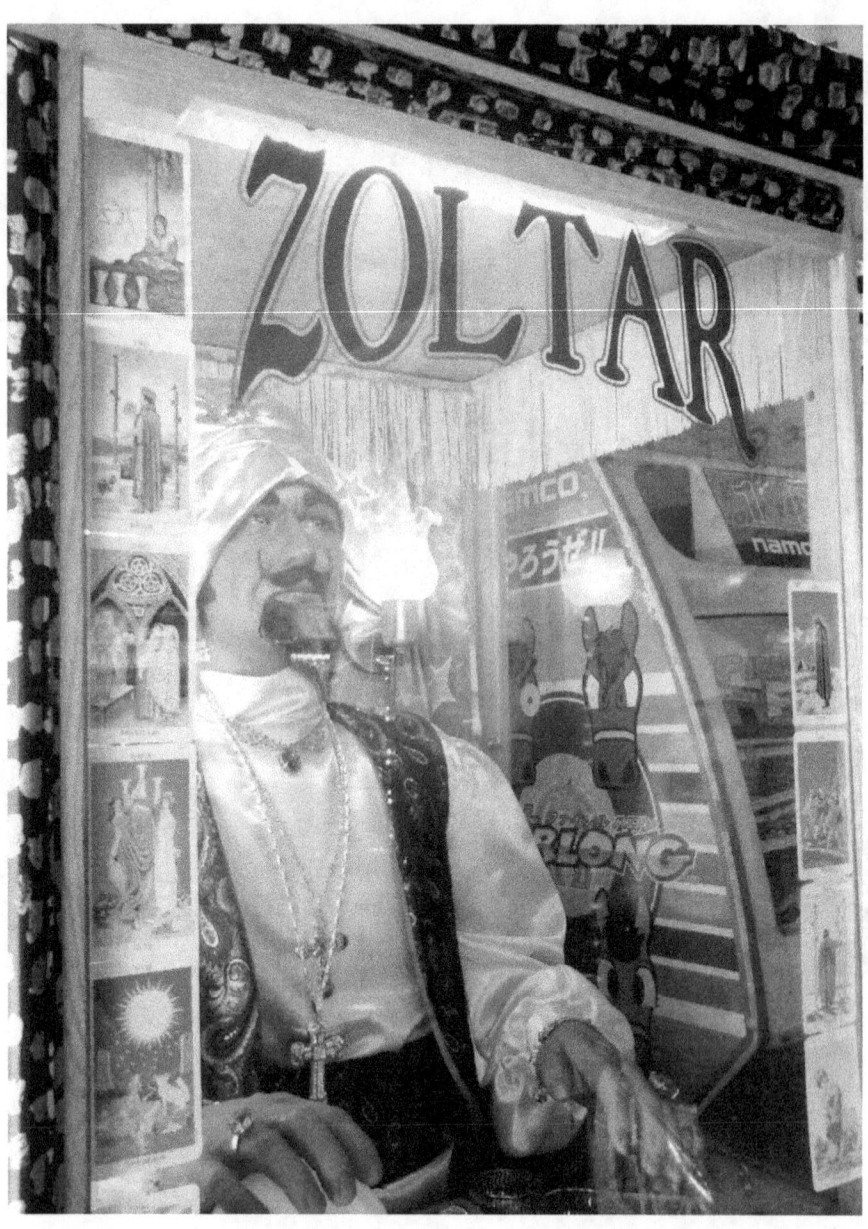

THEATRE DISTRICT

744 S. Broadway

South of the Sassony Arcade, the Globe Theatre (formerly the Morosco Theatre, which opened in 1913) was closed for decades, hidden away behind retail shops. But a new owner has vowed to revitalize the Globe to the tune of a staggering $5 million.

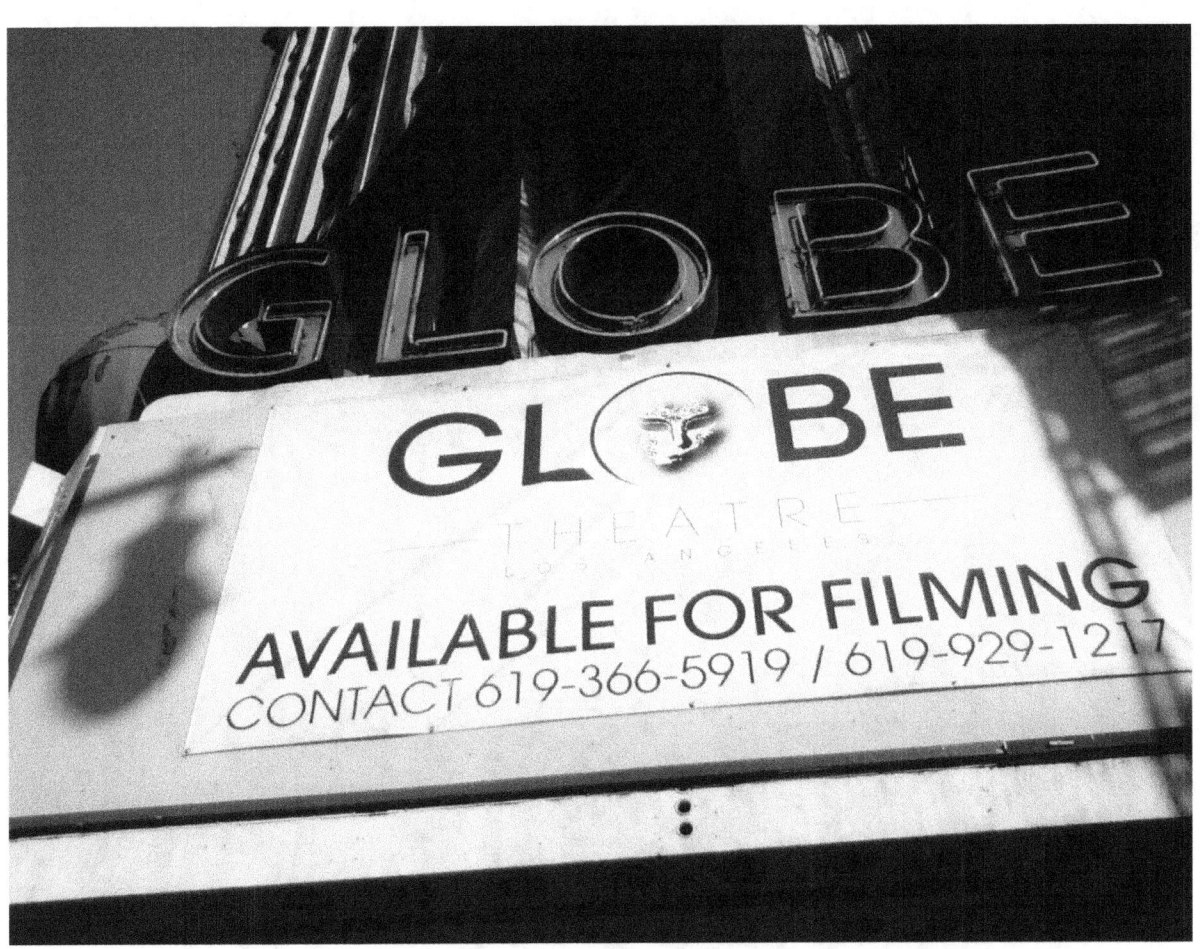

THEATRE DISTRICT

744 S. Broadway

Entering the space is a somewhat unnerving but fascinating experience. Well-preserved decorative ceilings contrast with bare walls and exposed pipes. The Globe is in a state of transition.

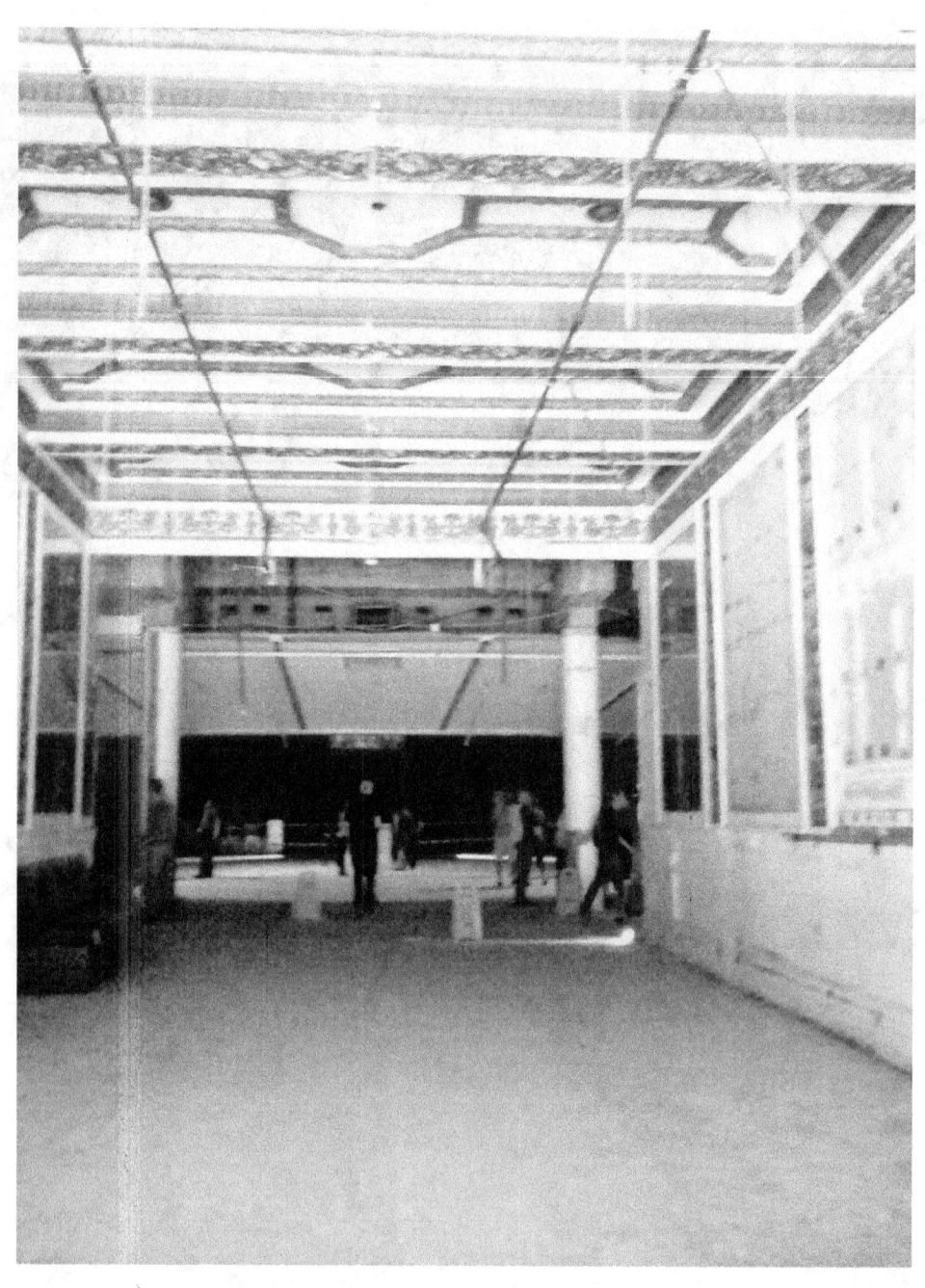

THEATRE DISTRICT

744 S. Broadway

There certainly seems to be $5 million dollars-worth of work to complete—and preservationists can be pleased someone has pledged to undertake the Herculean task.

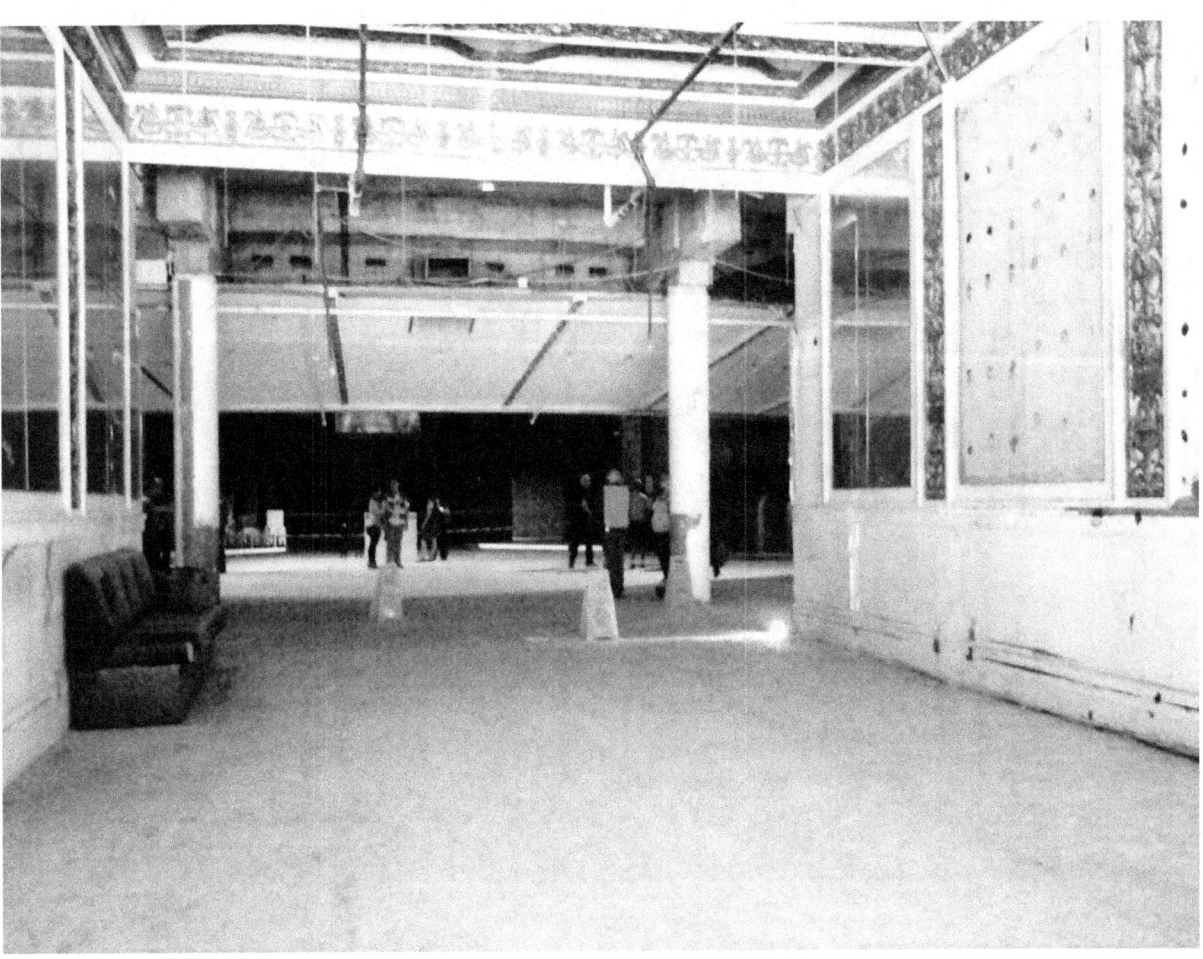

THEATRE DISTRICT

744 S. Broadway

Intact elements contrast strongly with features that are broken, decayed, or betwixt-and-between ...

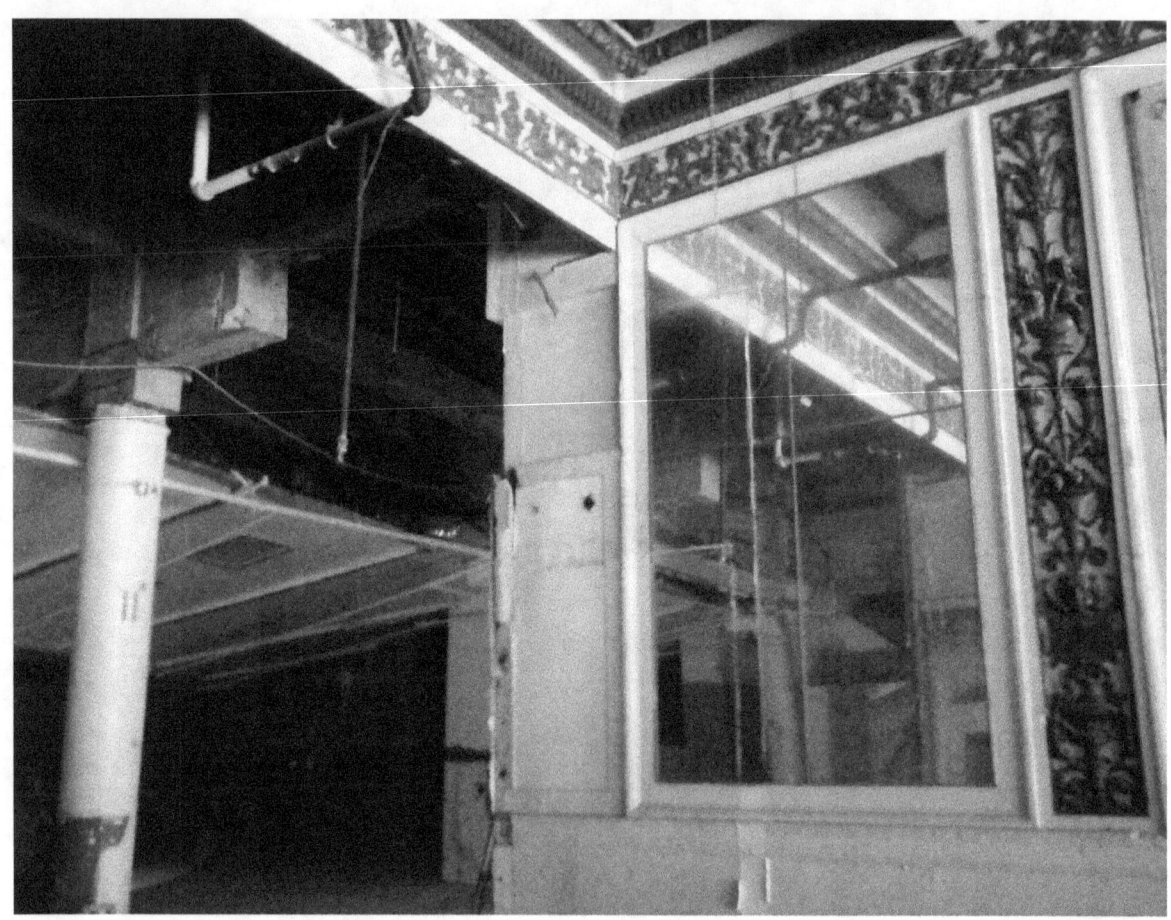

THEATRE DISTRICT

744 S. Broadway

... and the only occupants of the stage are tables and stacks of boxes lit by a lonely light.

THEATRE DISTRICT

744 S. Broadway

The lower balcony is accessible via flanking staircases ...

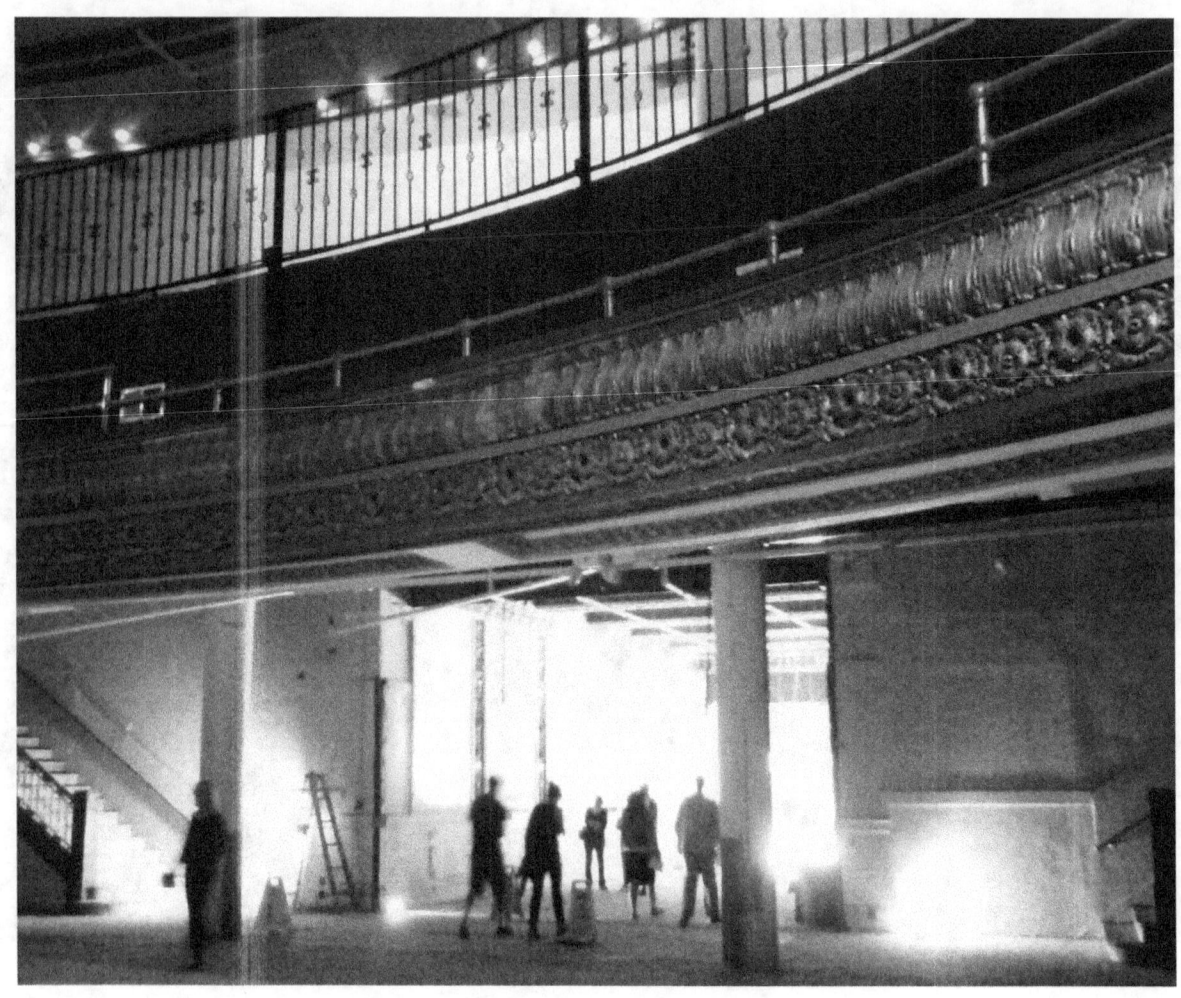

THEATRE DISTRICT

744 S. Broadway

... and viewed from above, the possibilities for this historic treasure are clear, even though ...

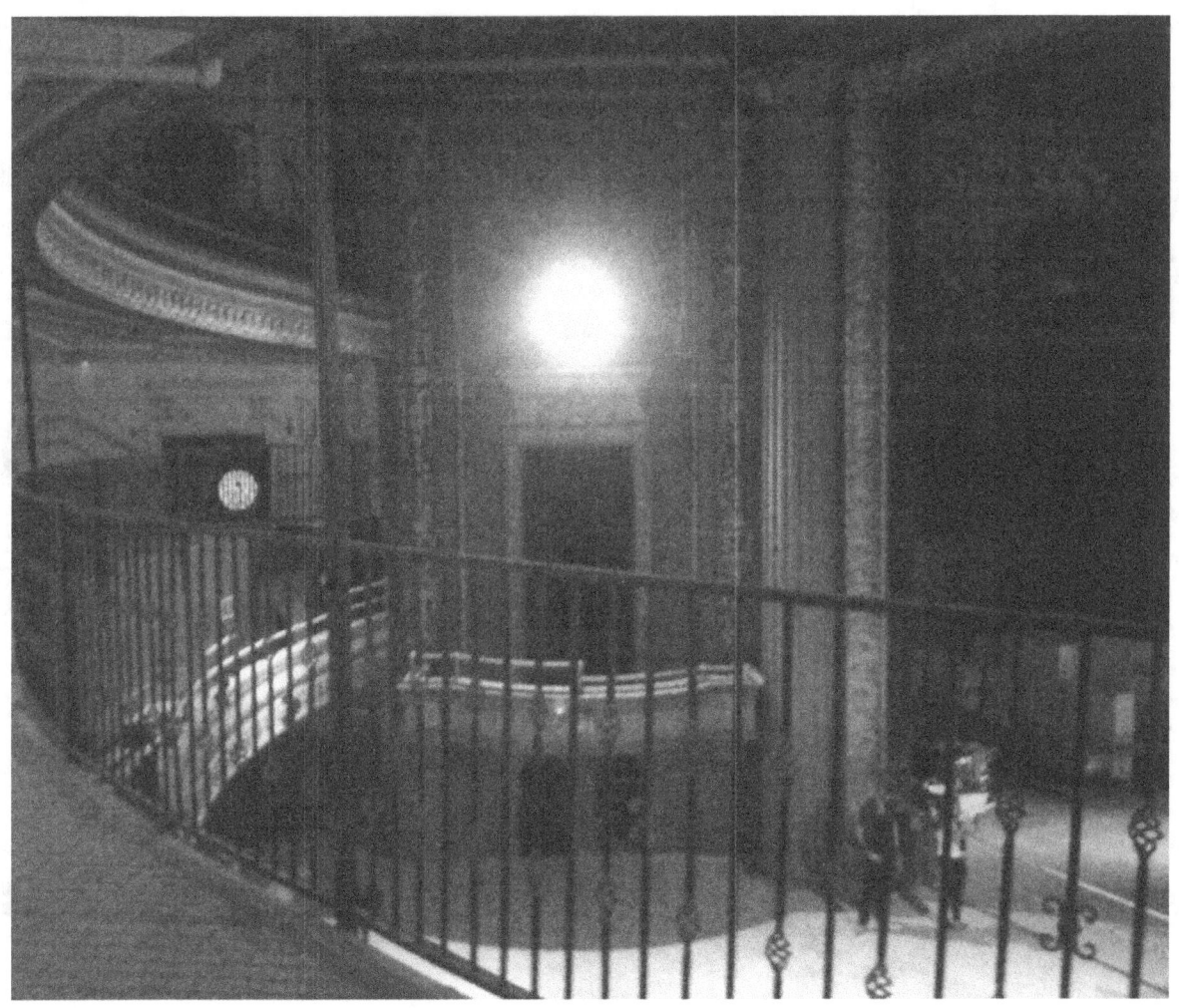

THEATRE DISTRICT

744 S. Broadway

... the upper balcony is presently closed and littered with rubbish.

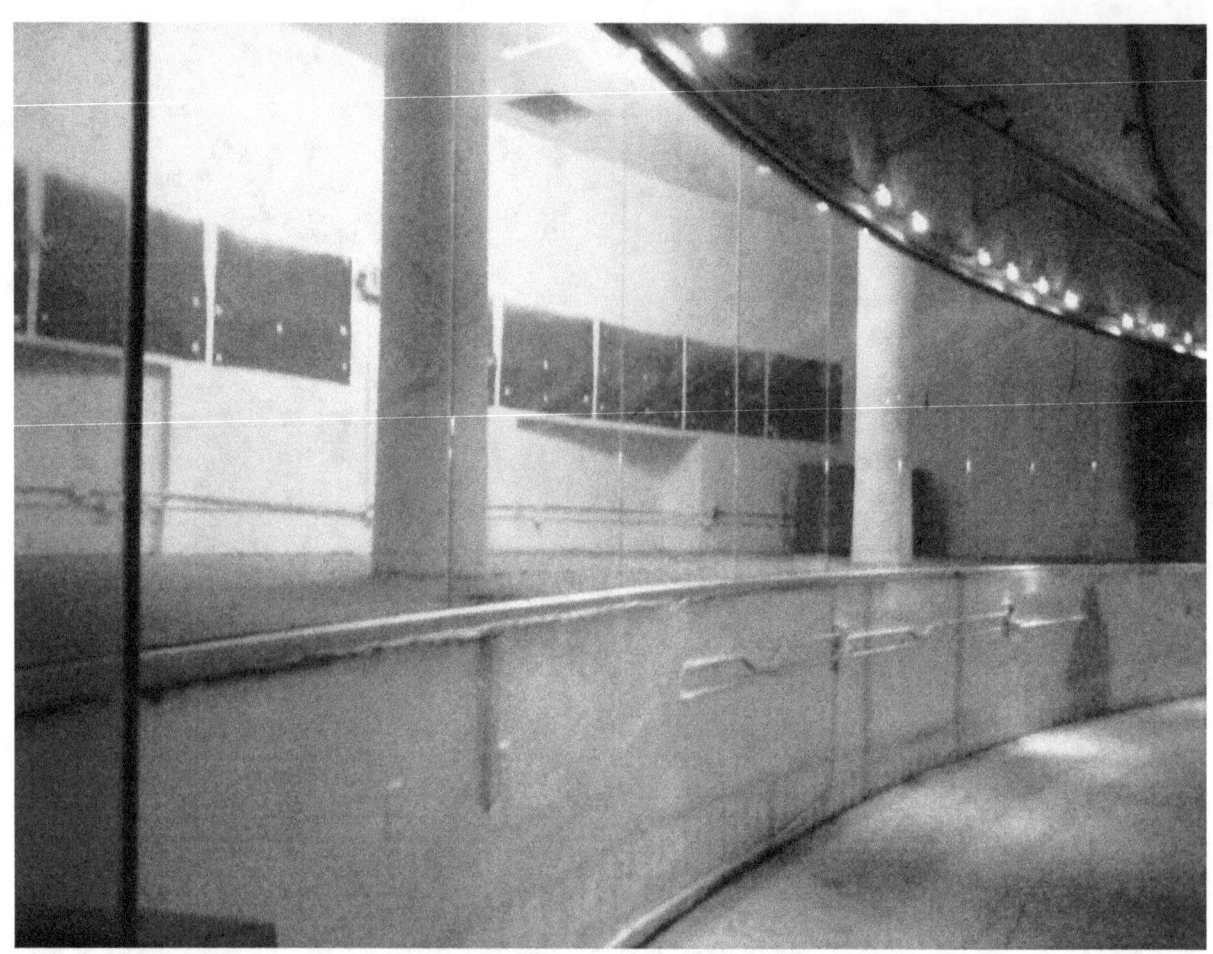

THEATRE DISTRICT

744 S. Broadway

Restoration work is needed at every turn.

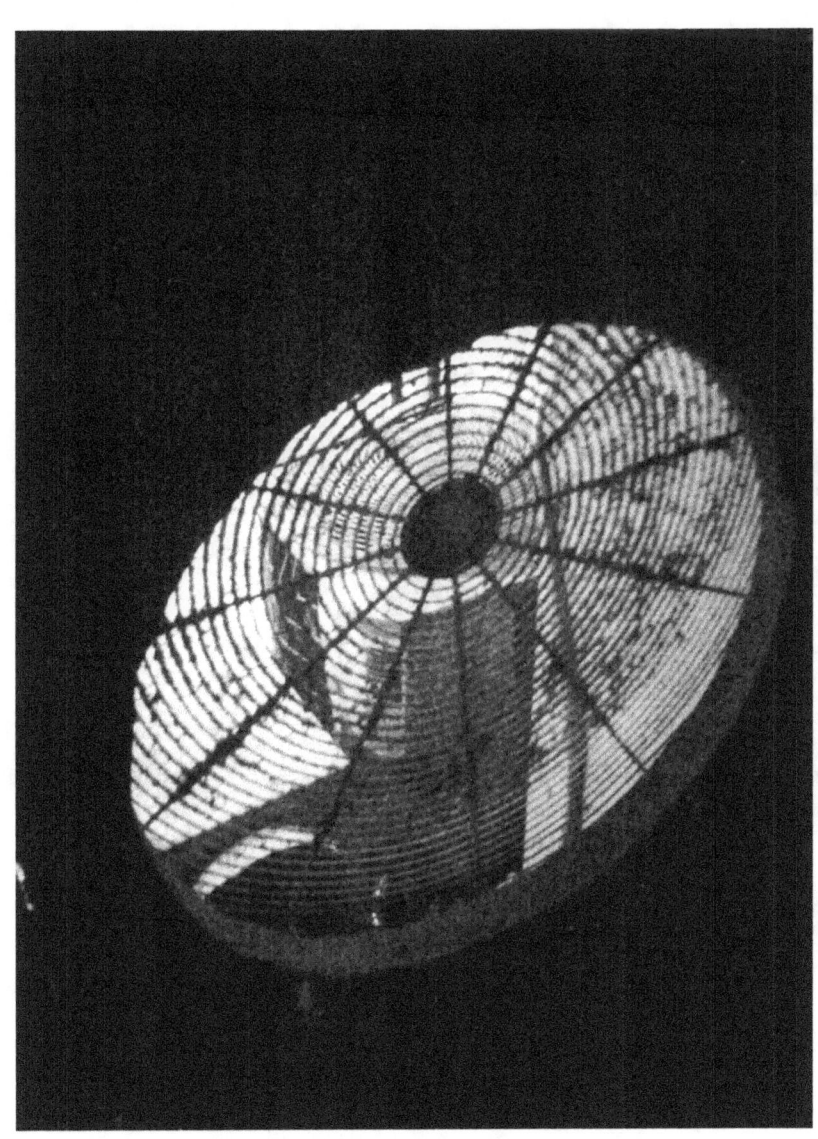

THEATRE DISTRICT

744 S. Broadway

Once the infrastructure, and the elegant touches—like marble staircases—have been revived and restored...

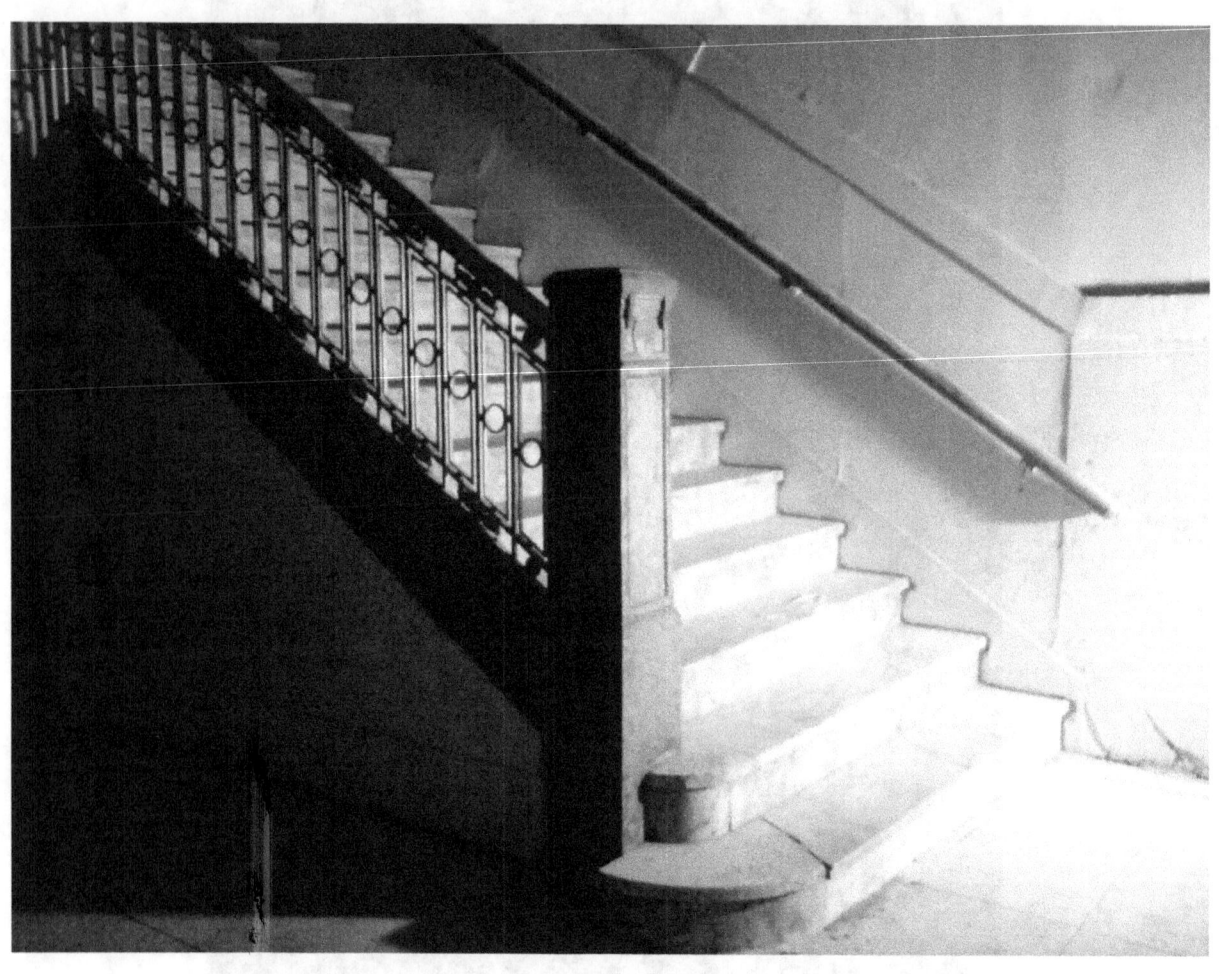

THEATRE DISTRICT

744 S. Broadway

... the presently Spartan—even spooky—theatre will become a stellar venue for concerts, plays, and film shoots.

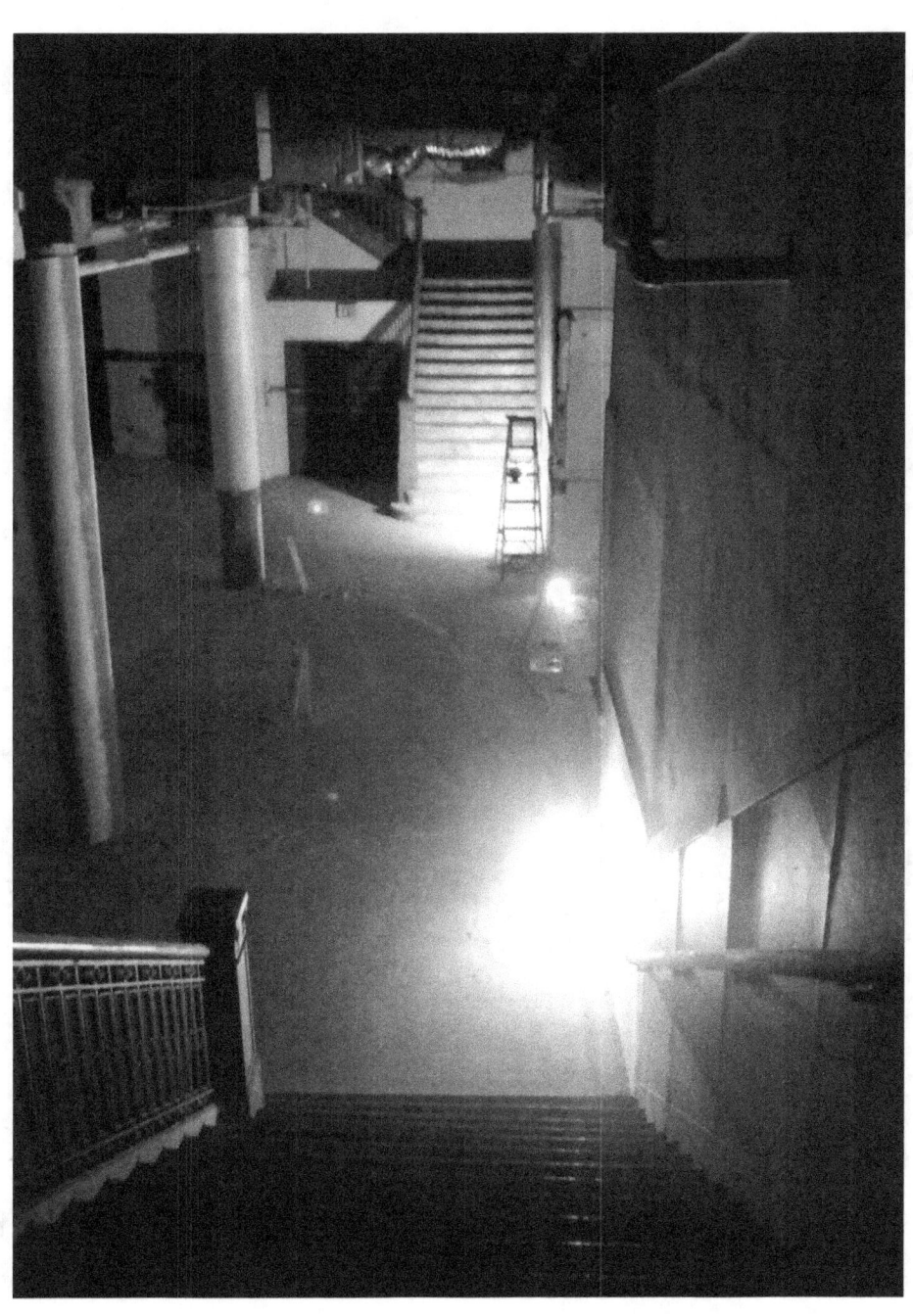

THEATRE DISTRICT

744 S. Broadway

For now, the Globe–which has been a stage theatre, movie house, and swap meet–is available for filming if you call the telephone number on the marquee.

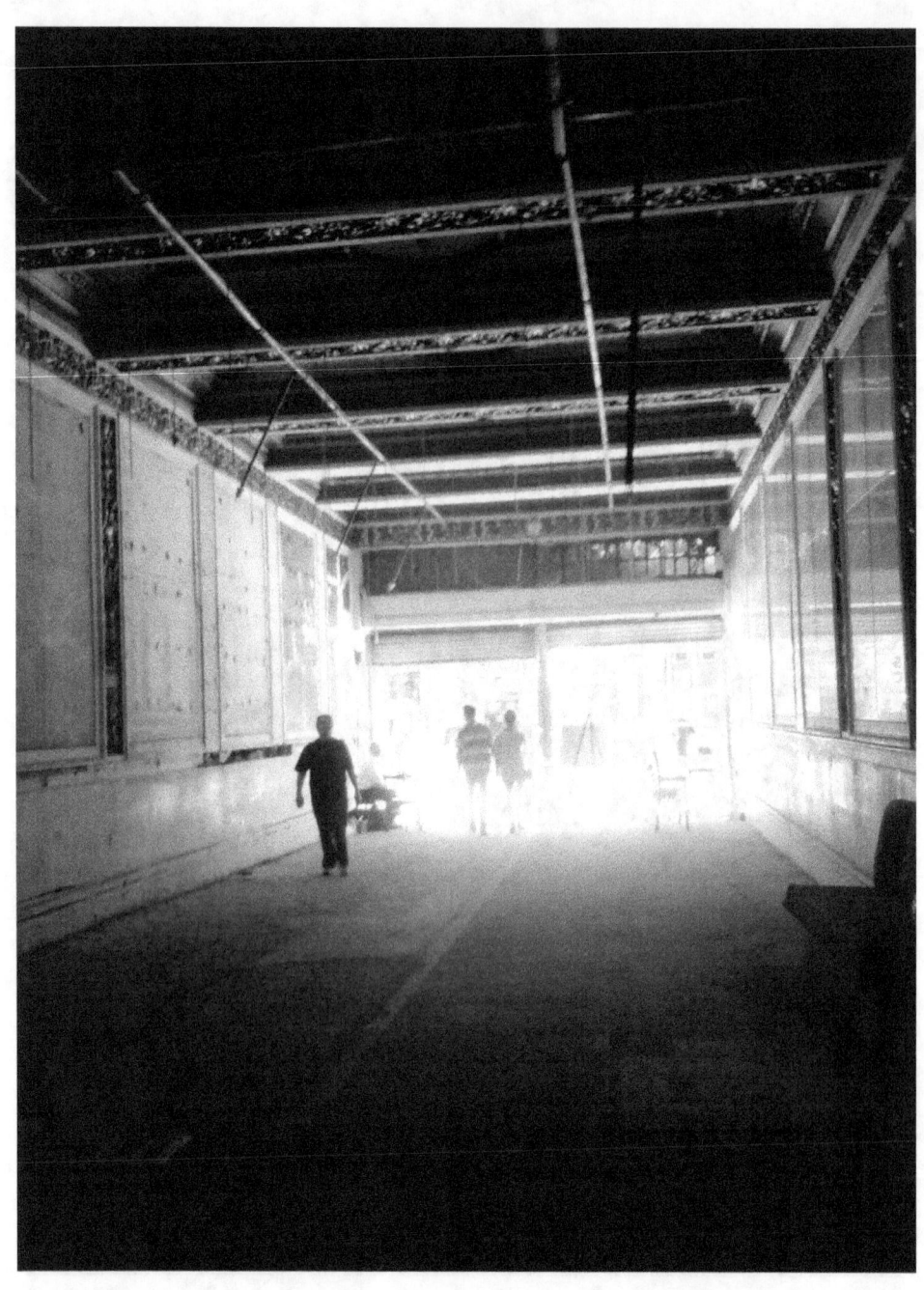

THEATRE DISTRICT

802 S. Broadway

Pictured here is the northern exterior (Eighth Street side) of the Tower Theatre, which opened in 1927. Note the stained glass windows and ornamental terra cotta reliefs which have drawn the attention and admiration of passers-by for almost ninety years. The original Tower Theatre was high-tech for the time in that it was the first movie palace in Los Angeles able to present "talkies". Warner Brothers' "The Jazz Singer," recognized as the first talky, premiered here at the Tower Theatre.

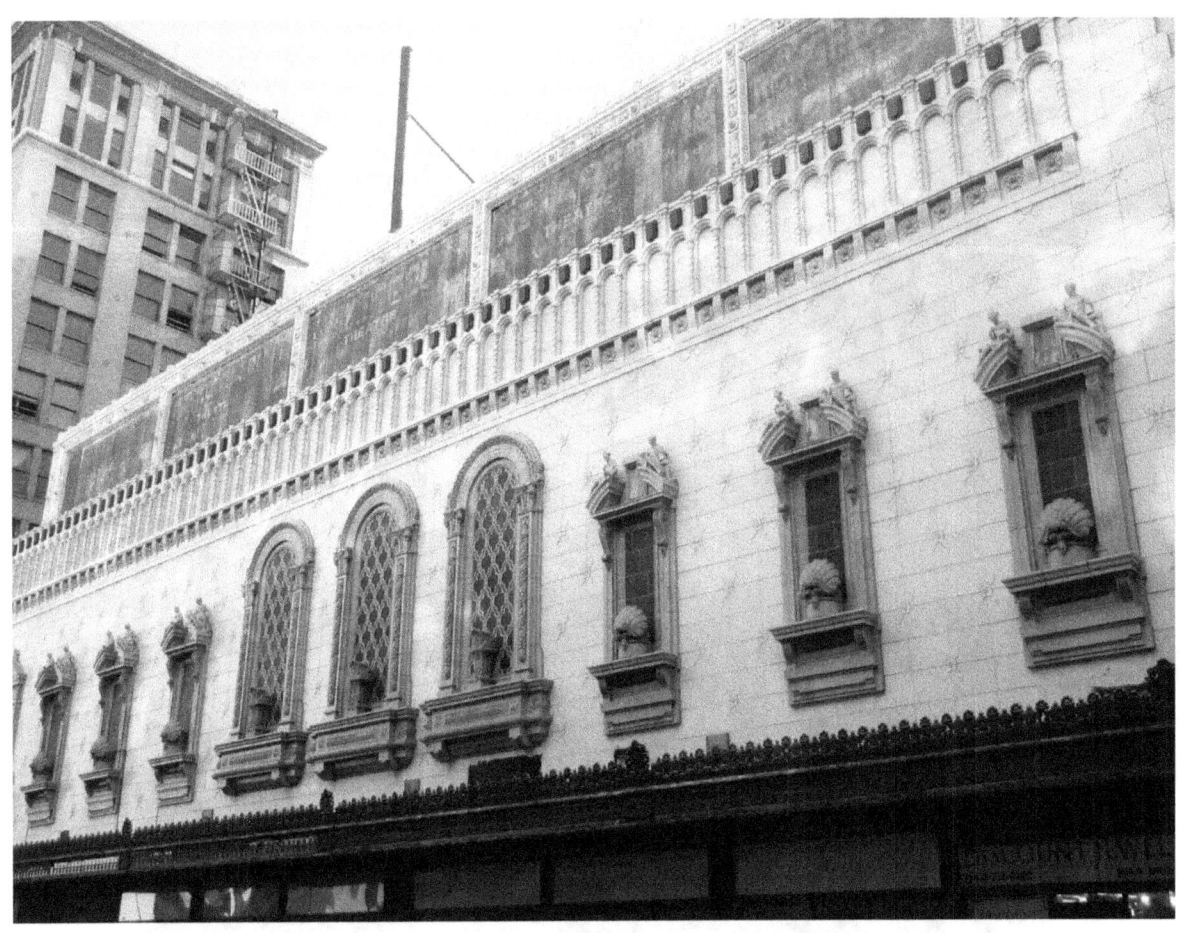

THEATRE DISTRICT

802 S. Broadway

At this time, the Tower is not open to the general public. It's used for church services, filming, and private events.

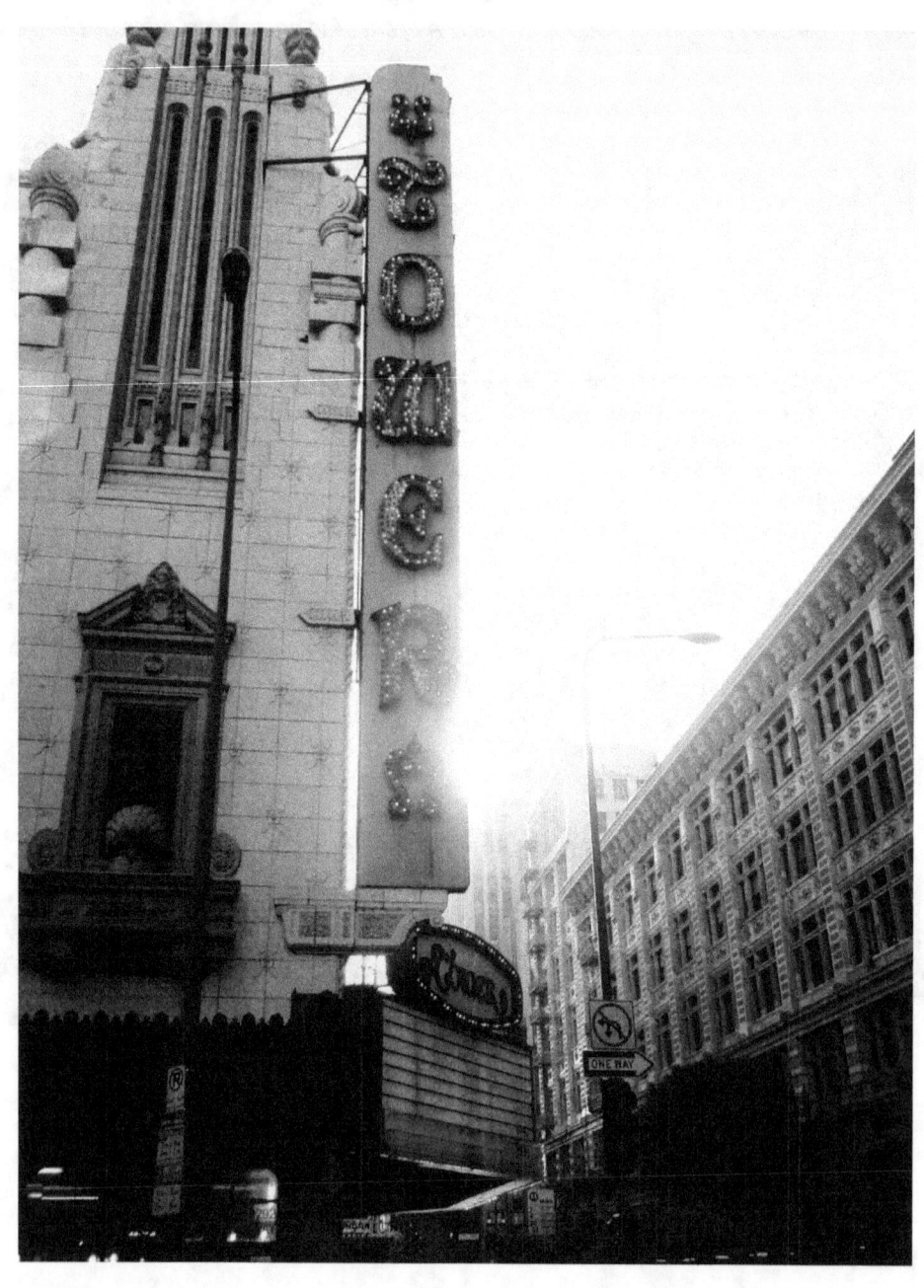

THEATRE DISTRICT

812 S. Broadway

The Rialto Theatre, which opened its doors in 1917, is one of the grand old movie palaces that has been spared destruction. It has, however, been converted to retail space. It's an Urban Outfitters—but the long marquee is in beautiful working order, the neon shining as brightly as in the Rialto's heyday.

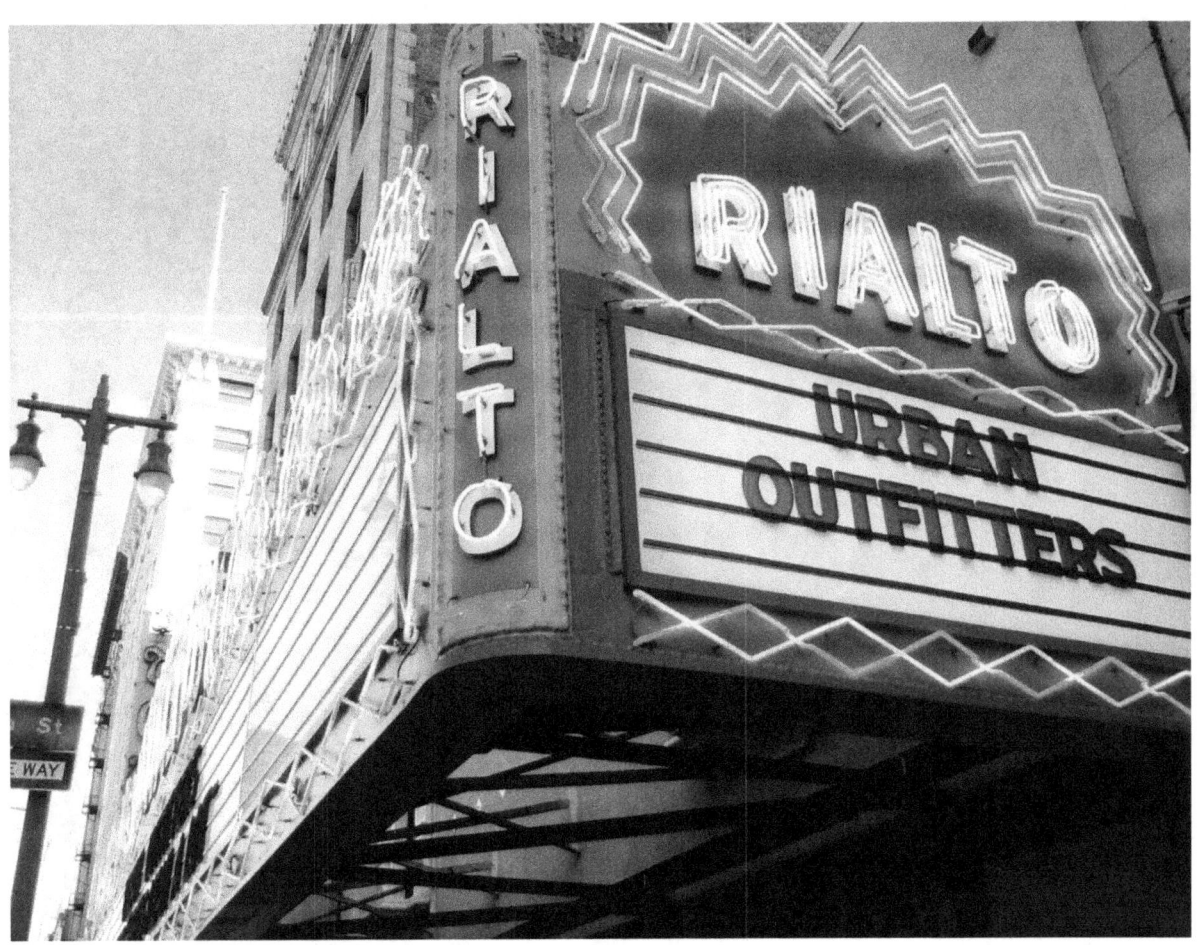

THEATRE DISTRICT

812 S. Broadway

The Rialto Theatre's entrance doors now lead to a high-ceilinged retail space where the young hipsters moving to Downtown LA in droves can purchase urban chic clothing and youthful necessities like retro-turntables—as well as vinyl albums to play on those old-school record players.

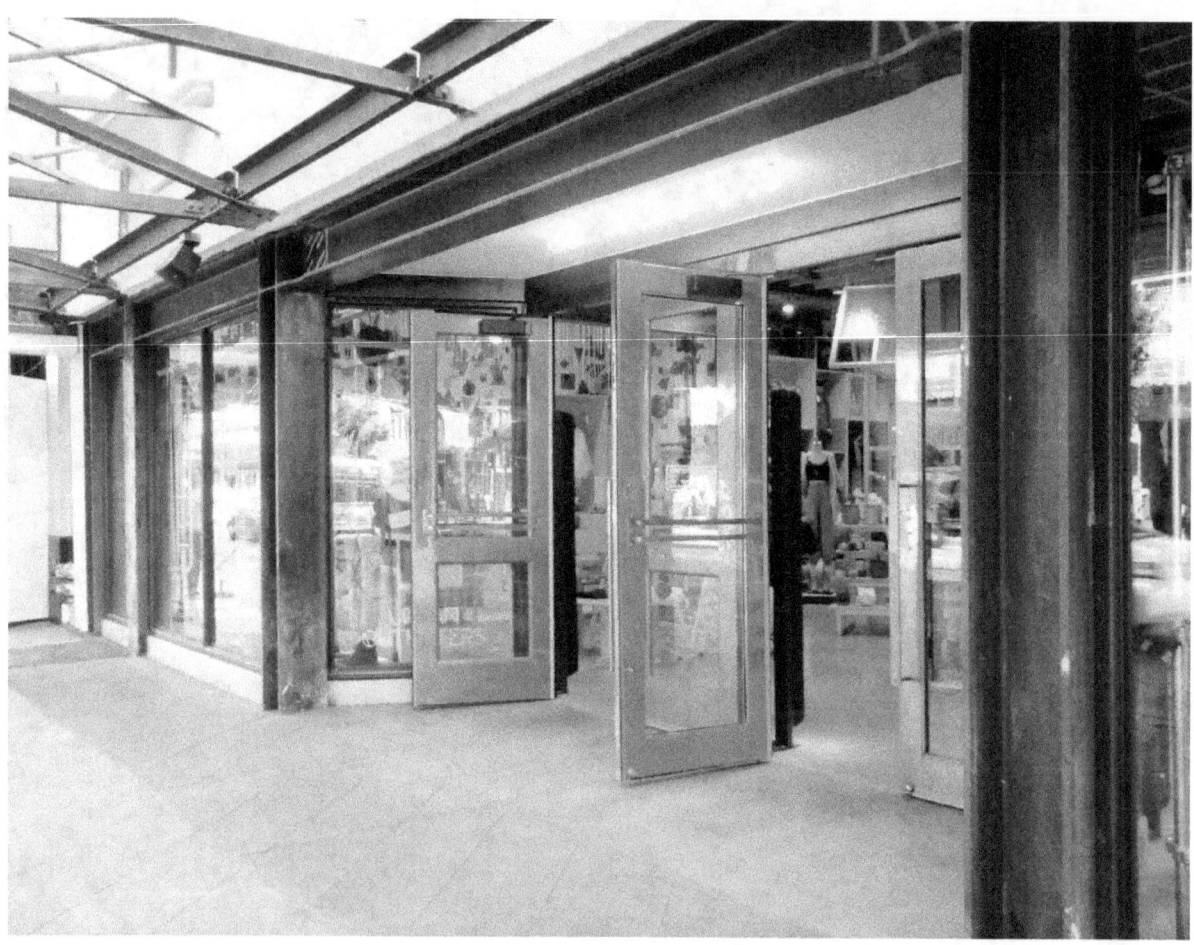

THEATRE DISTRICT

830 S. Broadway

Old-timers and history-loving young hipsters alike frequent the Broadway Bar between the Rialto Theatre and the Orpheum Theatre. At the classic Broadway Bar, with its iconic circular bar (and a patio where you can smoke), it's 1940 (or 1950, or 1960) all over again, every day. How authentic is the décor? "Mad Men" has shot here. The Broadway Bar is located in the historic Platt Building (completed in 1927). Drop in for a Manhattan or Vodka Gimlet after a show at the Orpheum next door but bring your money and be prepared for standing-room only depending on the night and the entertainment.

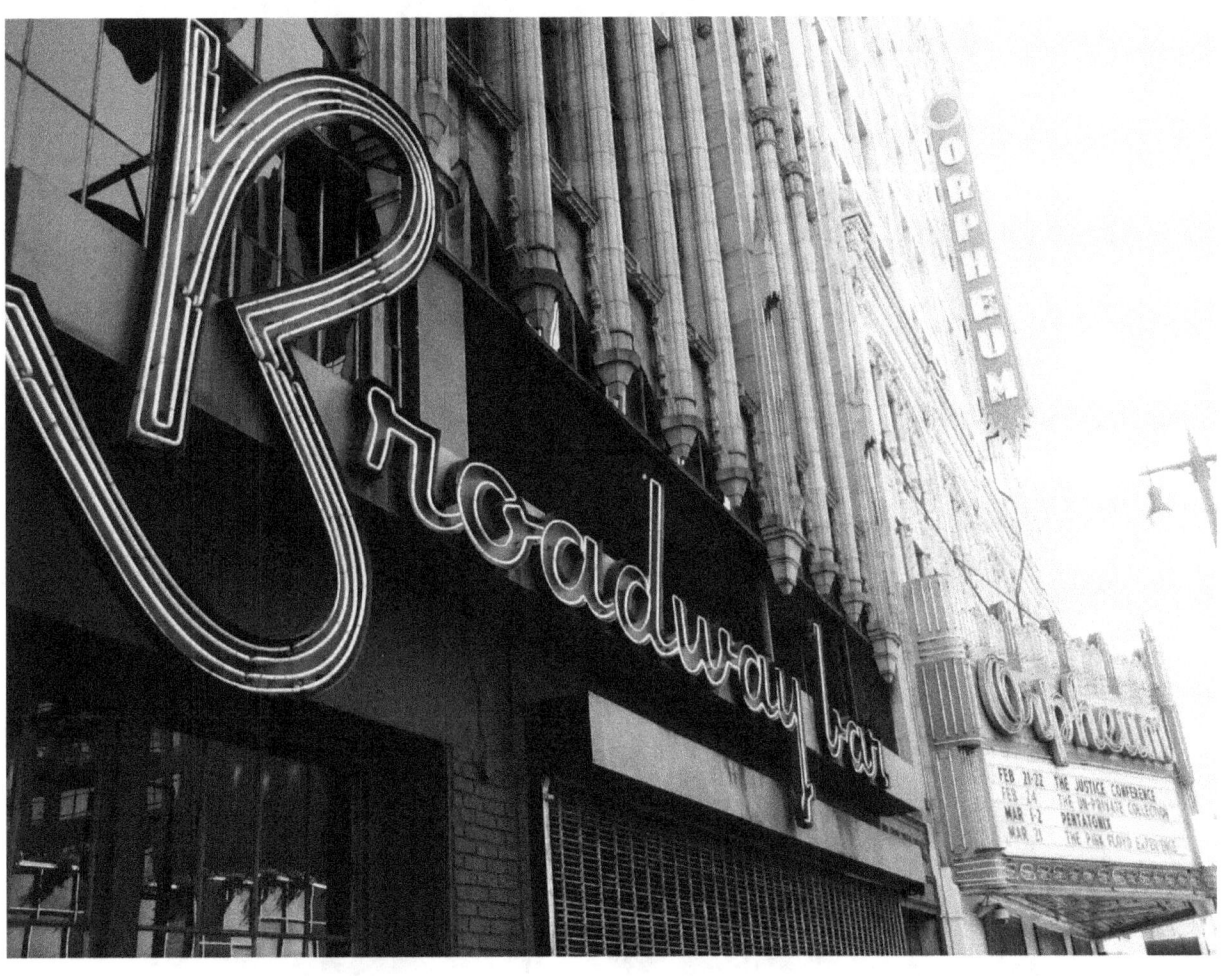

THEATRE DISTRICT

842 S. Broadway

In 1926, the year before the Tower Theatre opened up the block, the Orpheum Theatre debuted. Originally, it was part of the Orpheum vaudeville circuit. (As previously noted, two blocks north, the Palace Theatre at 630 S. Broadway was first known as the Orpheum (1911) and still bears the name above its marquee.) The Orpheum Theatre is next door to the Broadway Bar.

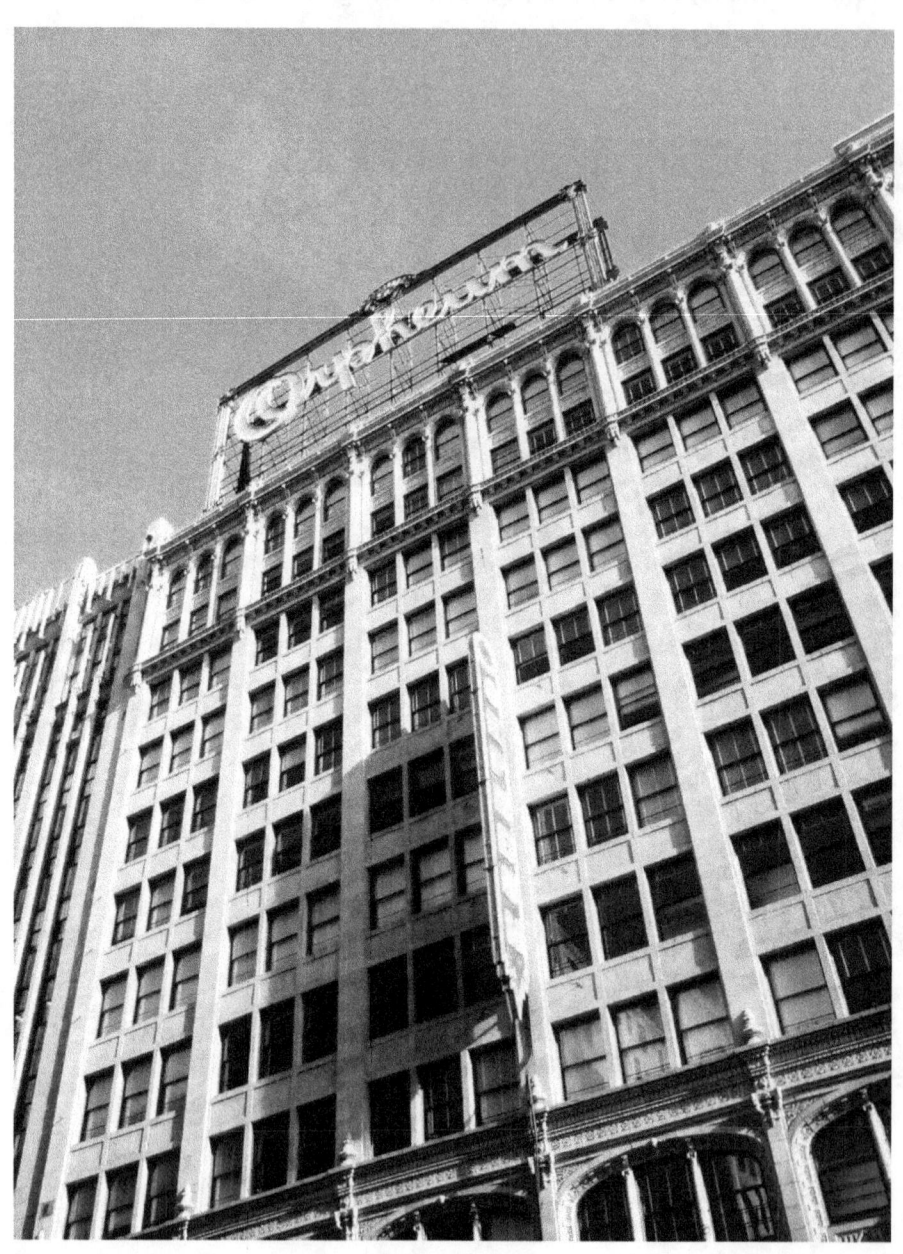

THEATRE DISTRICT

842 S. Broadway

The Orpheum Theatre is perhaps the best looking, best preserved venue of all of the S. Broadway theatres, with the (possible) exception of the Los Angeles Theatre.

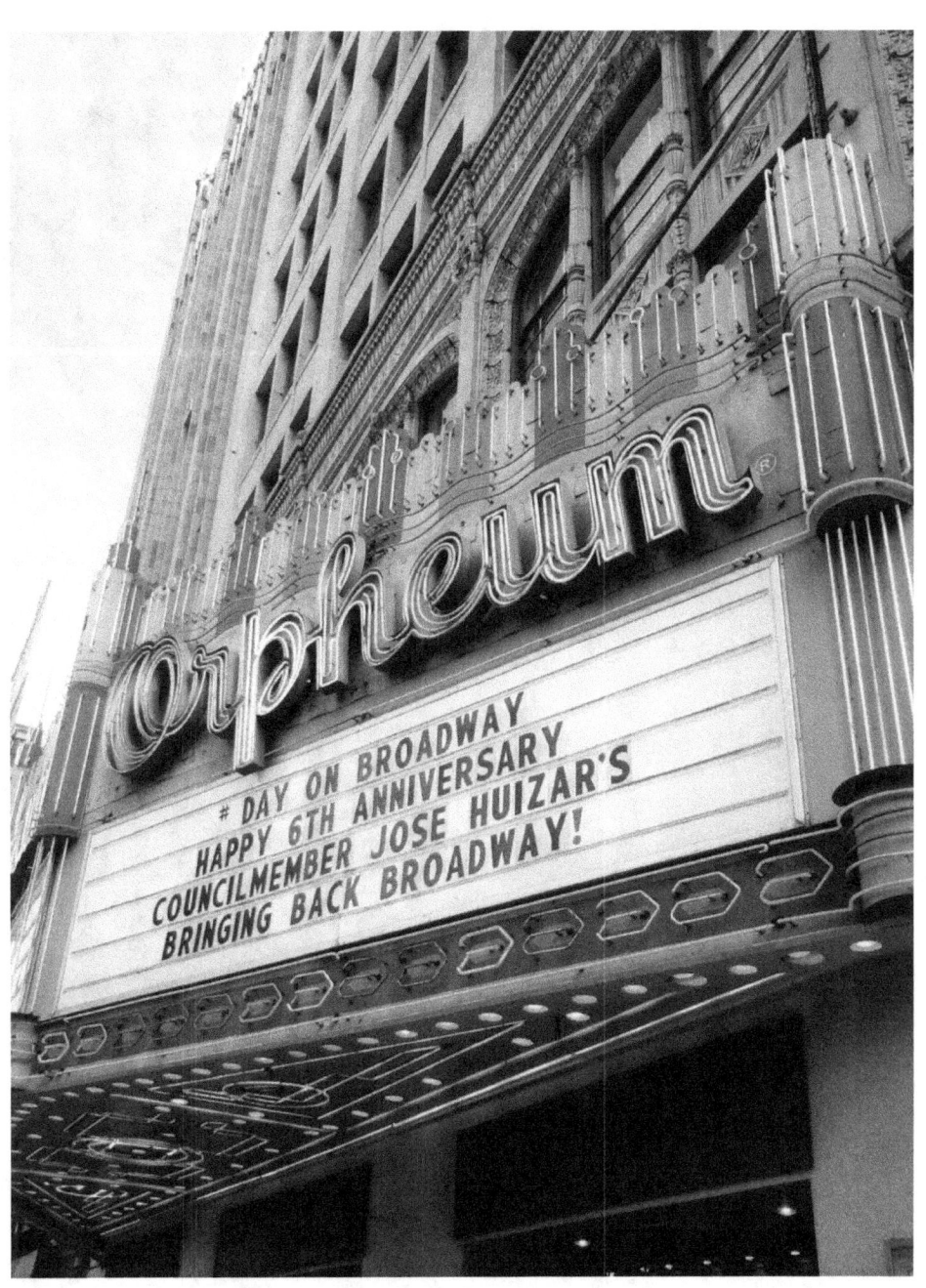

ORPHEUM THEATRE

842 S. Broadway

Its sumptuous interior—rich reds and golds, expanses of gilt and marble—mesmerizes. Pictured here is the Orpheum's lobby.

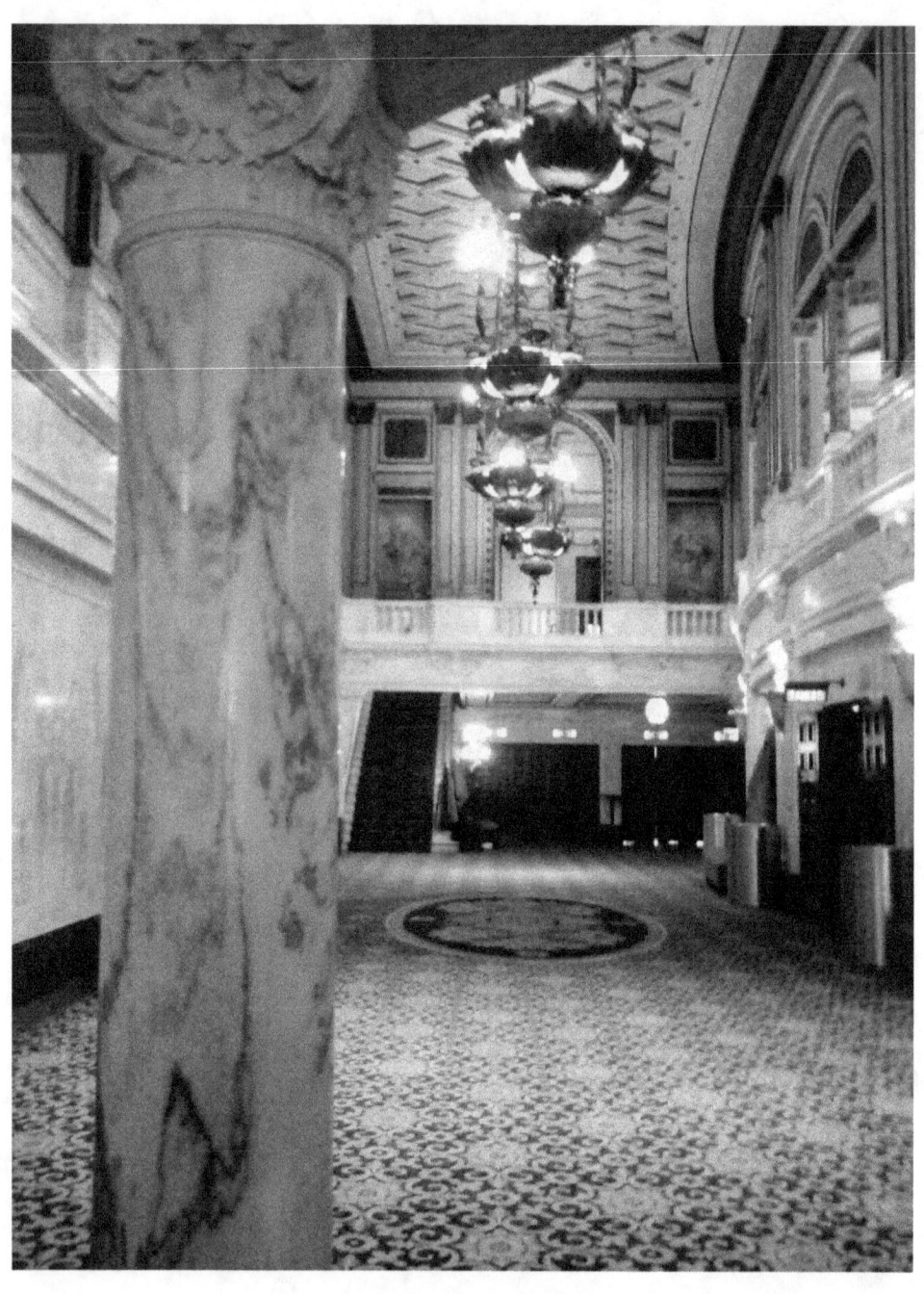

ORPHEUM THEATRE

842 S. Broadway

The Orpheum Theatre continues to present special events, theatrical productions and concerts, and also hosts film and TV shoots. Superstars from Lena Horne to Jack Benny and Stevie Wonder have performed at the Orpheum. Contemporary performance shows like "American Idol" and "So You Think You Can Dance" have held auditions here because of the Orpheum's capacity and excellent condition.

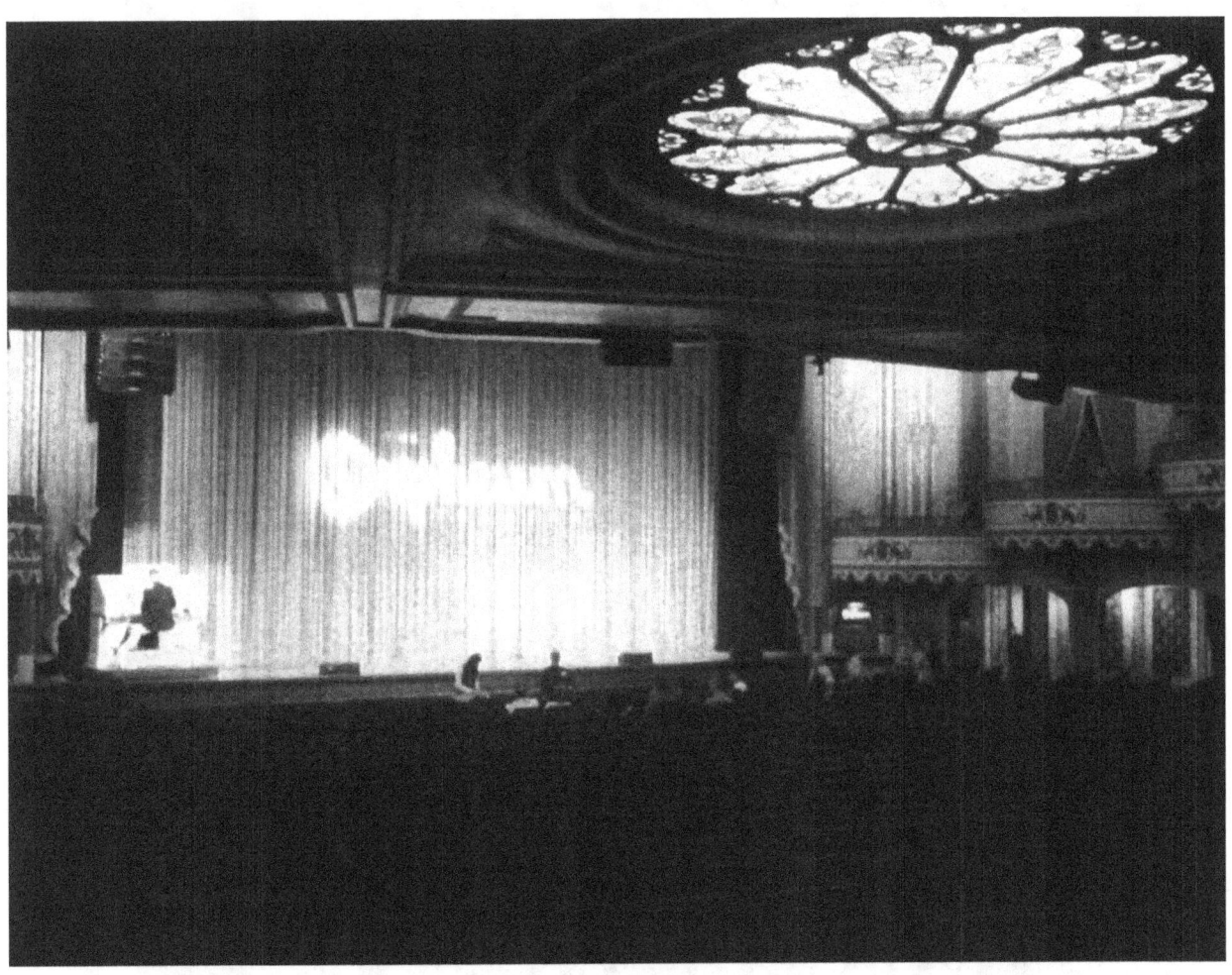

ORPHEUM THEATRE

842 S. Broadway

Note the intricacy of the décor of the arches, boxes, and organ pipe screen.

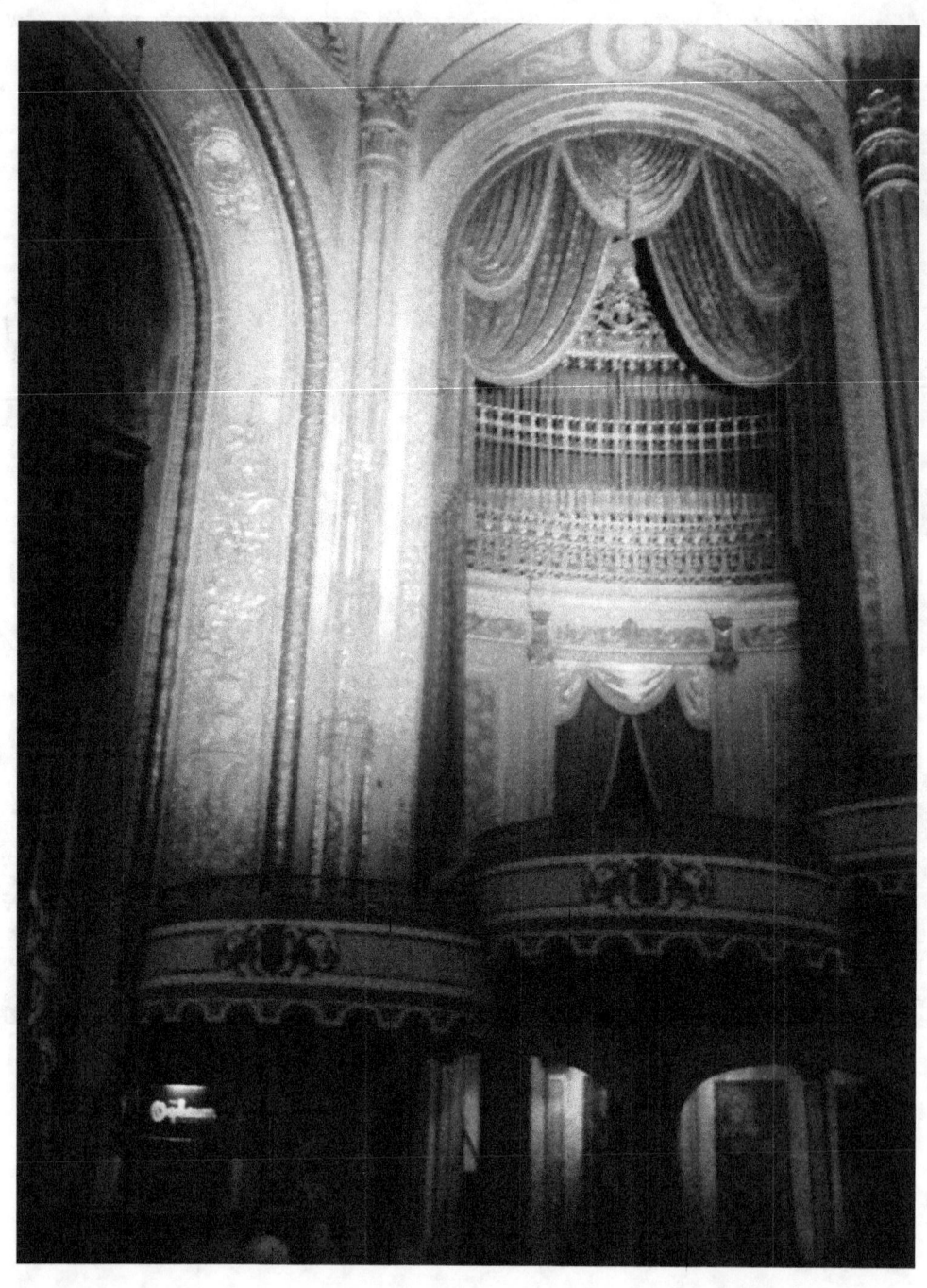

ORPHEUM THEATRE

842 S. Broadway

A view of the mezzanine gallery overlooking the lobby and the lobby's signature chandeliers.

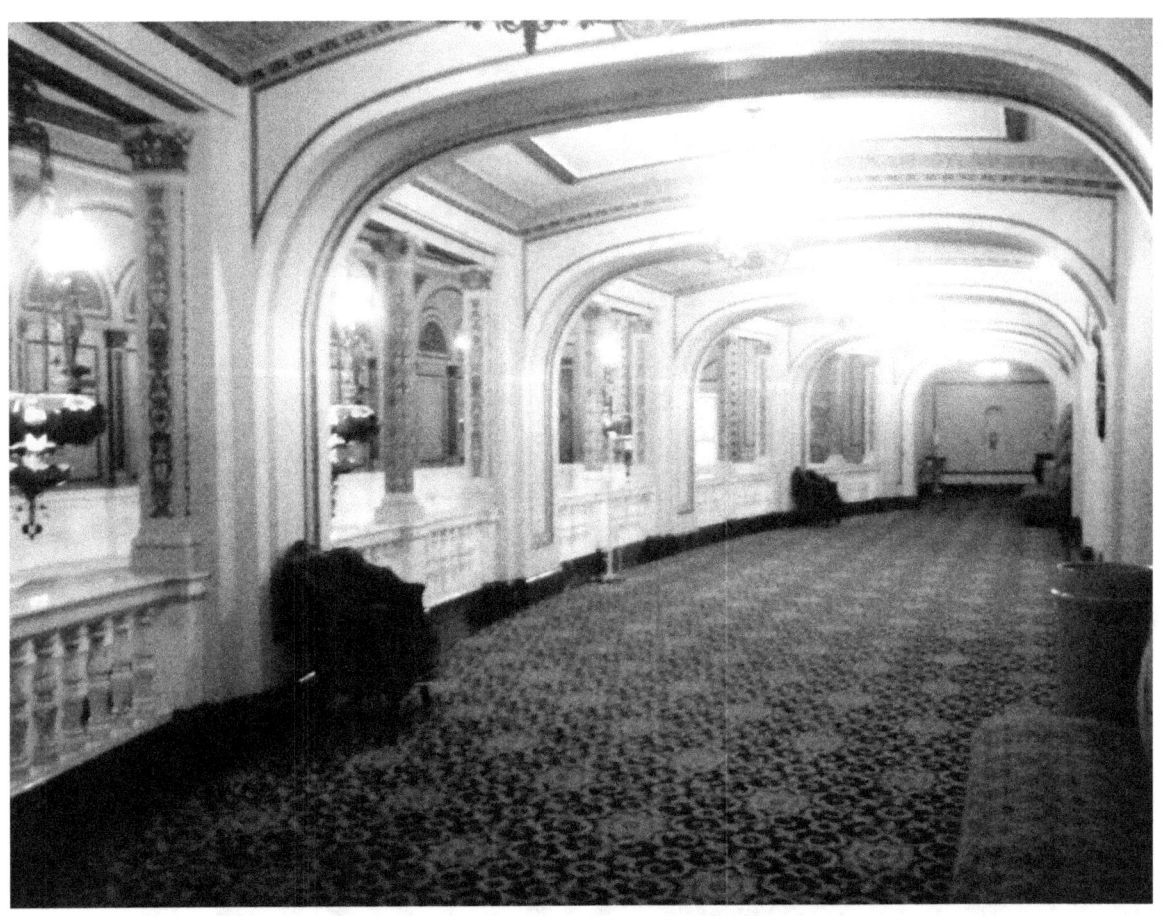

ORPHEUM THEATRE

842 S. Broadway

Marble-clad staircases lead up and up (and up) to multi-tiered balconies ...

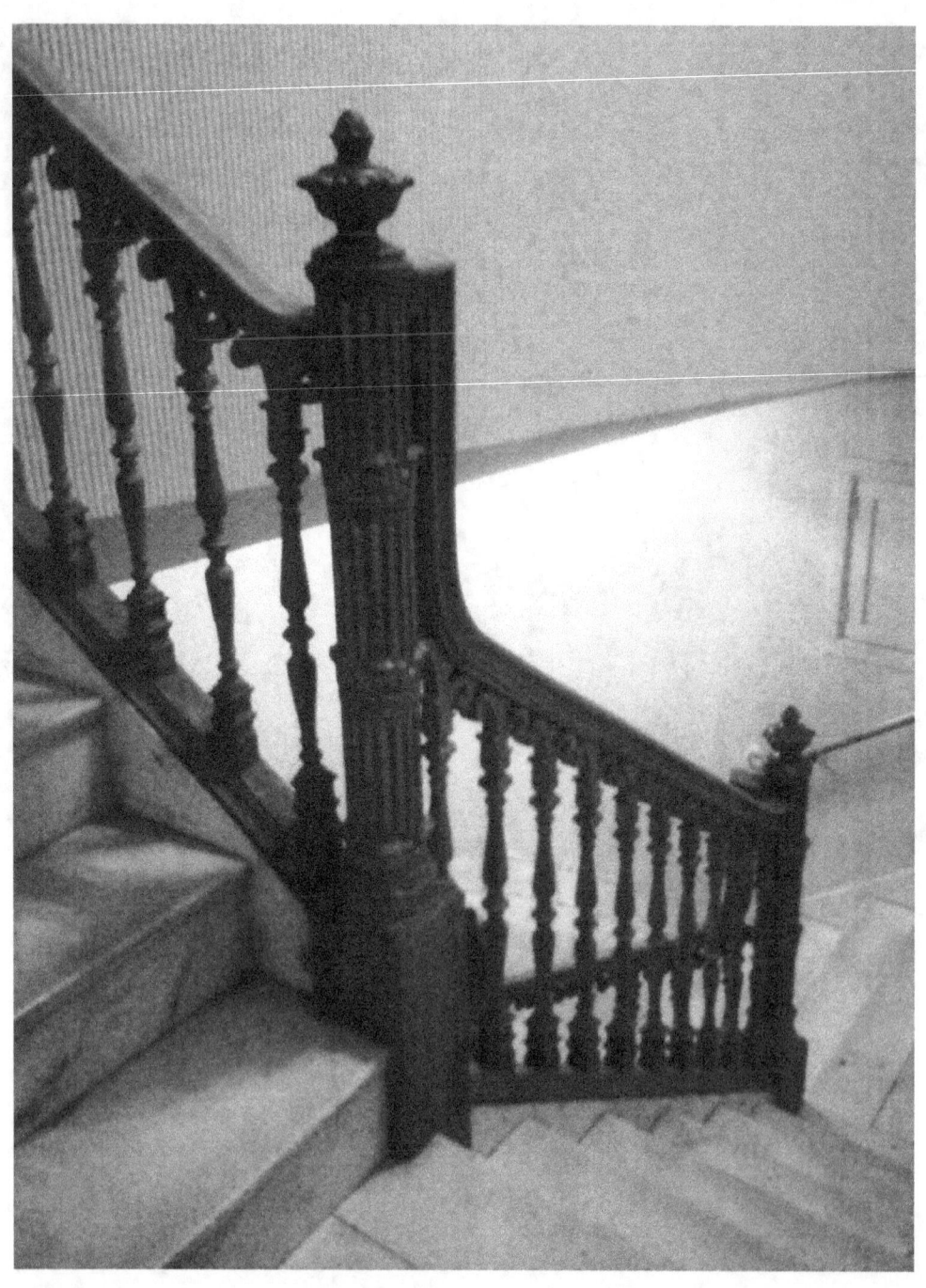

THEATRE DISTRICT

842 S. Broadway

... and stunning aerial views of the Orpheum Theatre's stage and auditorium. (If you're going to audition for "American Idol," what better setting could you ask for?). Note the dark figure playing the organ (bottom left), a kind volunteer letting attendees hear the instrument's tone.

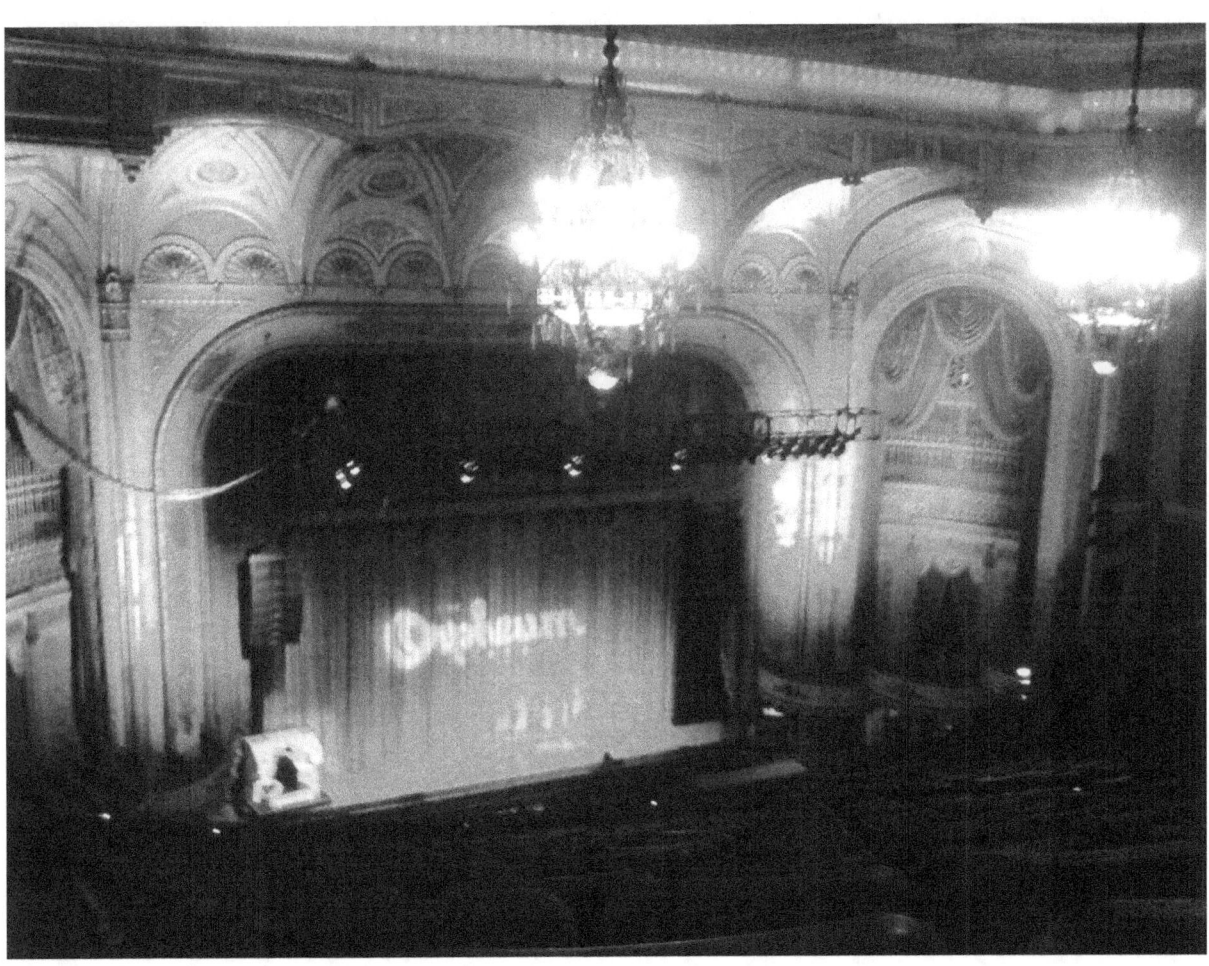

THEATRE DISTRICT

849 S. Broadway

Across the street from the Orpheum stands the Eastern Columbia Building. This Art Deco treasure, which was completed in 1930, had fallen on hard times by the end of the last millennium. The building's clock tower and the distinctive blue and gold exterior still drew attention, but the office building was a scabrous, water-damaged eyesore. Developers rescued it, spending over $80 million to restore the colorful terra cotta exterior to its former glory, converting the interior to contemporary (and reasonably priced) residential lofts. The views are excellent, there's a pool on the roof, and the clock tower is working once again.

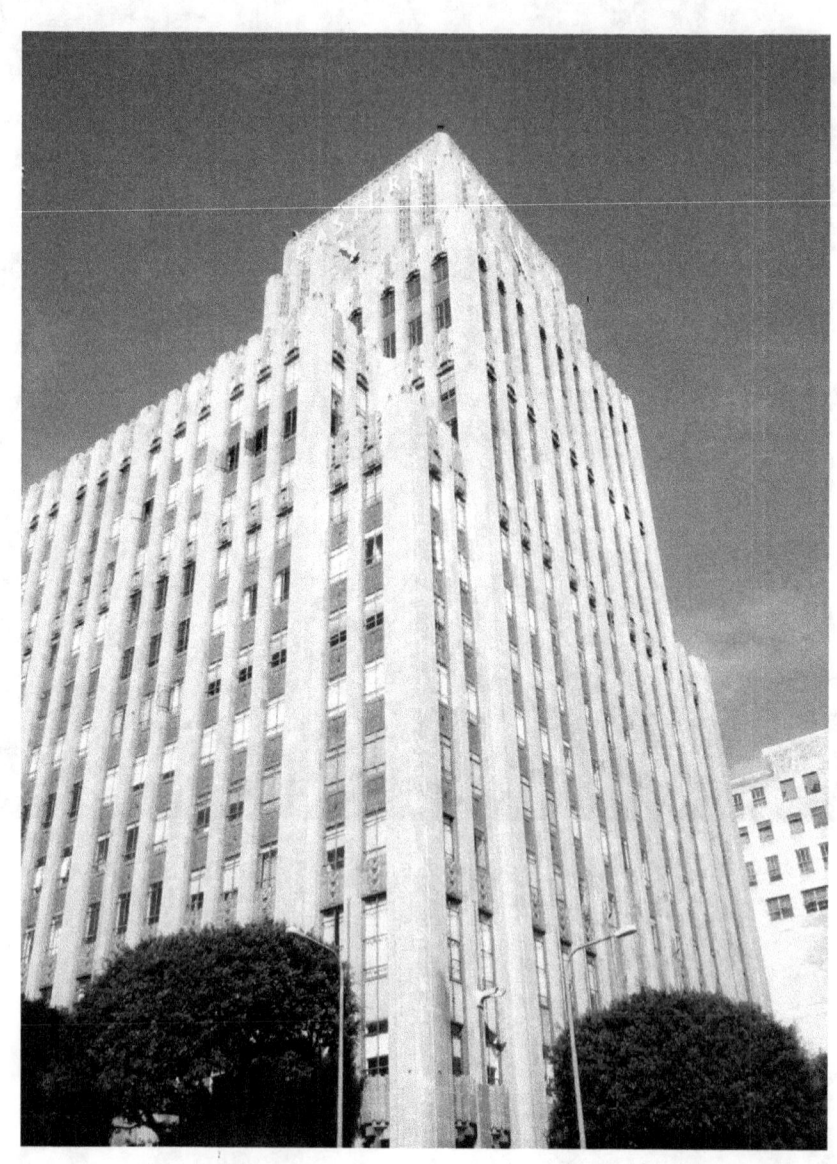

THEATRE DISTRICT

849 S. Broadway

The entrance vestibule of the Eastern Columbia Building is a visual poem of Art Deco design—vertical lines, bold geometric elements, balanced symmetry—from the chevrons high above to the terrazzo pavement. Retail and restaurant venues anchor the ground level (note the diners [bottom left]). Theatrical note: From 1908 until its demolition in 1933, the Majestic Theatre stood at 845 S. Broadway, just north of the Eastern Columbia Building.

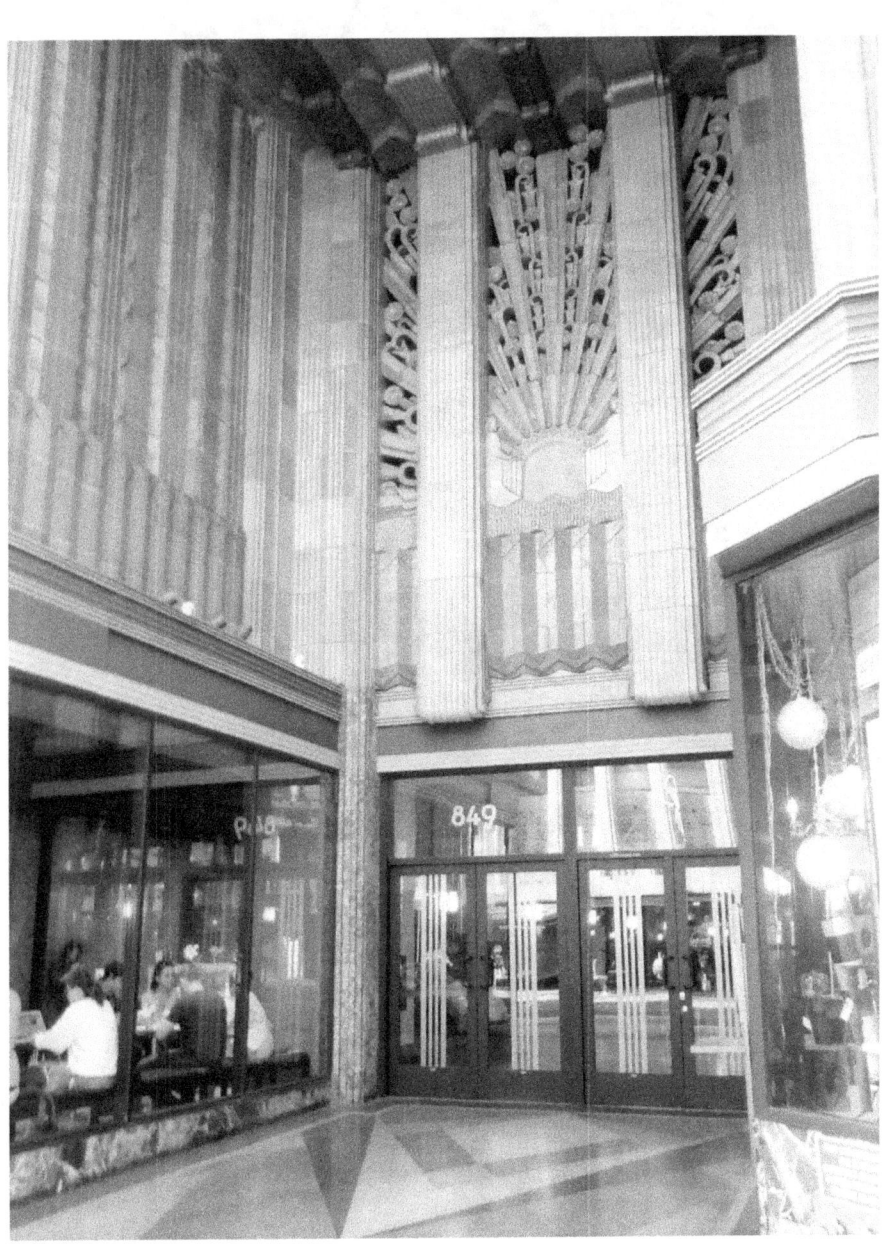

FASHION DISTRICT

849 S. Broadway

Looking for fashion-forward glad rags? Check out the gold and silver suits in the window of a high-end European designer on the ground floor of the Eastern Columbia Building.

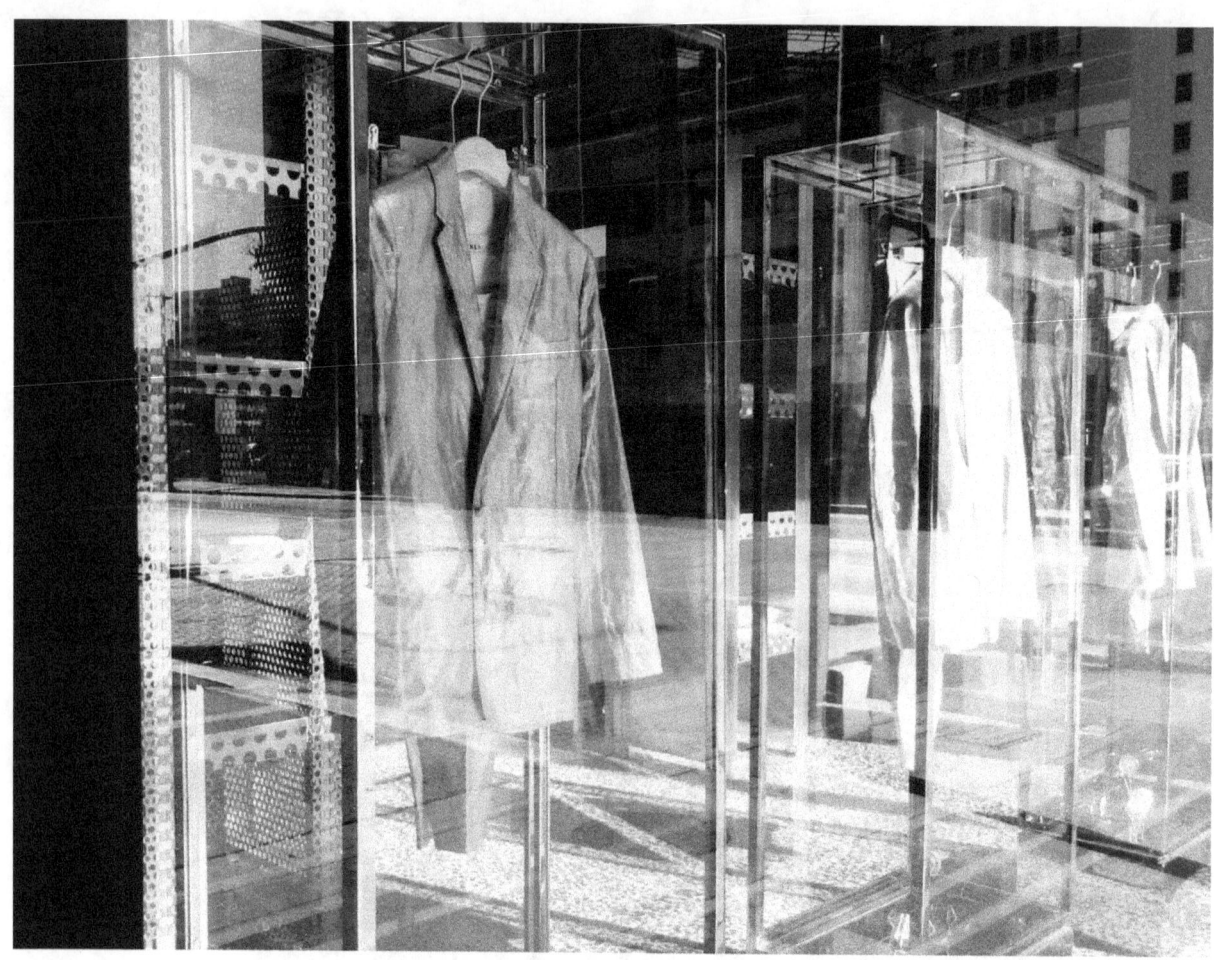

FASHION DISTRICT

800 – 900 Blocks of S. Broadway

Proceeding south on S. Broadway, visitors enters an "overlap" region where the Theatre District ends and the Fashion and Commercial/Industrial Districts begin. This photo was taken on the 900 block of S. Broadway, looking north toward the Eastern Columbia Building (top center).

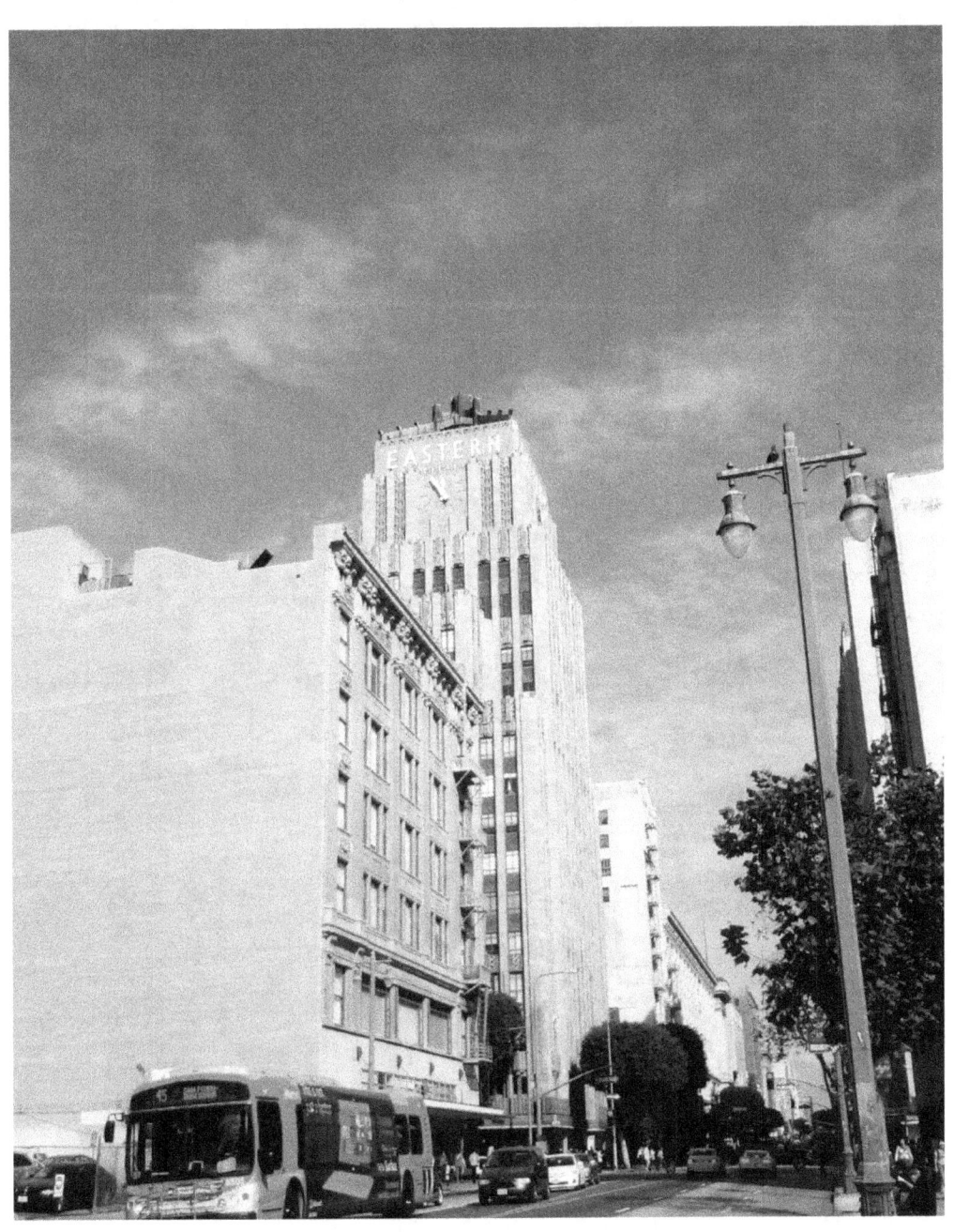

FASHION DISTRICT

850 S. Broadway

Like the Eastern Columbia Building across the street, the Ninth and Broadway Building opened in 1930 and is sheathed in terra cotta. The dominant decorative motif: grapevines. The Ninth and Broadway Building bears the words "Anjac Fashion Buildings" in gold lettering on its doors. Anjac Fashion Buildings is a downtown real estate investment firm that has roots in LA's garment/fashion district. Anjac Fashions was launched in Los Angeles in the mid-20th century by Jack Needleman. (The name "Anjac" combines Jack's name with that of his wife Annette.) Anjac Fashions created ab-fab women's fashions in the stylish 1950's and 1960's—then Needleman shifted his attention to real estate. One of Anjac's great designers, Ilse Metchek, founded LA's California Fashion Association.

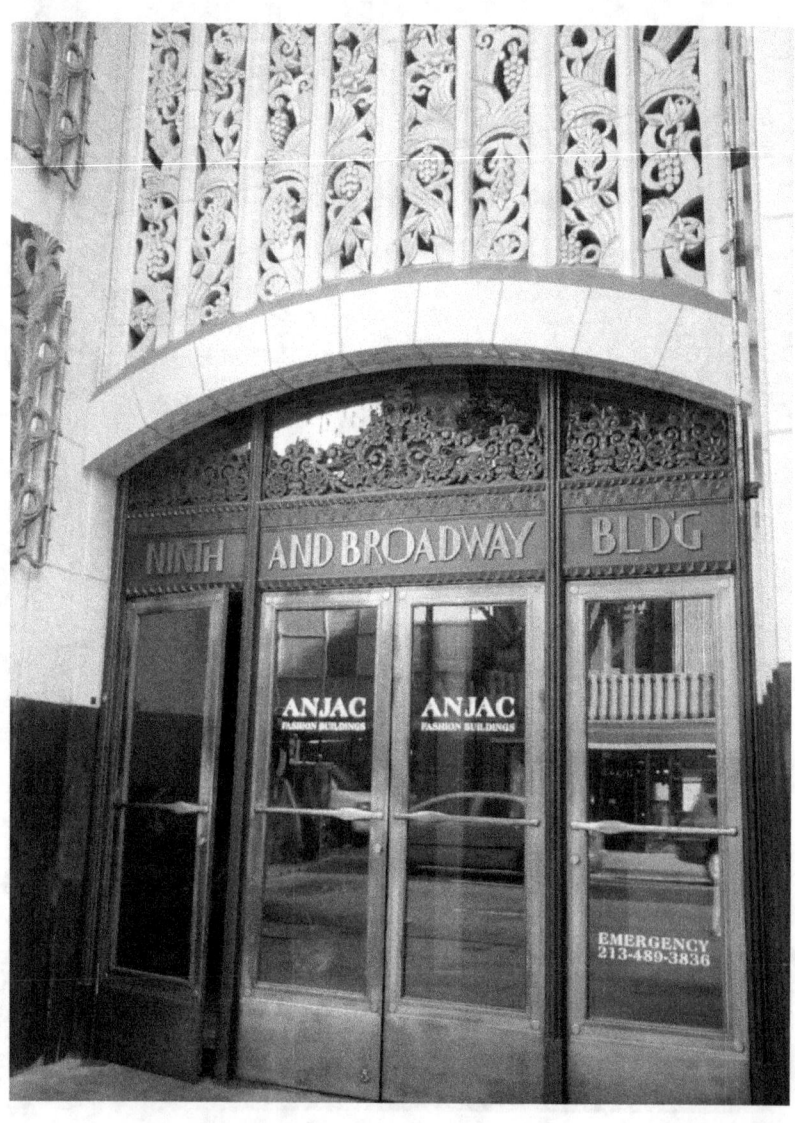

FASHION DISTRICT

900 Block of S. Broadway

Not every structure in the Fashion District is as elaborate as the Ninth and Broadway Building. For example, the Apparel Mart Building, as viewed looking northeast from the 900 block of S. Broadway, is composed of clean, simple lines. The concrete high-rise (located at 112 W. 9th Street) was completed in 1914 and presently serves as office space.

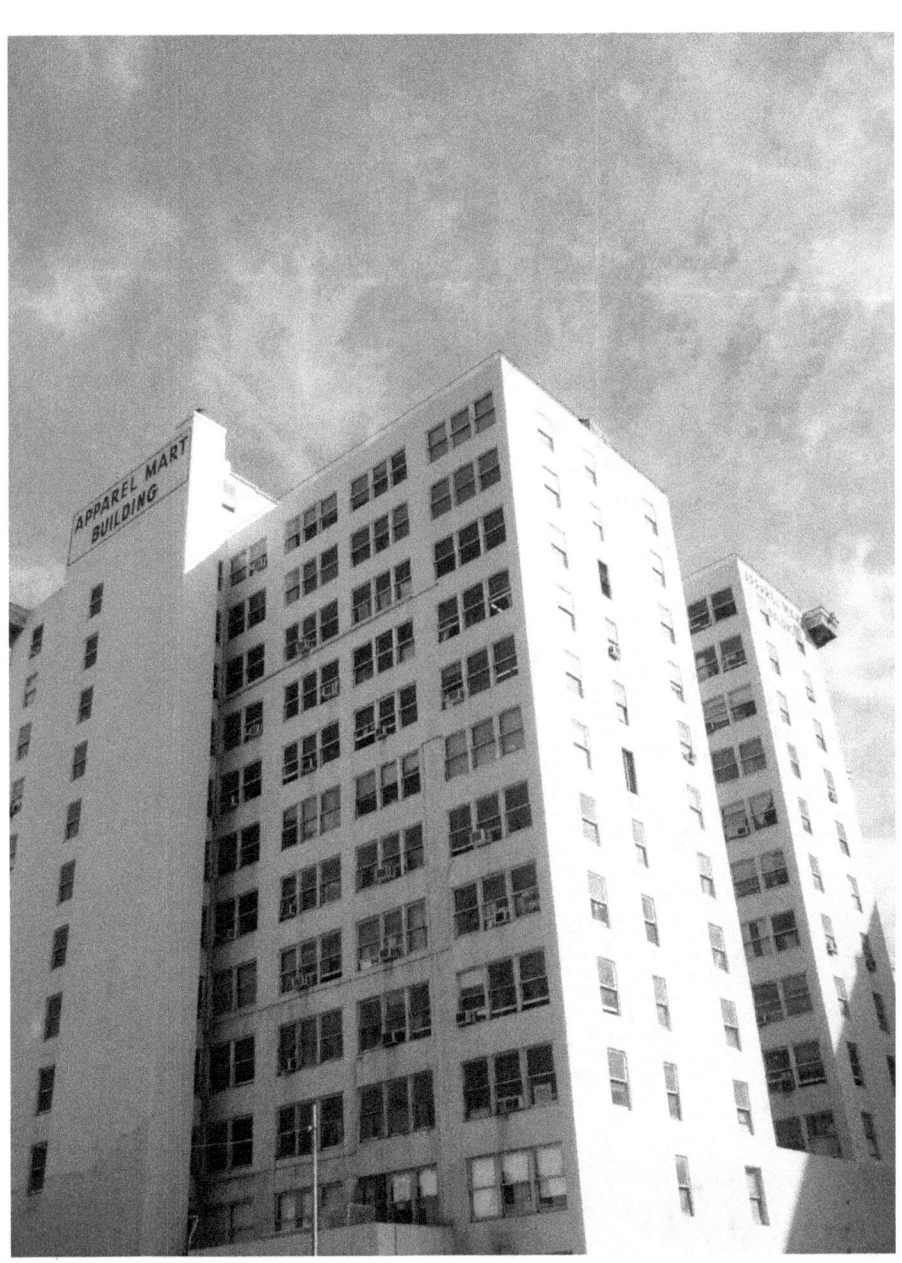

THEATRE DISTRICT

933 S. Broadway

In contrast to the plain lines of the Apparel Mart Building on the next block, the United Artists Theatre, completed in 1927, boasts a façade easily as complex and charming as that of the Million Dollar Theatre six blocks north. The Million Dollar Theatre anchors the Theatre District's north end, while United Artists anchors its southern termination.

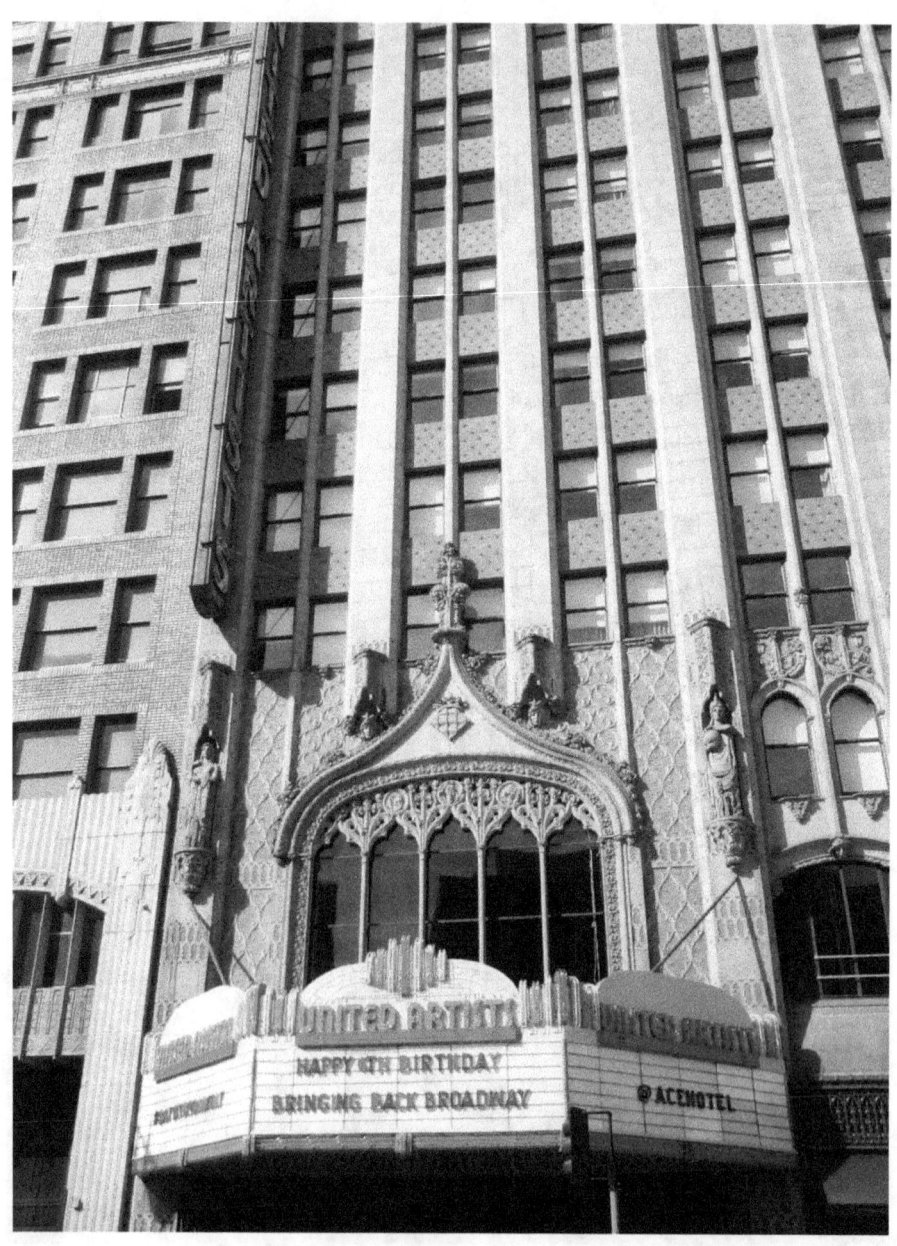

THEATRE DISTRICT

933 S. Broadway

In 1927, "talkies" hadn't yet gained traction, so the United Artists Theatre opened with a silent film starring Mary Pickford, then America's sweetheart and—not incidentally—one of the founders of United Artists. (The other founders were Charlie Chaplin, Douglas Fairbanks (Pickford's husband), and DW Griffith). Pickford had a screening room in the basement of the United Artists Theatre.

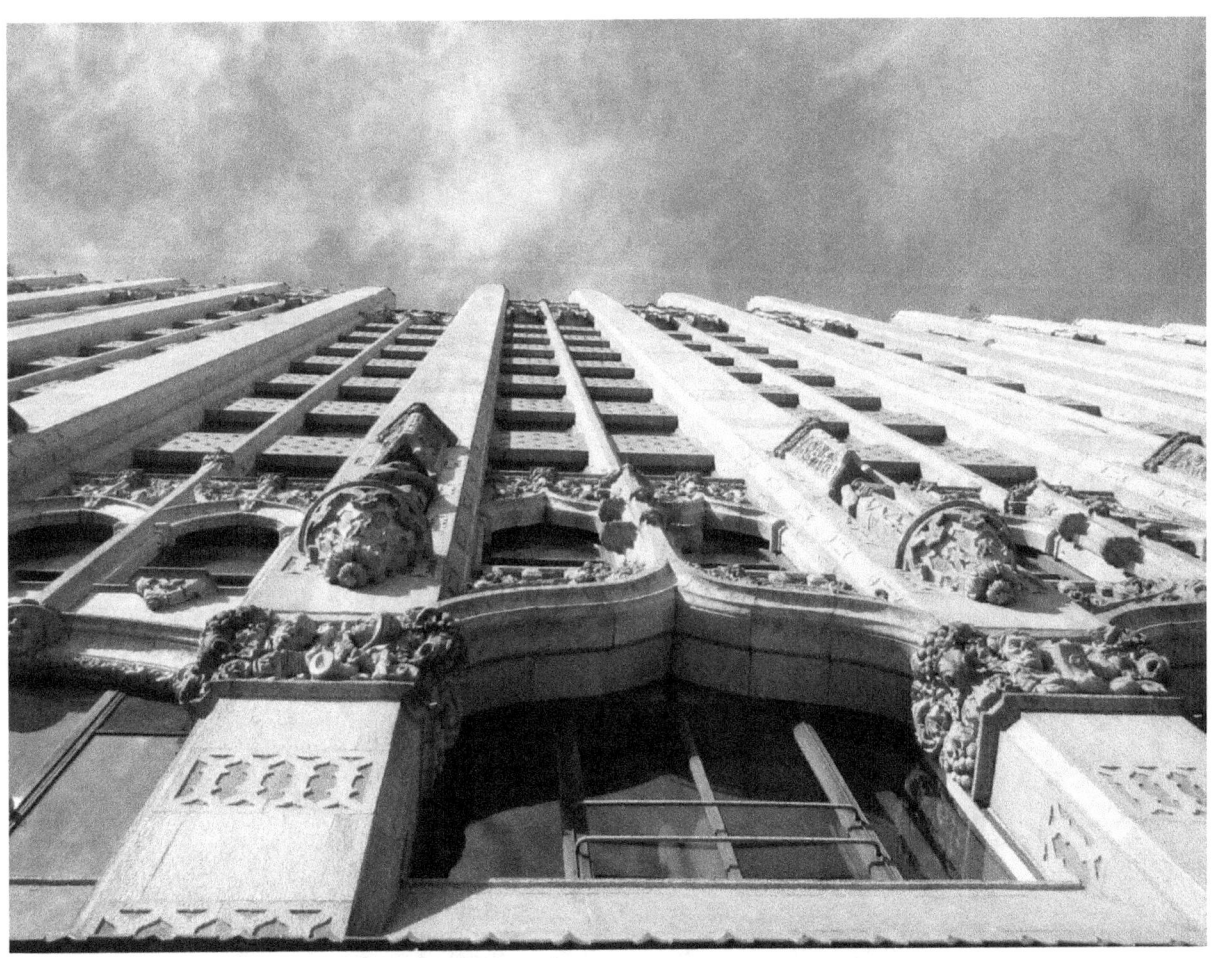

THEATRE DISTRICT

933 S. Broadway

United Artists Theatre closed in 1989, and for the next twenty years was used as a church—hence the origins of the giant "Jesus Saves" signs atop the building and its striking tower. In 2010 the church moved out; they took most of their signs with them, so today only one "Jesus Saves" sign remains on the west side of the building. Pictured here: An entrance vestibule of the United Artists Theatre lobby. The theatre is presently being renovated and can be secured for filming and private events.

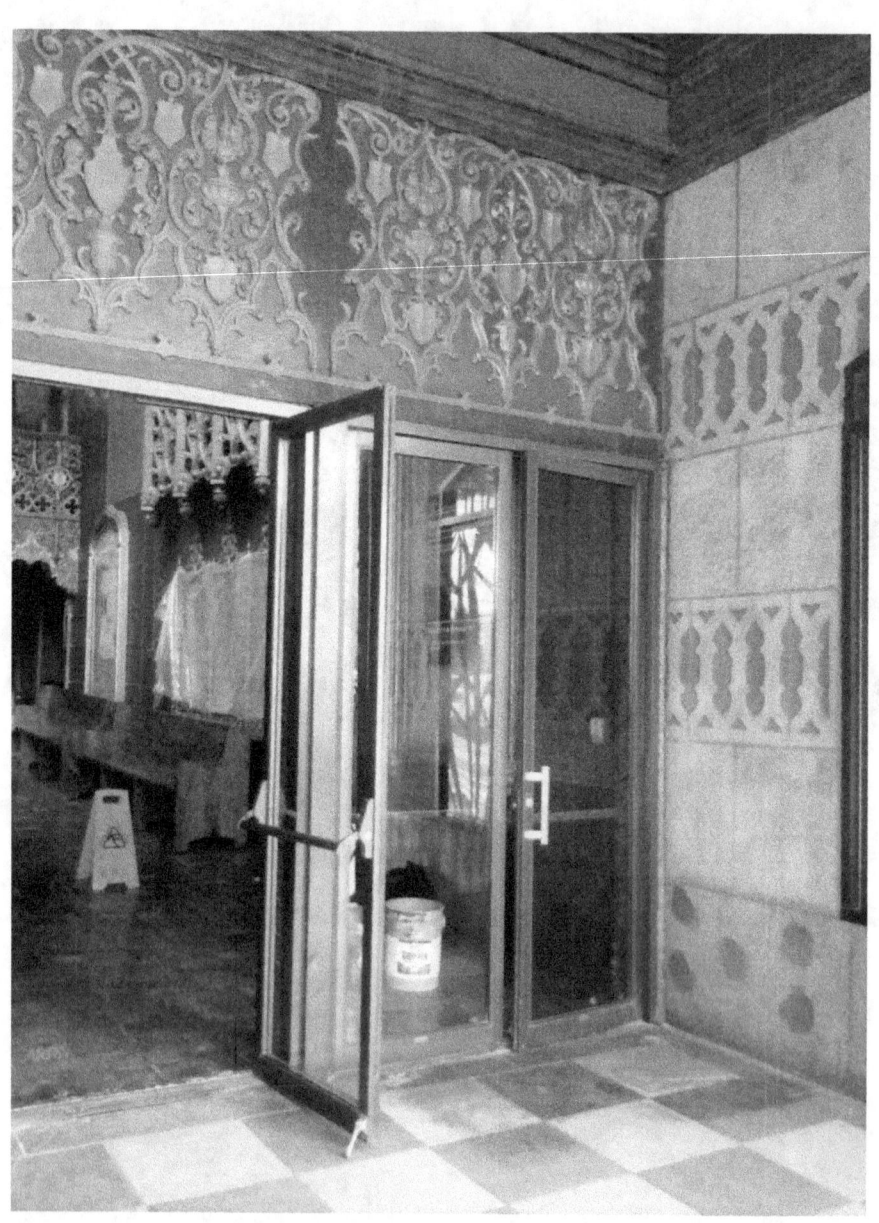

THEATRE DISTRICT

933 S. Broadway

The theatre is being restored, but most of the United Artists Theatre building already has been transformed into the hipster-cool Ace Hotel. Catering to the preservation-minded Millennials that are flooding the district, the Ace Hotel retained and restored much of the original décor while adding a rooftop pool and a ground-level café that includes handsome awnings, sidewalk tables, and a coffee bar. The mochas are tasty here, even if the service is sometimes hit-or-miss. Vive le hipster-chic!

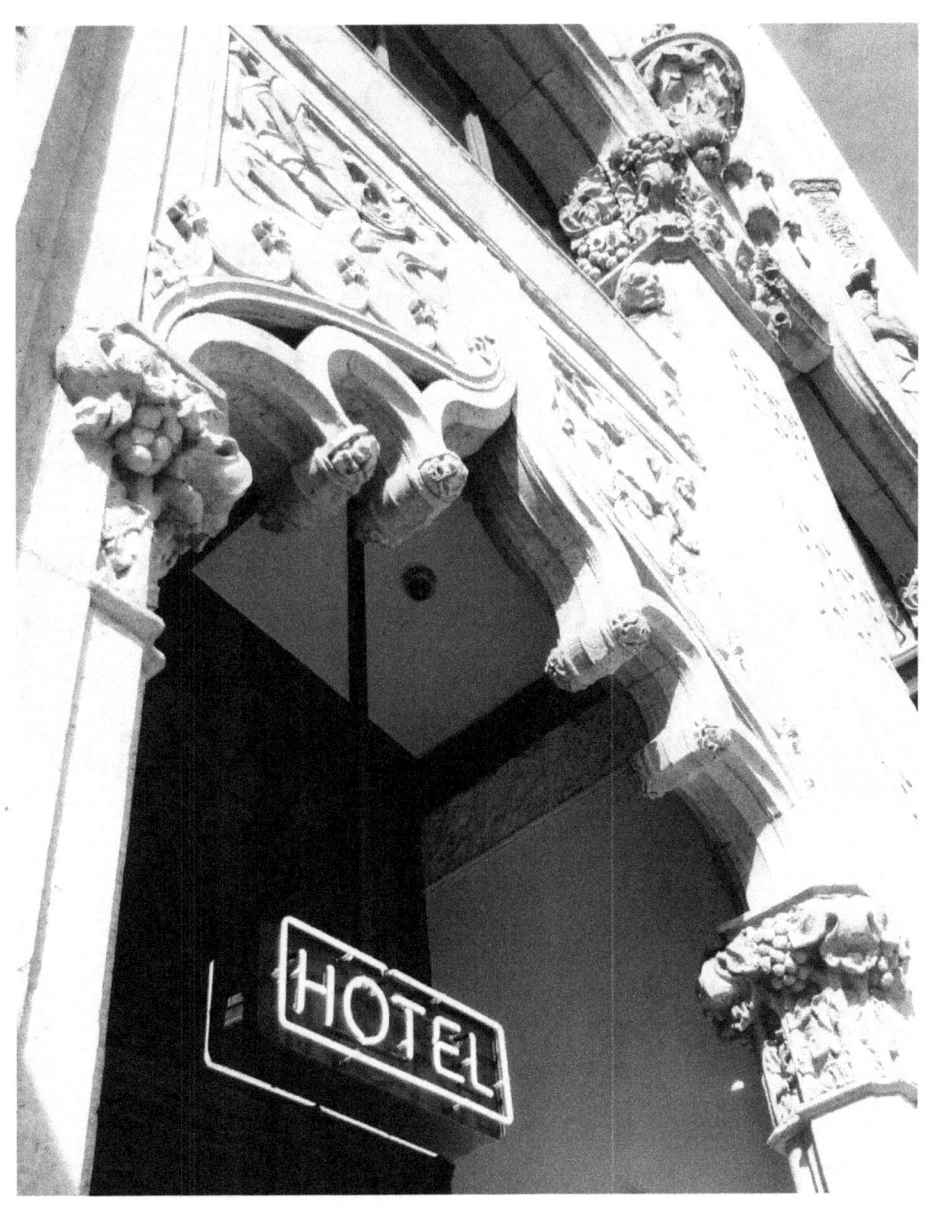

THEATRE DISTRICT

933 S. Broadway

One of the decorative touches at the Ace: A collage of books decorates the west wall of the lobby.

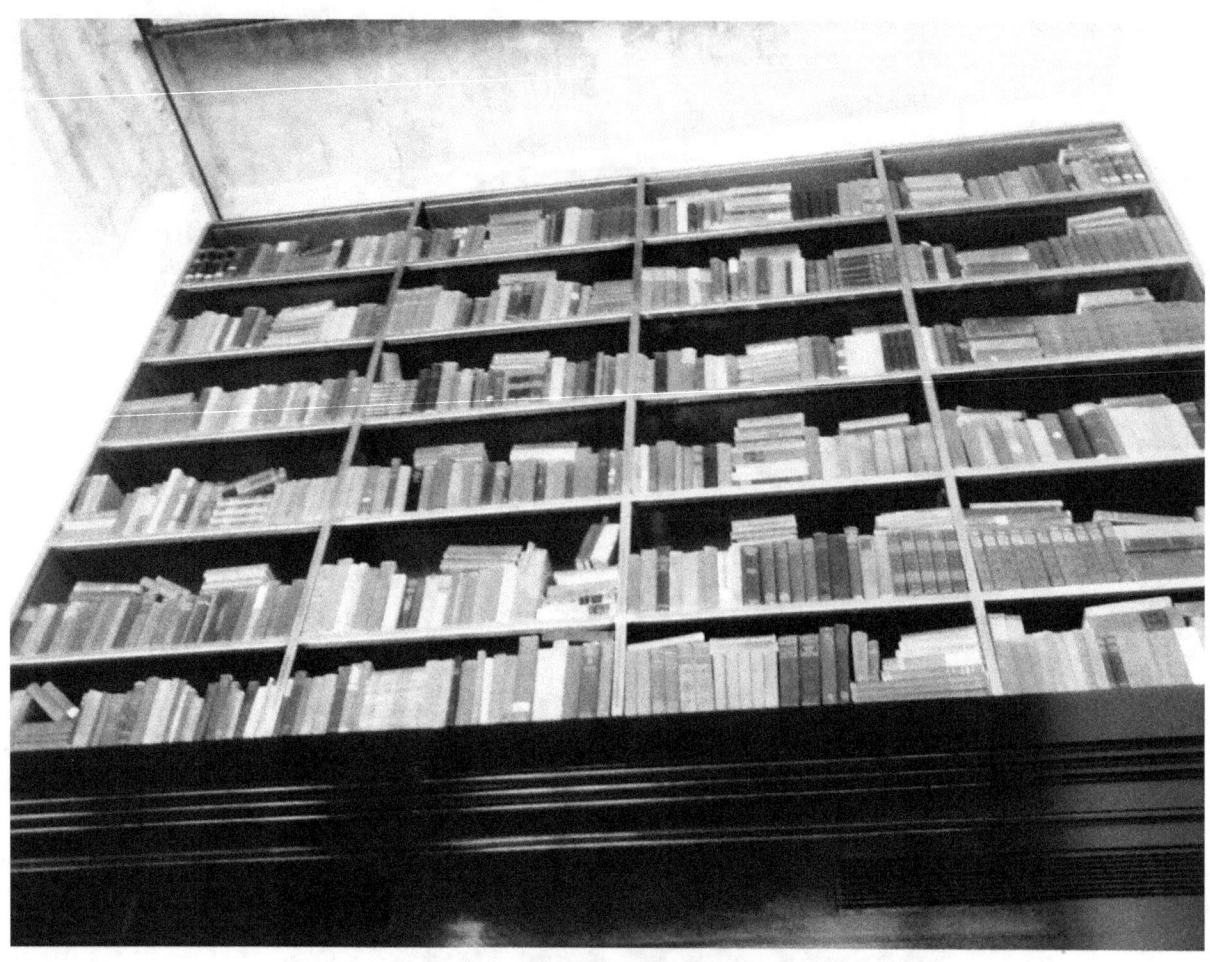

THEATRE DISTRICT

933 S. Broadway

A view of the United Artists Theatre/Ace Hotel from the Hill Street side, looking east. Note the tower—a well-known feature of the downtown skyline—and the remaining "Jesus Saves" sign.

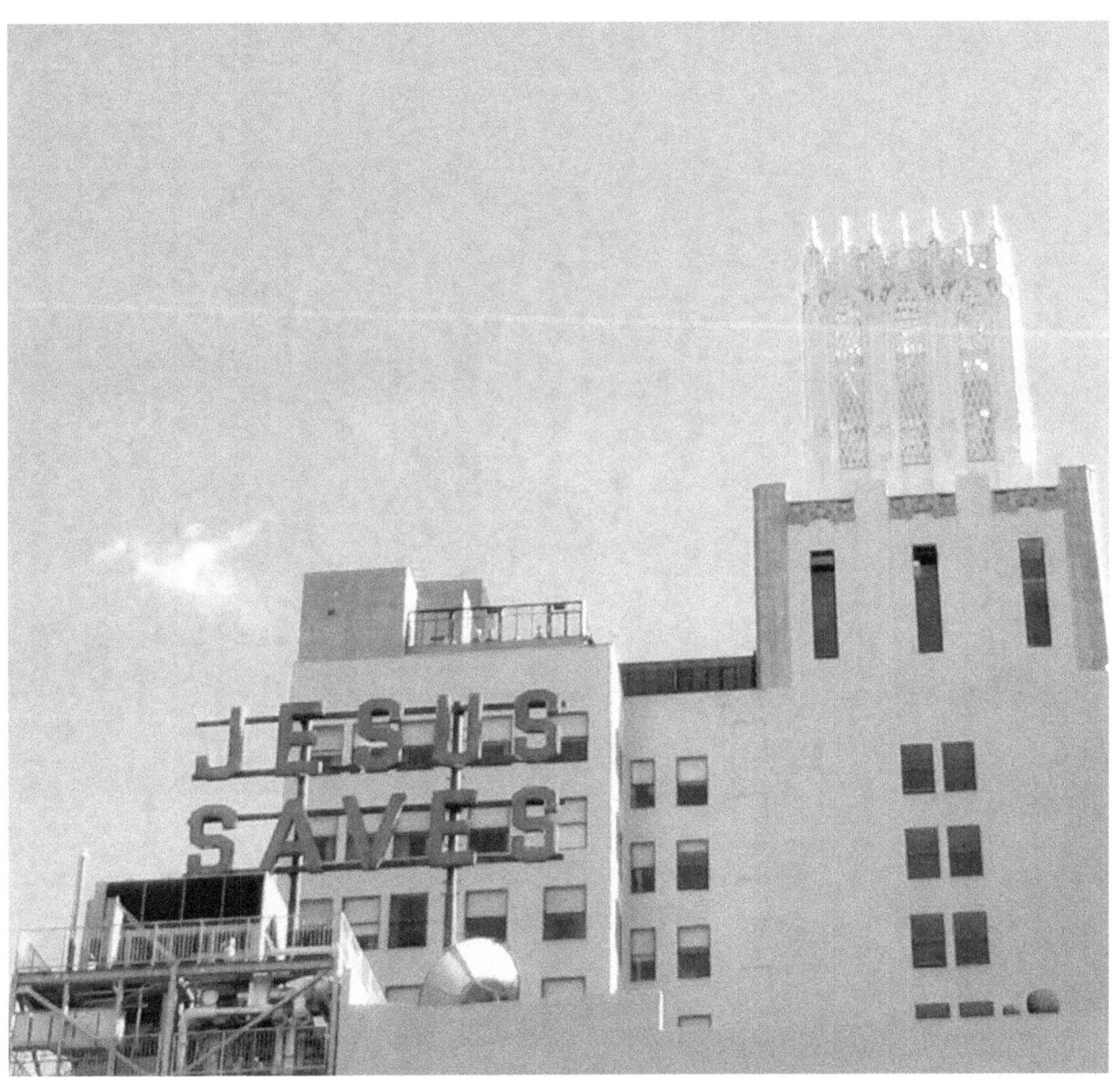

COMMERCIAL/INDUSTRIAL DISTRICT

S. Broadway and Olympic

South of Olympic, Broadway once again becomes a job lot of restaurants, mom-and-pop stores, parking lots, garment shops, offices, and industrial locales, not to mention abandoned storefronts and abandoned buildings. The view here is looking southwest. One attractive building in the landscape, between Olympic and Eleventh Street, is a well-maintained Anjac Fashion Building (center). In the distance (bottom left) is the main dome of the "Herald-Examiner" building.

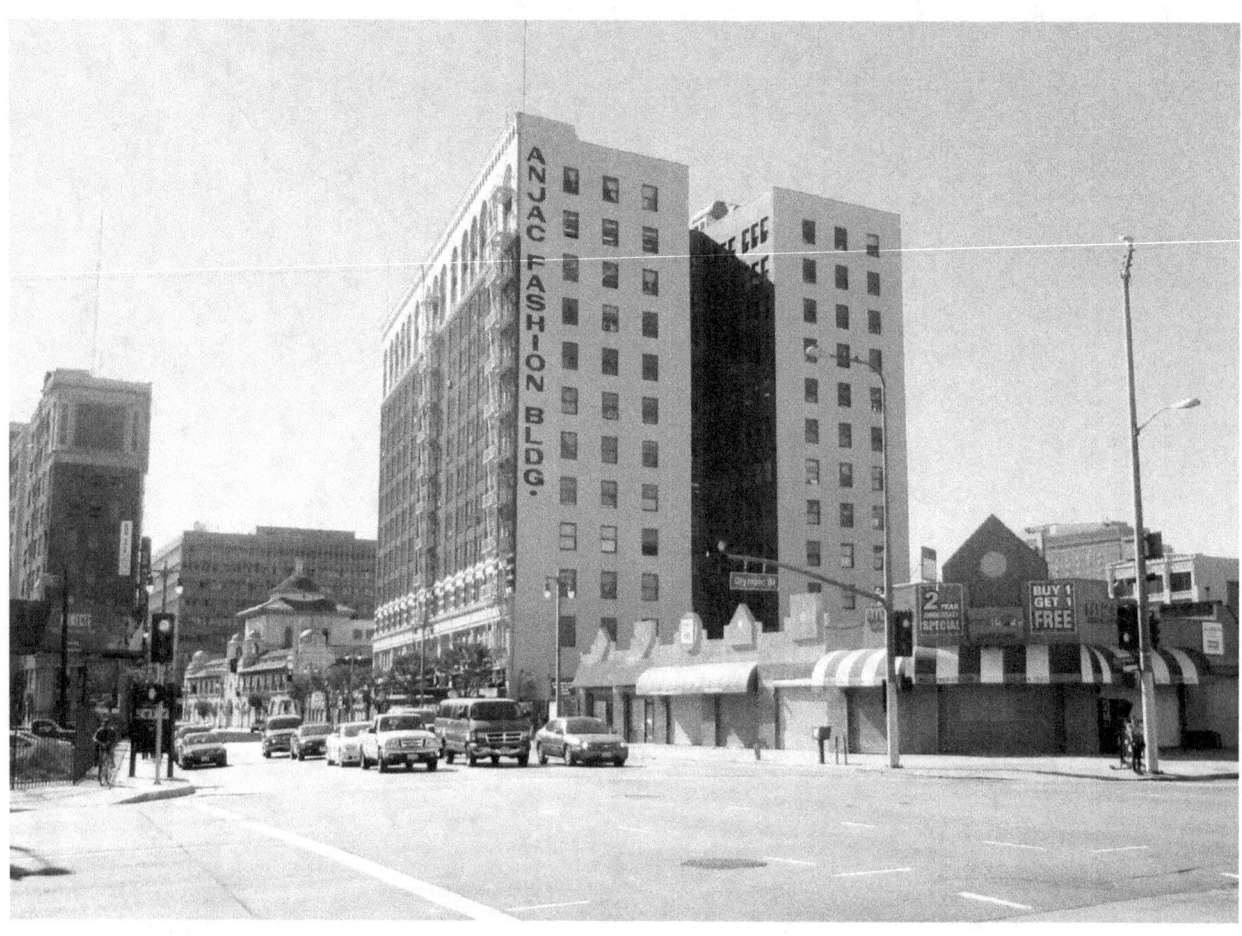

THEATRE DISTRICT

1000 Block of S. Broadway

Standing on the 1000 block of S. Broadway, just south of the Anjac Fashion Building, the back wall of the Mayan Theatre is visible to the west. This is the southernmost theatre in the downtown theatre district, though it fronts on S. Hill Street, not S. Broadway.

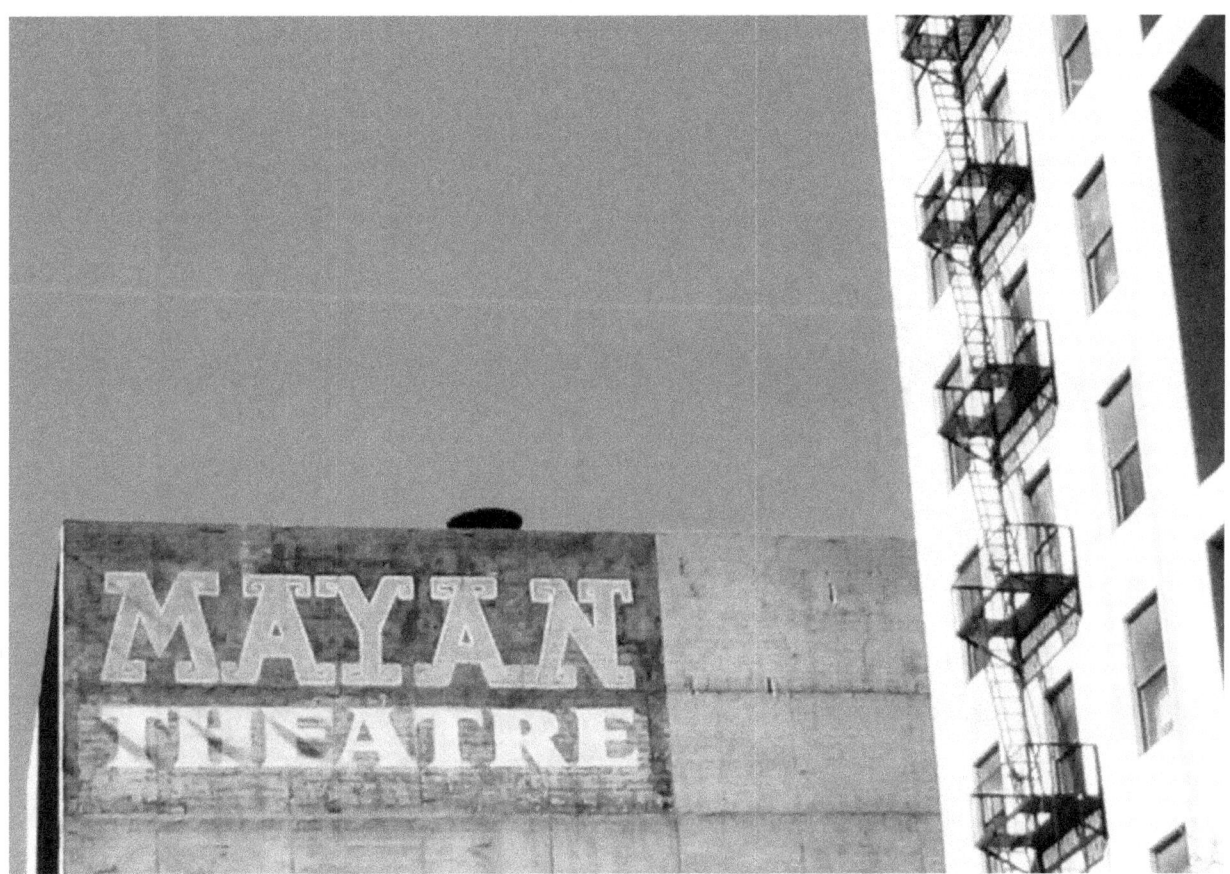

THEATRE DISTRICT

1038 S. Hill Street

Pictured here: The Mayan Theatre as viewed from its S. Hill Street entrance. The Mayan launched in 1927, and was unique from the beginning because of its elaborate Mayan Revival design, both the interior and the exterior. This distinctive style set the Mayan apart from competitors.

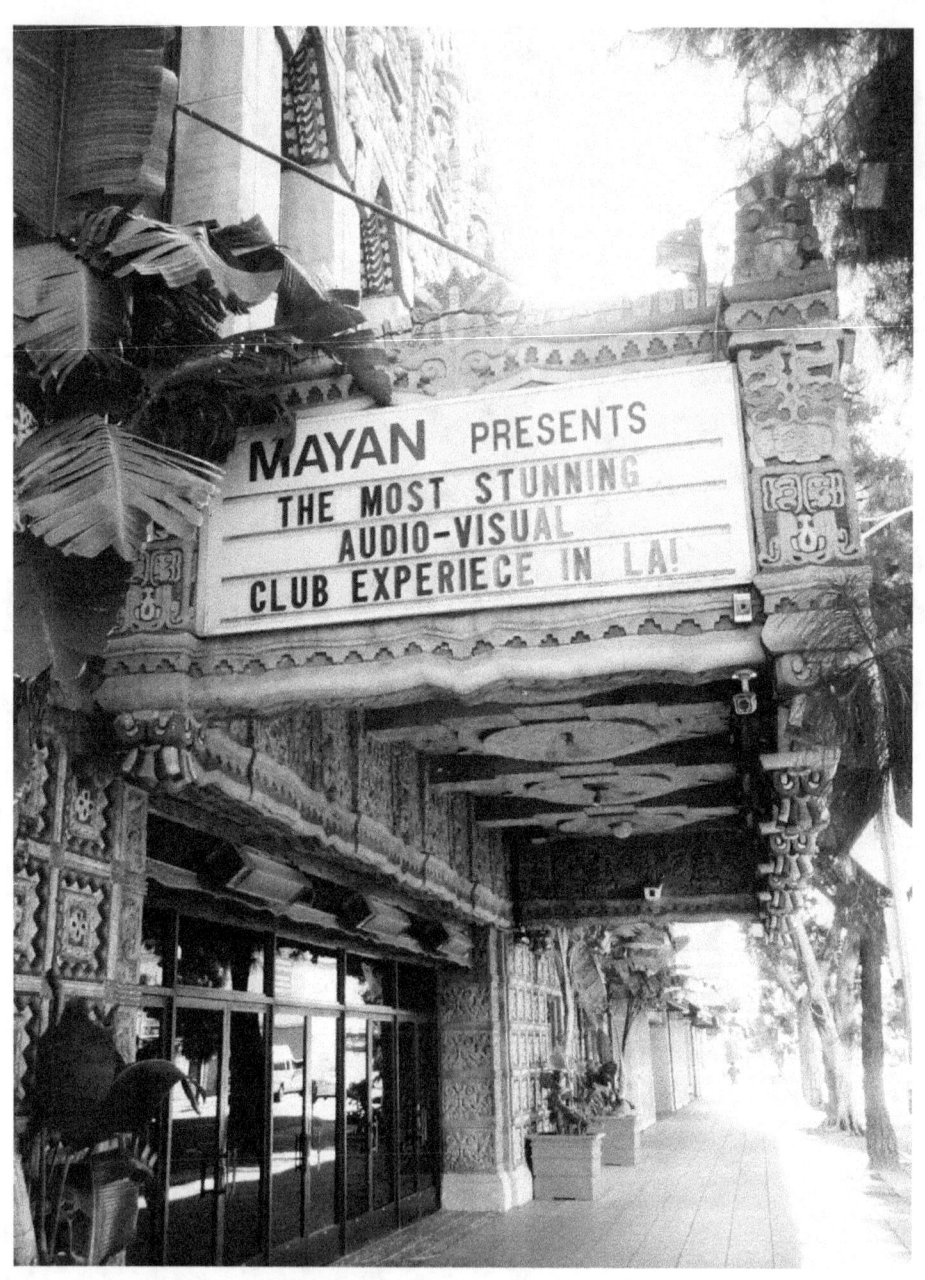

THEATRE DISTRICT

1038 S. Hill Street

This photograph provides a more detailed view of the Mayan Revival sculptural elements decorating the Mayan Theatre. The sculptor was Francisco Cornejo, a Mexican artist who lived, worked, and exhibited in California from 1911 until the 1930's. Today, the Mayan is a nightclub, as well as a treasured cultural monument.

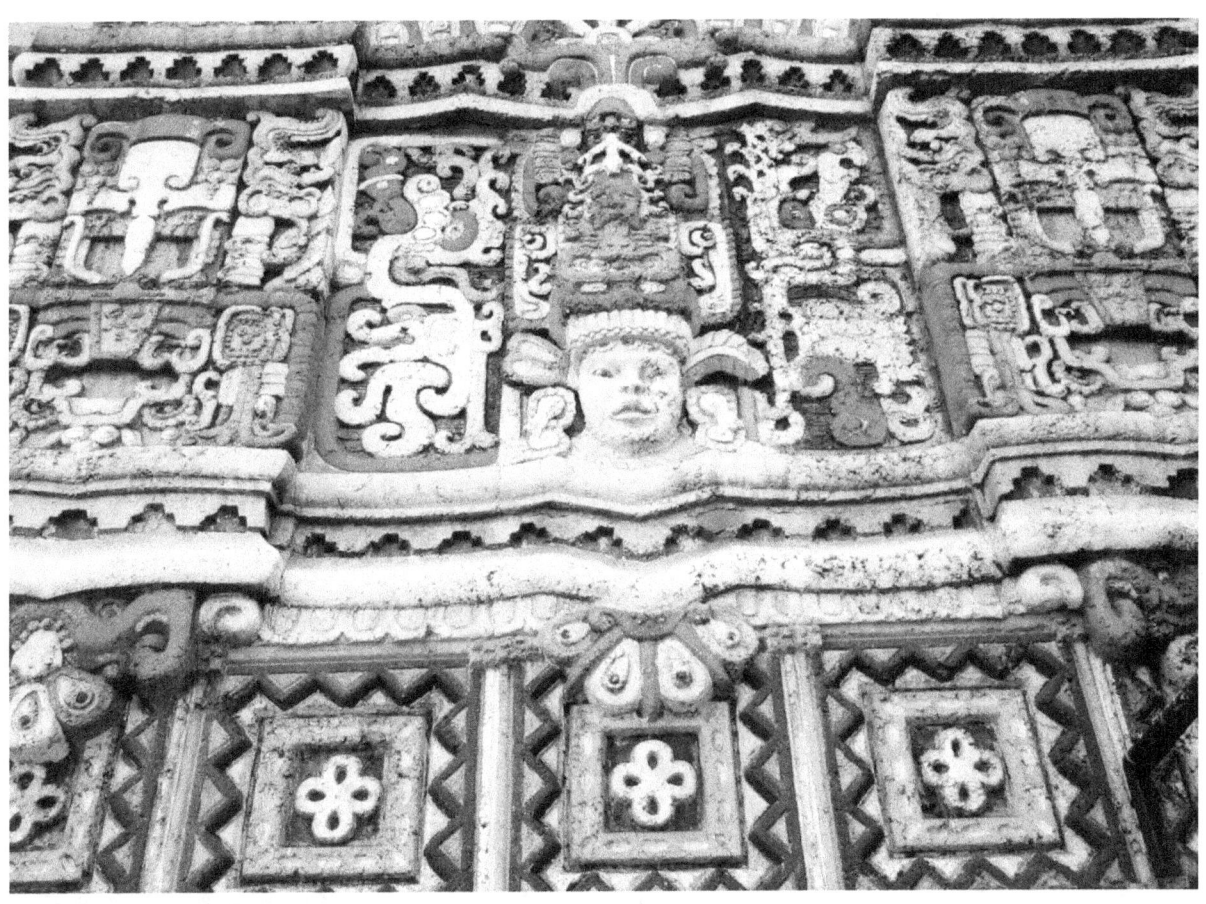

COMMERCIAL/INDUSTRIAL DISTRICT

1060 S. Broadway

South of Olympic, the area becomes less tourist and pedestrian-friendly as one enters the Commercial/Industrial District that stretches southward from the downtown core. Consider, for example, this handsome 1925 building with the outward-swinging windows (as seen in 1920's-set classics like "Thoroughly Modern Millie"). It looks like a lovely gem of a building, and it is, but ...

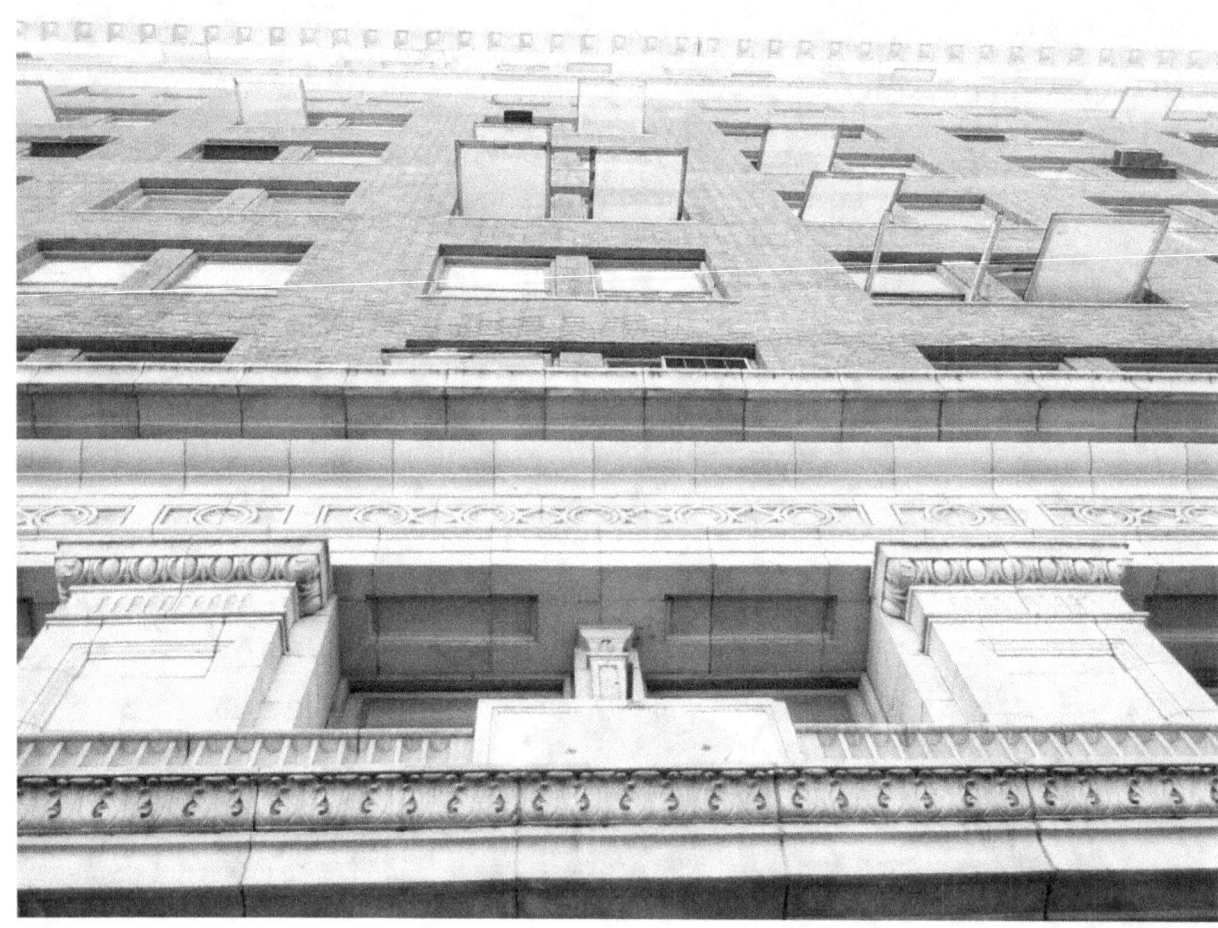

COMMERCIAL/INDUSTRIAL DISTRICT

1060 S. Broadway

... despite several small businesses on the ground level, the classic building is padlocked, forlorn, and in search of a buyer who needs commercial/industrial space. It's unfortunate to see a historic building in such straits. What was its significance in days gone by? 1060 S. Broadway was the Los Angeles Railway Building (called, in later years, the Los Angeles Transit Lines Building). From here, LA's far-flung rail and transit systems were managed.

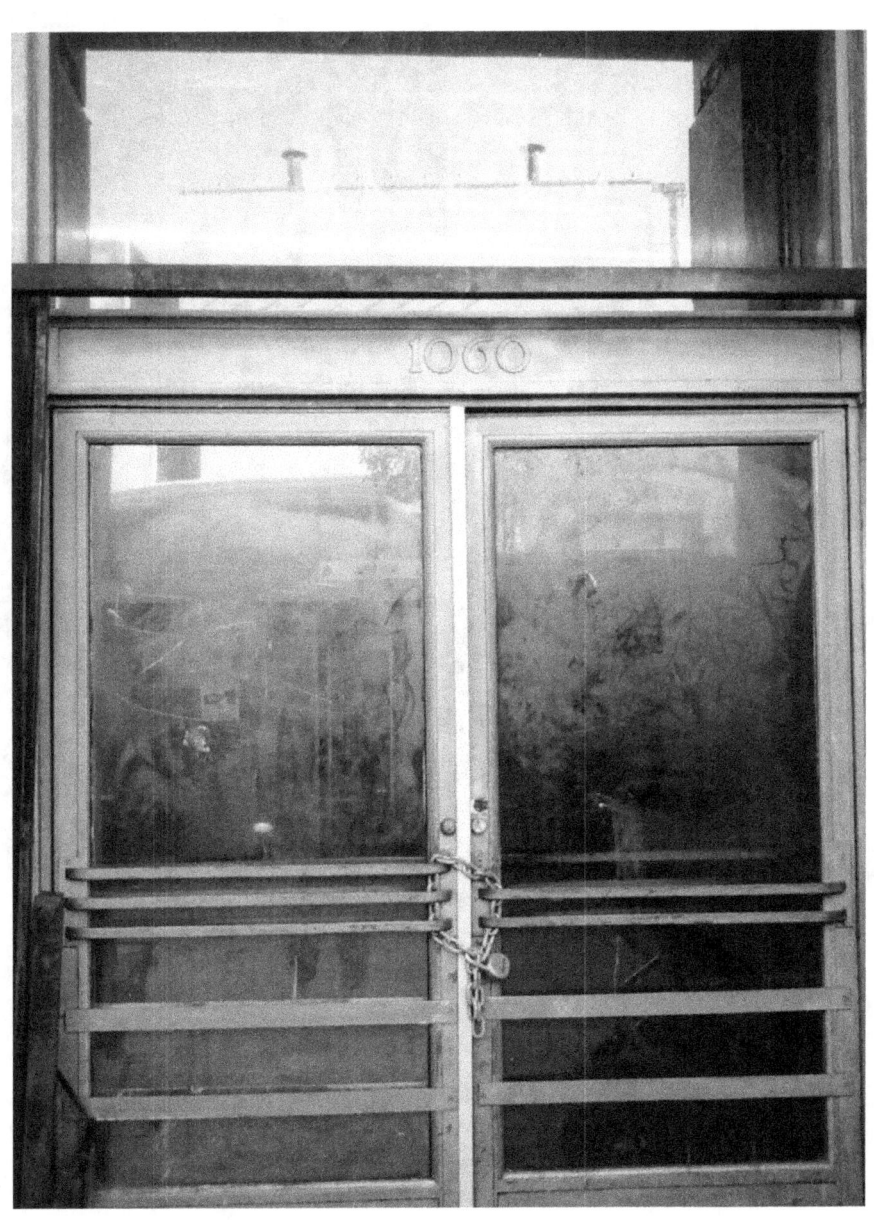

COMMERCIAL/INDUSTRIAL DISTRICT

1060 S. Broadway

A , shattered, graffiti-tagged pay phone outside the south end of the building is yet another clue that this is an area that would benefit from the revitalization that has swept S. Broadway to the north.

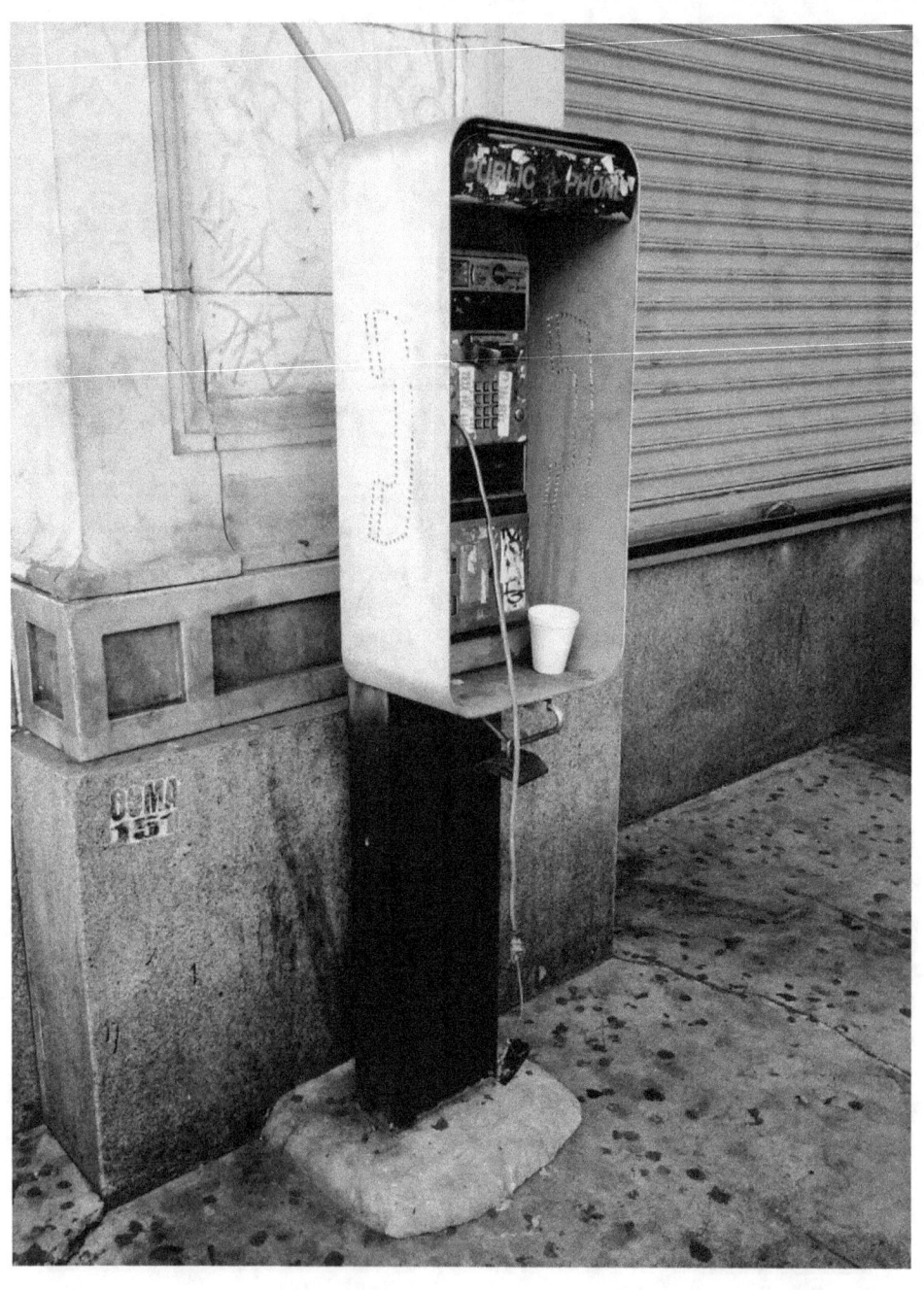

COMMERCIAL/INDUSTRIAL DISTRICT

1111 S. Broadway

On the southwest corner of S. Broadway and Eleventh Street stands a fantastical structure that locals recognize instantly as the Herald-Examiner Building. Looking particularly exotic in the shadow of the modern AT&T (formerly Transamerica) tower behind it, this domed, arched, ornate Spanish Colonial Revival masterpiece housed LA's "Herald-Examiner" operations until the newspaper folded in 1989.

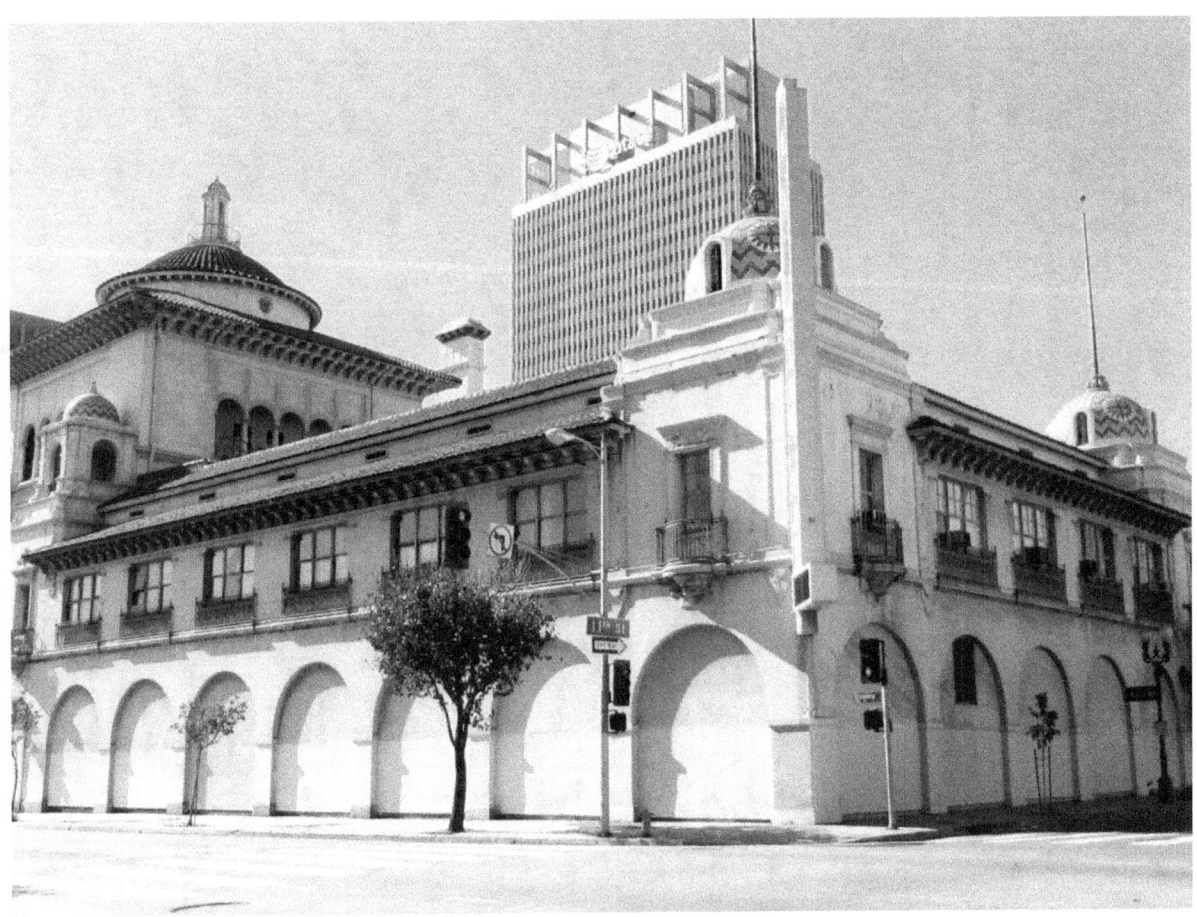

COMMERCIAL/INDUSTRIAL DISTRICT

1111 S. Broadway

No one who has seen "Citizen Kane" will be surprised to learn that this exotic building was commissioned by William Randolph Hearst (upon whom the character of "Charles Foster Kane" was based). The whimsical structure was designed in the main by architect Julia Morgan, who later designed Heart Castle. Opening in 1914, this gorgeous building housed Heart's "Herald-Examiner". (The "Los Angeles Examiner" was founded by Hearst in 1903 and was located at 509 S. Broadway).

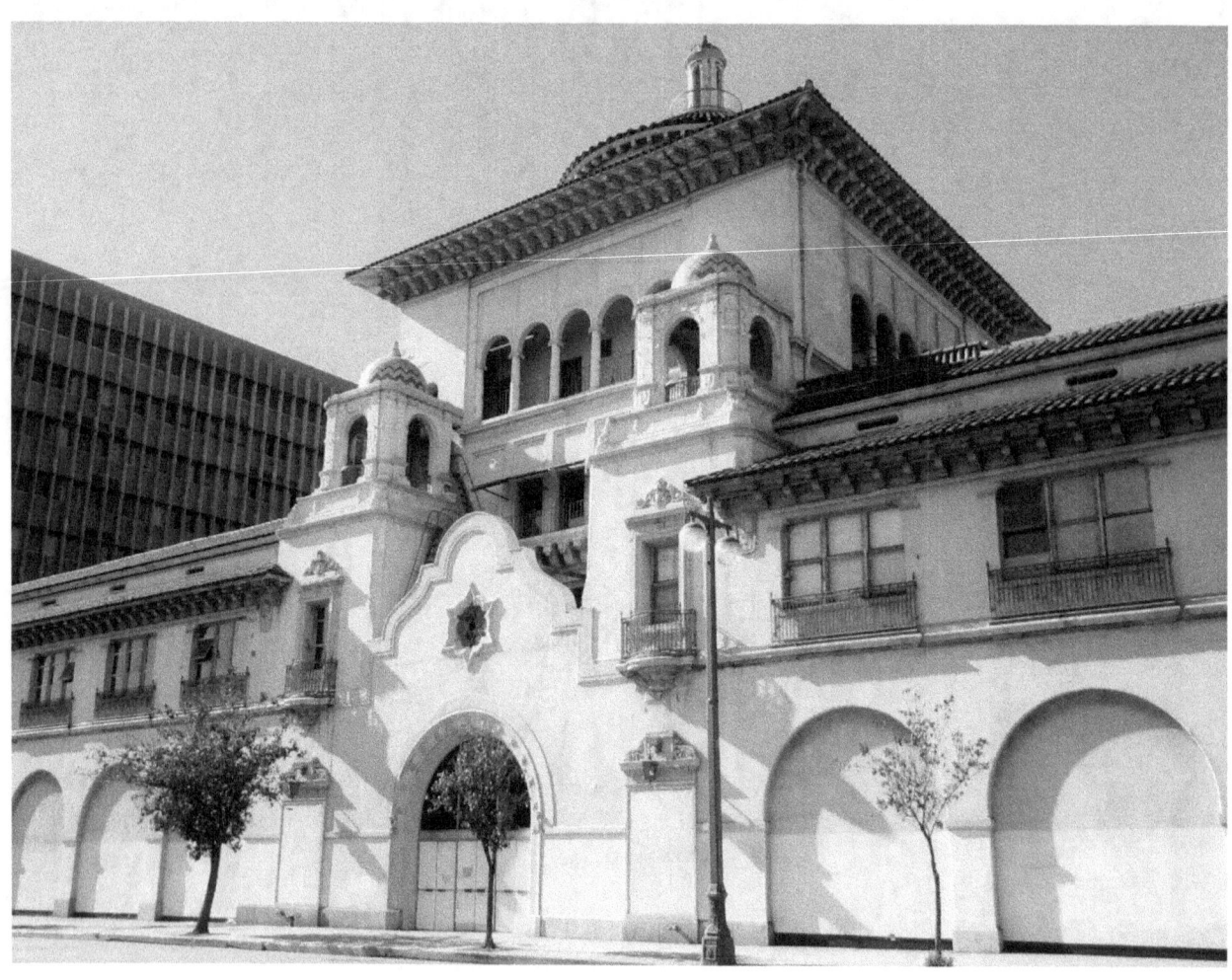

COMMERCIAL/INDUSTRIAL DISTRICT

1111 S. Broadway

The "LA Examiner" was a powerhouse in its day. Hollywood gossip columnist Louella Parsons wrote for Hearst's "LA Examiner". (Her famous rival, Hedda Hopper, wrote for the "LA Times".) The "LA Examiner" constantly scooped the "LA Times" in its coverage of the Black Dahlia murder. But over the decades, mergers, a lingering strike, distribution issues, and decreased ad revenues were among the factors that doomed the paper. Since the "Herald-Examiner" folded in 1989, the building has been unused except for film shoots. A variety of redevelopment and restoration plans have been proposed (and rumored) but nothing is solid—yet. For now, it continues to serve as an active film location.

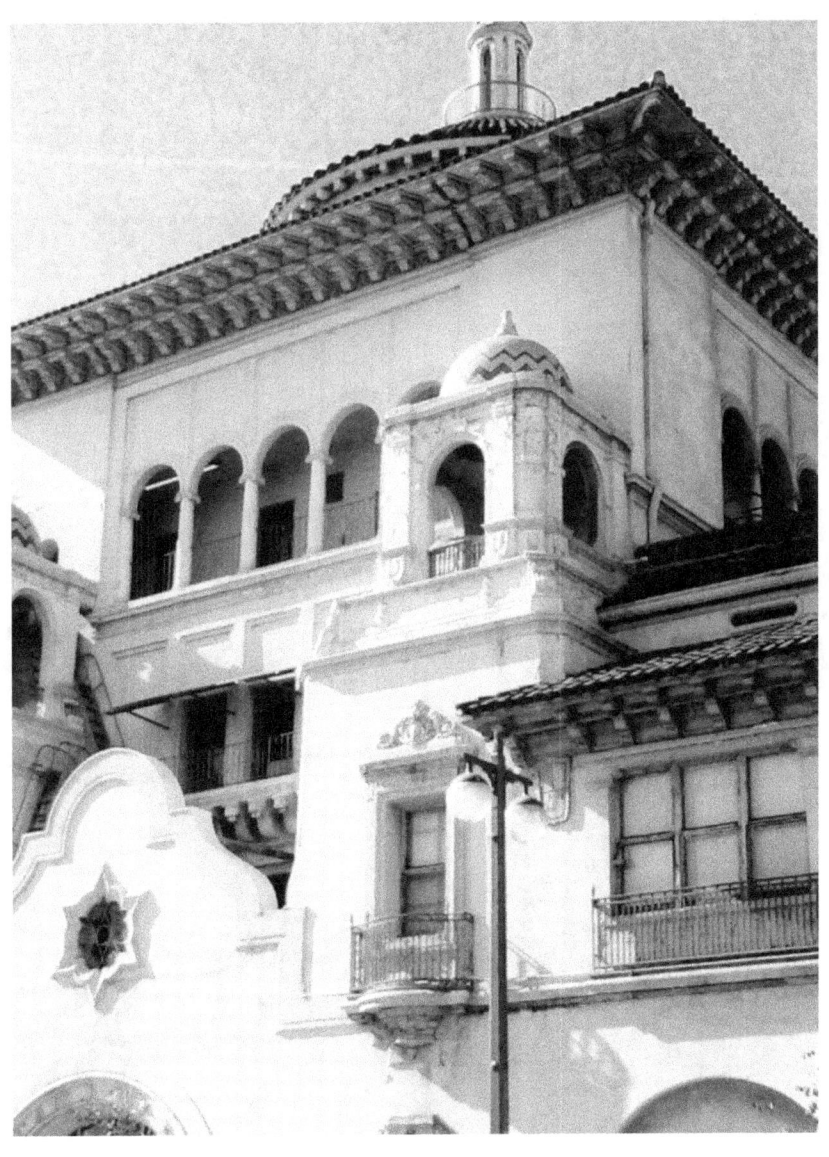

COMMERCIAL/INDUSTRIAL DISTRICT

S. Broadway and Twelfth Street

And so our tour of Broadway in Downtown Los Angeles concludes at the corner of S. Broadway and Twelfth, looking southeast, where the landscape is dominated by factories and warehouses, parking lots and office buildings. The FW Braun Building (right center), for example, housed FW Braun industrial textiles. FW Braun was an important figure in early Los Angeles. He started his career in the pharmaceutical business in the late 1800's. Braun originally worked in the (now) landmark Brunswig Building at 501 N. Main Street. Lucien Brunswig was another significant figure in LA's formative years, although he didn't move to LA until 1903. Among many achievements, he was responsible for USC's School of Pharmacy, and contributed to the construction of historic Olvera Street. That's Downtown Los Angeles, in a nutshell—nearly every building has a story to tell, a tale of LA's history. Each story connects to another story of how LA became the metropolis we know today.

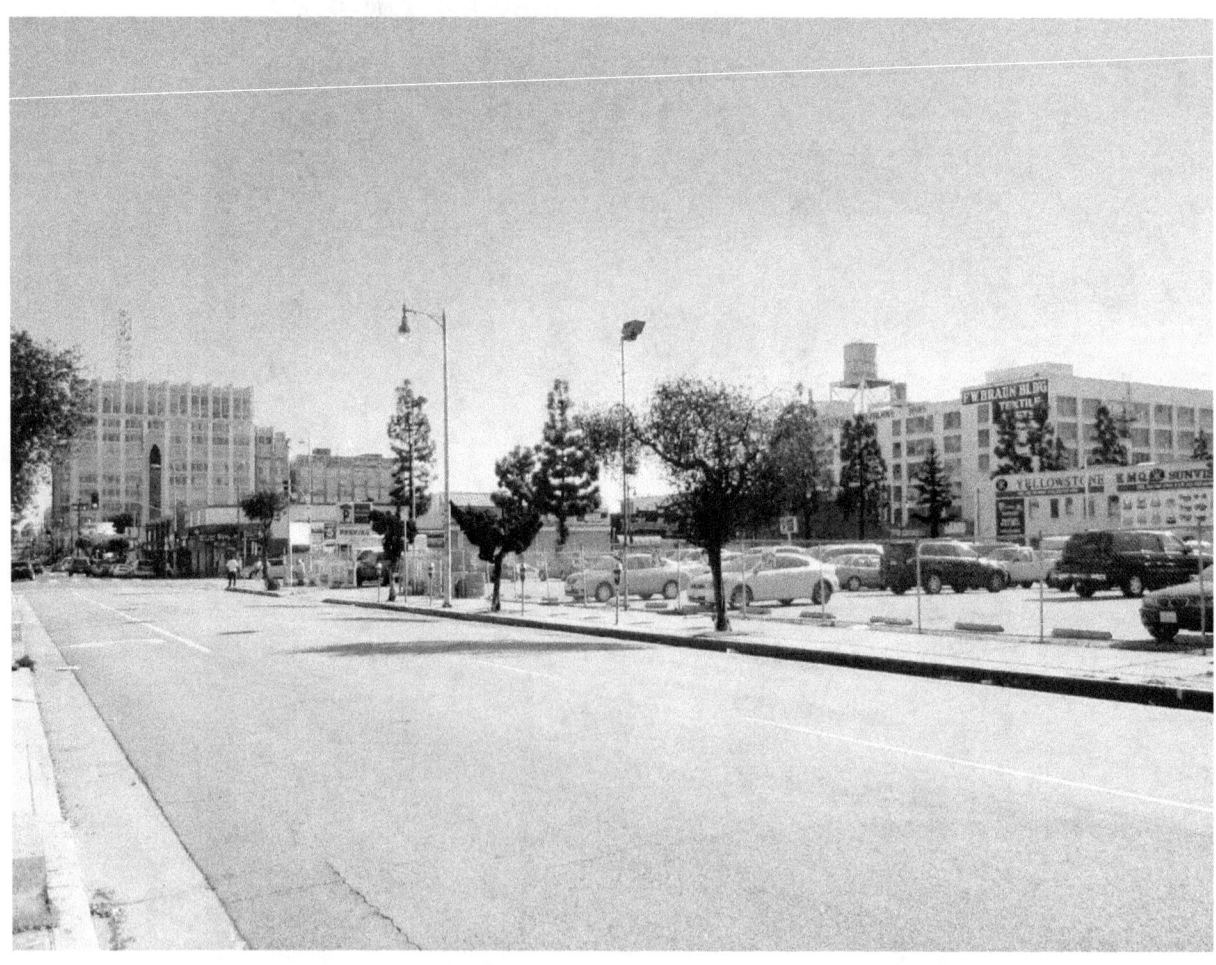

THANK YOU

Thank you for taking this photographic journey. We've followed Broadway through Downtown Los Angeles, from its northern reaches in Little Italy to the commercial and industrial zone. Our tour has concluded for now, but there are more tours ahead in new photograph collections.

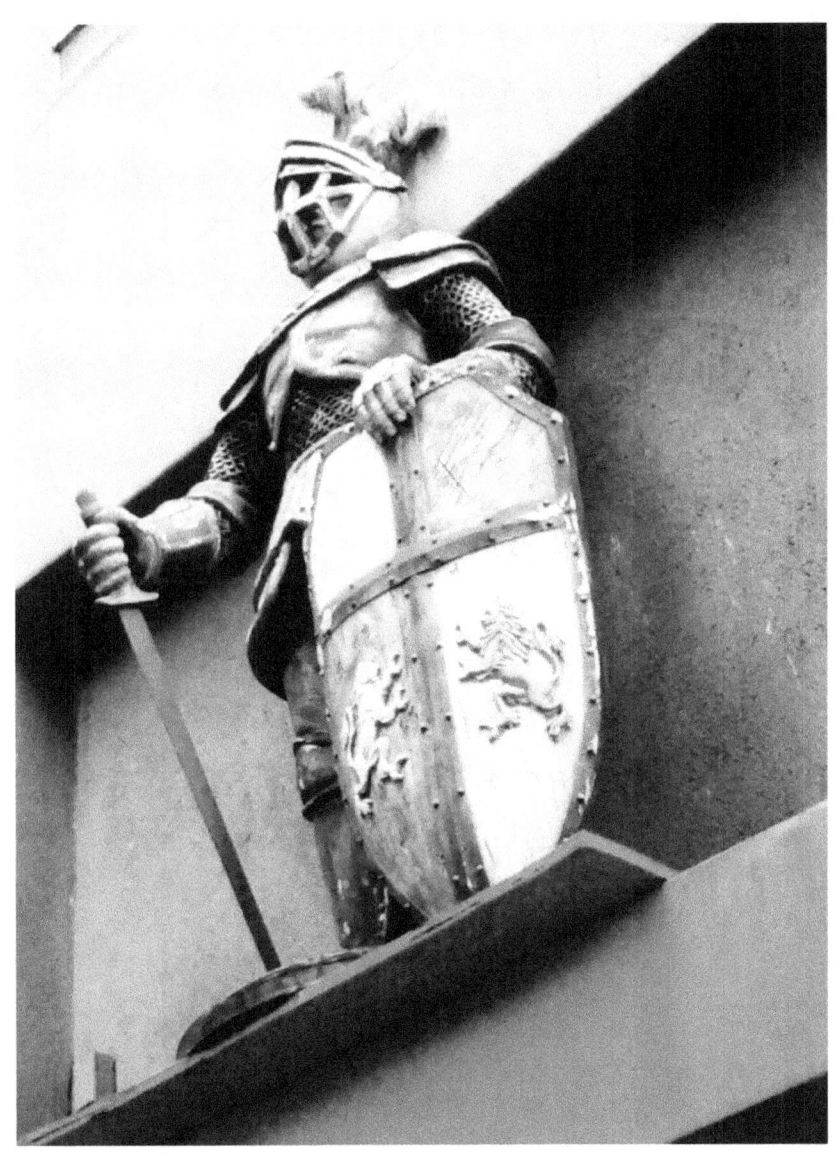

RESOURCES & RECOMMENDATIONS

Learn more about Los Angeles. The author recommends (but is not affiliated with) the following:

Explore
Secret City Tours
www.facebook.com/SecretCityTours
https://twitter.com/SecretCityTours

LA History Blogs and Articles
www.kcet.org

Follow
Vintage Los Angeles
Twitter: @alisonmartino

Help
Union Rescue Mission
545 S. San Pedro Street, LA CA 90013
(213) 347-6300
http://urm.org

Join/Learn
LA Conservancy
523 W. 6th Street, Suite 826, LA, CA 90014
(213) 623-2489
www.laconservancy.org

Los Angeles Historic Theatre Foundation (LAHTF)
PO Box 9122, LA, CA 90014
www.lahtf.org

Read
LA Noir: The City as Character (Book)
Silver, Alain and James Ursini
Santa Monica Press, 2005

ABOUT THE AUTHOR

Leslie Le Mon is an author, artist, and manager who has lived in Los Angeles since 1992.

She is an amateur historian.

Reader feedback is welcome and appreciated.

Please email her at les.lemon.author@gmail.com.

You can visit her website at www.leslielemonauthor.com and follow her on Twitter @leslemonauthor.

OTHER BOOKS BY THE AUTHOR/PHOTOGRAPHER

If you enjoy photographs, consider the author's other collections, such as *Downtown Los Angeles in Photographs 2013*, a photographic walking tour of some of Downtown LA's notable sites.

Sircus of Impossible Magicks: Chosen is an epic fantasy following the adventures of three young heroes time traveling in and around Los Angeles and Pasadena. Available as a paperback and as a digital book at booksellers like Amazon.com and BarnesandNoble.com.

Fans of chilling tales are invited to read *Cold Dark Harbor and Other Tales of Ghosts and Monsters*, available as a paperback and a digital book at booksellers such as Amazon.com and BarnesandNoble.com.

COPYRIGHT INFORMATION

All content—including all photographs, maps, and text—is copyrighted by Leslie Le Mon.

Copyright Questions: Contact the author at les.lemon.author@gmail.com.

© 2014 Leslie Le Mon